PLYMOUTH ARGYLE FOOTBALL CLUB

OFFICIAL YEARBOOK 2006/07

Editorial
Rick Cowdery, Tim Herbert

Sidan Press Team
Simon Rosen, Julian Hill-Wood, Marc Fiszman, Mark Peters, Karim Biria, Rob Cubbon,
Anette Lundebye, Marina Kravchenko, Gareth Peters, Janet Calcott, Trevor Scimes, John Fitzroy,
Jenny Middlemarch, Anders Rasmussen, Lim Wai-Lee, Emma Turner, Charles Grove, Tim Ryman

Photography
Dave Rowntree

Copyright © 2006 Plymouth Argyle Football Club

Sidan Press, 63-64 Margaret St, London W1W 8SW
Tel: 020 7580 0200
Email: info@sidanpress.com

sidanpress.com

Copyright © 2006 Sidan Press Ltd

Maps redrawn and based on Collins Town and Country series
Copyright © 2006 Bartholomew Ltd
Reproduced by permission of Harpercollins Publishers

Club Directory

Contacts

Argyle Box Office
Tel: 0845 338 PAFC (7232)
Fax: 01752 606167
Email: tickets@pafc.co.uk
https://eticketing.co.uk/pafc/index.asp

Argyle Superstore
Tel: 01752 558292
Fax: 01752 606167
Email: argyle.shop@pafc.co.uk
www.argylesuperstore.co.uk

Hospitality
Tel: 01752 519762
Fax: 01752 606167
Email: dan.thomas@pafc.co.uk

Commercial/Marketing
Tel: 01752 302204
Fax: 01752 606167
Email: argyle.sales@pafc.co.uk

Communications
Tel: 01752 302207
Fax: 01752 606167
Email: rick.cowdery@pafc.co.uk

The Board

Chairman
Paul Stapleton

Vice-chairman
Robert Dennerly

Directors
Phill Gill, Damon Lenszner,
Nic Warren, Tony Wrathall

Chief executive
Michael Dunford

Plymouth Argyle Football Club
Home Park
Plymouth PL2 3DQ

Tel: 01752 562561
Fax: 01752 606167
Email: argyle@pafc.co.uk

CONTENTS

Chairman's Message 5
Chief Executive's
Message 6
Captain's Message 7
Club Information 8
How to Read the Stats 18

Season Review 2005/06
06.08.05 Reading (A) 22
09.08.05 Watford (H) 24
19.10.87 Derby (H) 26
02.05.04 C Palace (A) 28
23.08.05 Peterborough (H) 30
27.08.05 Hull City (H) 32
29.08.05 Brighton (A) 34
10.09.05 Norwich (A) 36
13.09.05 Crewe (H) 38
17.09.05 Burnley (H) 40
20.09.05 Barnet (A) 42
24.09.05 Southampton (A) 44
27.09.05 Sheff Utd (A) 46
01.10.05 Stoke (H) 48
15.10.05 Sheff Wed (H) 50
18.10.05 QPR (A) 52
22.10.05 Luton (A) 54
30.10.05 Millwall (H) 56
05.11.05 Ipswich (A) 58
19.11.05 QPR (H) 60
22.11.05 Sheff Wed (A) 62
26.11.05 Reading (H) 64
03.12.05 Coventry (A) 66
10.12.05 Watford (A) 68
17.12.05 C Palace (H) 70
26.12.05 Cardiff (A) 72
31.12.05 Wolves (A) 74
02.01.06 Leeds (H) 76
07.01.06 Wolves (A) 78
14.01.06 Norwich (H) 80
21.01.06 Crewe (A) 82
24.01.06 Leicester (H) 84
31.01.06 Southampton (H 86

04.02.06 Burnley (A) 88
11.02.06 Sheff Utd (H) 90
14.02.06 Stoke (A) 92
18.02.06 Coventry (H) 94
25.02.06 Derby (A) 96
04.03.06 Brighton (H) 98
07.03.06 Preston (H) 100
11.03.06 Hull City (A) 102
18.03.06 Cardiff (H) 104
25.03.06 Preston (A) 106
01.04.06 Wolves (H) 108
08.04.06 Leeds (A) 110
15.04.06 Millwall (A) 112
17.04.06 Luton (H) 114
22.04.06 Leicester (A) 116
30.04.06 Ipswich (H) 118

End of Season Review 120

Player Profiles
Romain Larrieu 126
Luke McCormack 128
Rufus Brevett 129
Mathias Doumbe 130
Nuno Mendes 132
Elliott Ward 133
Anthony Barness 134
Hasney Aljofree 136
Paul Connolly 138
Taribo West 140
Akos Buzsaky 141
Bojan Djordjic 142
Bjarni Gudjonsson 143
Tony Capaldi 144
Lee Hodges 146
Lilian Nalis 147
Jason Jarrett 148
Keith Lasley 149
Paul Wotton 150
Anthony Pulis 152
Luke Summerfield 153

David Norris 154
Leon Clarke 156
Chris Zebrowski 157
Matt Derbyshire 158
Vincent Pericard 159
Nick Chadwick 160
Reuben Reid 162
Scott Taylor 163
Micky Evans 164

2006/07: The Opposition
Barnsley 168
Birmingham City 169
Burnley 170
Cardiff City 171
Colchester 172
Coventry City 173
Crystal Palace 174
Derby County 175
Hull City 176
Ipswich Town 177
Leeds 178
Leicester 179
Luton Town 180
Norwich City 181
Preston 182
QPR 183
Sheffield Wed 184
Southampton 185
Southend 186
Stoke City 187
Sunderland 188
West Brom 189
Wolves 190

Fixture List 2006/07 191

OFFICIAL PARTNERS

CHAIRMAN'S MESSAGE
Paul Stapleton

Welcome to another season of Coca-Cola Championship football. I hope you all enjoy our third successive campaign at this level, and that this yearbook proves an invaluable source of reference throughout the campaign.

In many ways, this is a momentous time for our club: we are completing the purchase of Home Park from the City Council, which means, for the first time in its history, Argyle will own their own ground, and Phase II is on the horizon. A state-of-the-art stadium will highlight to the rest of the football world the fact that we are highly ambitious.

Also, we will shortly be setting out a new five-year plan, for which we will seek the thoughts, ideas and opinions of the Green Army.

We all want to continue our progress of recent years and move higher up the Championship table, a task which becomes increasingly harder to maintain. It inevitably takes a greater effort and resource to maintain that forward momentum, which makes last season's 14th-placed finish such a noteworthy achievement.

Everyone at Home Park is deeply committed to ensuring that progress continues.

If we can match the efforts of the past five seasons, on and off the pitch, during the next few seasons – and, crucially, continue to enjoy your support – we will not be far away from achieving the dream of everyone connected with the club: playing in the top flight for the first time in our history.

CHIEF EXECUTIVE'S MESSAGE
Michael Dunford

Welcome to the beginning of another Coca-Cola Championship campaign.

Once again, thanks to the hard work and commitment of everyone last season, we are competing in one of the hardest leagues in the world: the likes of Birmingham, West Brom, Sunderland, Leeds United, Wolves, Southampton, Norwich, Leicester and Crystal Palace have all played in the Premiership in the last three years.

We have a decent platform from which to challenge these big-name clubs. We ended last season with more points than the previous season and in our best position for two decades.

The challenge this season is to improve on that new benchmark. Our aim as a club must be to improve year on year, as we have done – on and off the pitch – for the last five years.

We cannot promise you what will happen over the next nine months or so. What we can promise is that everyone connected with Plymouth Argyle will work as hard as they can to build on what we have already achieved.

As ever, your support will be vital if we are to push on. To give ourselves a chance of getting to be where we all want to go, we will have to stand together.

Please be part of the team and get behind the lads.

Best wishes.

CAPTAIN'S MESSAGE
Paul Wotton

On behalf of the dressing-room, I'd like to thank you for again showing your support for the lads.

I can't emphasise enough how vital your continued backing is, not only for the team on the pitch, but the club as a whole.

For me, the atmosphere at Home Park is second to none, especially on the big occasions – memories of afternoons like the final day of last season, when the stands rose to acclaim my good mate Michael Evans, will live with me forever.

You really can raise us up.

As a Plymothian, I've been proud and privileged to see how Argyle have progressed, both on and off the field, during my time at Home Park.

It's my desire and the hope of everyone who loves the Pilgrims, from the Boardroom to the Barn Park, that we keep up this forward momentum.

Nobody knows what the coming campaign will bring – who could have predicted the twists and turns of last season? – but I can promise you that no-one who pulls on the green shirt will be found lacking in the attitude and commitment you demand of your team.

Keep it Green.

FOOTBALL IN THE COMMUNITY

Football in the Community is a non-profit making organisation funded by the Professional Footballers' Association. Our aim is to help children become more actively involved in football at a young age, and to develop and promote closer links with both the football club and the local community.

The Plymouth Argyle Community Scheme has improved tremendously over the last five years and continues to grow from strength to strength under the leadership of Community Scheme manager Mark Rivers and his team of coaches. All our coaches are fully UEFA qualified and CRB checked.

We currently provide football coaching to schools in Devon and Cornwall. We run in-school-hours curriculum sessions, lunch-time clubs, and after-school clubs, Inset Days, and Teacher Training Days, Match-day Packages and birthday parties.

We run many successful Development Centres across Plymouth, at the Mayflower Leisure Centre, Stoke Damerel Community College, Coombe Dean School, and, more recently, Ridgeway School, for boys and girls aged 5-7, 8-11, and 12-14.

In Spring 2006, we expanded into Cornwall, where we opened an office at St Blazey Football Club. We hope to develop our operation further into Cornwall and offer the children of the county the same opportunities available in Plymouth, to come along and participate in football coaching in a safe and fun environment.

Without doubt, our biggest source of income comes from our Football Courses, held every school holiday at various venues across Devon and Cornwall.

The courses are broken down in two sections. Mornings are usually used to practice skills and techniques, and so children will participate in various drills to help them learn the skills.

In the afternoons, there are opportunities to take part in small-sided matches. Children attending a course at Home Park are, on most occasions, offered an extra bonus of a day-trip out to another Stadium. Recent trips have included Chelsea, Manchester United and Reading, while visits to Anfield, the home of Liverpool, and Tottenham Hotspur's White Hart Lane were on the schedule of the FitC Summer 2006 courses.

Every child who attends one of our courses receives a certificate of attendance and medal. There are also lots of competitions run throughout the duration of the courses where prizes are up for grabs.

Unfortunately we cannot predict the weather, but courses continue to run in all conditions. We are fully prepared, with DVDs and other football related material, should the weather conditions mean we have to take the children inside for short periods during a session.

Call us on 01752 562561 for further details or visit our website (www.pafc.co.uk).

HOME PARK HOSPITALITY

Private Functions

Make your family occasion extra special at Home Park. With four different rooms to choose from and free parking for up to 200 cars, the Argyle function rooms will help any event go with a swing. Packages can be put together to suit every taste and budget.

Mariner's Marquee
(capacity: 180 seated; 225 buffet)

Ideal for businesses: conferences; large seminars; formal dinners; award ceremonies.

Popular for Christmas parties, balls, and other large-scale functions, such as large business meetings or conferences, Mariner's provides a unique atmosphere. With a full bar and drinks service to your table, you are guaranteed first-class hospitality and a night to remember.

Argyle Lounge
(capacity: 80 cabaret style; 120 theatre style)

Ideal for presentations, lunches, birthdays or anniversaries.

The dance-floor in the Argyle Lounge means guests can boogie the night away. We offer a resident DJ or choice of local bands to make your party an extra special evening. Let us take away the hassle of organising your event by doing it all for you – please contact us for details.

Green Room
(capacity: 60)

Ideal for businesses: informal meetings; lunches; syndicate room.

Perfect for smaller parties or informal meetings, the Green Room has the feel of a pub within a club. It is the main club bar on match days and can be set up entirely to meet your needs. You can use it in conjunction with the Argyle Lounge – book it for a large party and enjoy the use of two bars.

Boardroom
(capacity: 30 seated, 60 buffet)

Ideal for businesses: lunches, launches, meetings, seminars.

Where better to impress family and friends than the luxurious setting of the Boardroom? The Boardroom has provided the venue for many of the most important decisions in the club's history. With its plush carpet, wooden finish and views over the city, it is an ideal location for a small formal meeting or seminar, working lunch, formal interview, or Press launch. With full bar and facilities at hand, we can cater for up to 30 for dinner, or 60 for buffet or canapés.

Please note: Rooms are normally available prior to events for customers to decorate. Room hire is free where we cater for more than 50 guests.

Weddings

Enjoy one of the most important days of your life at Home Park. Now that Argyle holds a wedding licence, we can host civil ceremonies in the luxurious setting of the Boardroom.

When you book your wedding at Home Park, we will work with you to make sure your day is extra special. We will help you to devise your wedding breakfast, arrange your evening reception, and book additional services such as photographers, flowers and wedding cars.

We look forward to making your wedding day truly memorable.

Conferences and Seminars

Make your event stand out in the unique surroundings of Home Park. Whether a three-day conference for 200 delegates, a seminar for 50, or a business meeting for five, the excellent facilities on offer at Argyle are sure to meet your needs.

All seminar rooms have full bar facilities, where required. Our caterers offer numerous options, from finger buffets to four-course banquets. Bespoke packages are readily available – please ask us for details.

MATCH DAY HOSPITALITY

New for 2006-07

Mariner's

Treat yourself, your clients, friends or family to a fantastic match-day experience at Home Park for as little as £55 (inc. VAT) per person

Your day will include: VIP car-parking; pre-match celebrity guest speaker; award-winning match-day Pilgrim programme; superb three-course lunch; centre-grandstand seats, half-time refreshments, man-of-the-match presentations, exclusive use of Mariner's bar, Argyle TV

PLUS the chance to win a **FREE** Pontins holiday

Entertain your clients or staff with a Match-day Sponsorship

OUR premier package is for up to 24 people and includes: champagne reception; VIP car-parking; your own exclusive lounge for the whole day; stadium tour; pre-match lunch; programme advertising; and you will pick the man of the match and meet him after the game.

Your company will also be acknowledged as Match-day Sponsors on Argyle TV for the five hours of match-day broadcasts on more than 50 televisions around the stadium.

Shortly after your sponsorship day, you will also receive an Argyle photograph album containing a complete record of your memorable day.

Match-ball/Programme/Team picture Sponsorship (For up to 10 ten people)

Start your day with champagne, a stadium tour, and a three-course lunch in Mariner's, followed by: centre-circle presentations with the match officials; centre grandstand seats; and programme and TV messages - and take part in the man-of-the-match presentations after the game.

As with the Match-day Sponsorship, your company will also be acknowledged as Match-ball Sponsors on Argyle TV's match-day broadcasts around the stadium, and you will receive a photograph album of your memorable day.

Executive Box
(14-seater executive box on the halfway line)

Exclusive reserved VIP car-park places; match-day programmes; day membership of the Argyle Lounge with large-screen TVs and pre-match entertainment; a pre-match buffet - or upgrade to a three-course lunch in Mariner's; waitress service into your box leading up to, and during, the match. Only £75 per person, inc. vat (subject to availability)

To book, call Andy or Lesley on 01752 302204, or email **andy.budge@pafc.co.uk**

ARGYLE SUPERSTORE

You can find the perfect gift for the Argyle fan in your life at the Argyle Superstore.

Our friendly sales team are always on hand to help you find what you are looking for, and, with their extensive knowledge on everything Argyle, they can always point you in the right direction.

The Argyle Superstore at Home Park is right next to the stadium, with plenty of free parking for your visit to us. We are open Monday–Friday 9am–5pm; Saturday Match-days 9am–5.30pm; Saturday non Match-days 10am–3pm; and Sunday noon–3pm.

The Argyle Superstore is also pleased to offer fans the chance to shop 24 hours a day, 7 days a week, with the launch of our online store at **www.argylesuperstore.co.uk.**

Here, you can shop and have the items delivered to your door direct from the Superstore itself, as well as keeping up to date with kit launches and seeing new products as they come into the Superstore itself.

We can also offer you a mail-order facility – you can call us on 01752 558292 and place your order over the phone, our staff are always happy to help.

The Argyle Mobile Retail Unit is often out and about within the region. We try to spread our wings and meet you at several venues, including Liskeard Show, Honiton Show, Launceston Show,

Devon County Show and the Royal Cornwall Show, offering fans and Superstore staff a chance to meet away from Home Park. The Unit carries a selection of our merchandise and we can always take an order if we have not got what you require.

Official Argyle merchandise can also be purchased throughout Devon and Cornwall at several retail outlets:

Derry's 88 Royal Parade, Plymouth.
Launceston Sports 3-5 Market Street, Launceston, Cornwall. 01566 774127
Studs Sports 64 Bank Street, Newquay, Cornwall. 01637 873560
Studs Sports 56 Fore Street, Bodmin, Cornwall. 01208 78003
Trophy Textiles Unit 2 Dudnance Lane, Pool, Cornwall. 01209 713341
Whirlwind Sports 62 Meneage Street, Helston, Cornwall. 01326 564297
Whirlwind Sports 45 Market Jew Street, Penzance, Cornwall. 01736 363855
Whirlwind Sports 26 Commercial Street Camborne, Cornwall. 01209 612454

Whatever your requirements are, the friendly Argyle Superstore Staff will always endeavour to help.

BOX OFFICE

For the most up-to-date information on ticket availability, visit the official website at www.pafc.co.uk.

We would remind supporters to retain ticket-stubs for all home and away games that they attend this season in case they are needed for priority ticket allocation later in the campaign.

White and Pilgrim members can buy tickets for all home league matches. For full details of this season's fixtures and prices, please speak to someone at the Box Office or go to www.pafc.co.uk and follow the prompt.

If you are a White or Pilgrim member you can buy home tickets (for yourself) at any time during the season by 'phone, post or in person at the Argyle Box Office. Members must have their membership card with them or state their membership number when ordering.

Tickets for Argyle matches at Home Park are available from the following sources:

By Phone
0845 338 PAFC (7232)

For ticket-related enquiries, please call our new lower priced designated Box Office number. Credit and debit card bookings can be made using Mastercard, Visa, Switch or Delta. Please note that a 1.6% levy will be charged on all credit card orders.

Sale dates for telephone sales can be found at www.pafc.co.uk.

Online – e-ticketing

We are now able to process online orders. Please visit www.pafc.co.uk and follow the link to 'tickets' and then 'e-tickets'. All existing club members have been allotted a default user name and password. Please contact the Box Office if you are unaware of your log-in information.

By Post

Postal applications must be sent to Box Office, Plymouth Argyle FC, Home Park, Plymouth PL2 3DQ. You must include payment with an SAE and covering letter stating your name, address and which game you would like to book. Please make cheques payable to 'Plymouth Argyle FC'.

In Person

We sell tickets by personal application at the Box Office. The Box Office opening times are stated below. Payment will be accepted by cash, cheques, credit or debit card.

Ticket information for people with disabilities

Stand for Disabled Supporters

Ambulant (uncovered) – concession available (see price tariff below)

All other areas of the ground

Wheelchair (uncovered) – full price
Ambulant (covered) – full price

A free carer's pass will be issued if needed, if you are in receipt of the higher rate of Carer or Mobility Allowance from the Department of Work and Pensions or Department of Social Security.

Box Office opening times

Monday to Friday	9am-5pm
Saturday (non-home match)	10am-3pm
Saturday (home match)	9am-kick off and for a short time afterwards
Sunday	12pm-3pm
Monday before a Tuesday home match	9am-7pm
Friday before a Saturday home match	9am-7pm
Reserve night matches (at Home Park)	9am-7pm

The Box Office will not be open on non-match day Bank Holidays (except where advertised).

Memberships Available

Green Membership – Season Tickets for 2006-2007

Available areas:
Grandstand Seating
Mayflower Seating
Mayflower Terrace (Standing)
Devonport End (Seating) Blocks 1-5
Lyndhurst Stand (Seating) Blocks 6-16

White Membership – 6 Vouchers

Adult:	£142.00
Over 65:	£95
Student:	£95
Under 16:	£41

Pilgrim membership – priority available

Price for all groups - £25

Home match-day ticket prices

	Adult	Over 65	Student	Under 16
Seating	£24	£17	£17	£6
Standing	£20	£15	£15	£6
Disabled Enclosure	£15	£12	£12	£6

Pre match-day ticket prices

	Adult	Over 65	Student	Under 16
Seating	£22	£15	£15	£6
Standing	£18	£14	£14	£6
Disabled Enclosure	£15	£12	£12	£6

HOW TO READ THE STATS

This year's review is better than ever, packed with the sort of in-depth stats which really get you close to the action. If you'd like to know why a particular match turned out the way it did, how a player's form varied over the course of the season, or how Argyle have fared against their biggest rivals, you'll find all the info inside.

To make sure you're getting the most out of the stats, we're including this section to highlight the information presented by some of the charts and tables.

Colours

Argyle vs Opposition
There are lots of comparisons between Argyle and our opponents throughout the book. Argyle stats are shown in green; opponents are shown in grey:

Figure 1: Plymouth stats are in green; opposition stats are grey.

WDL, Scored, Conceded
When reviewing match results, wins, draws and losses are indicated by green, grey and orange blocks, respectively. For goals, green blocks indicate goals scored; orange blocks show goals conceded:

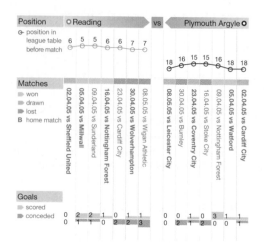

Figure 2: Wins, draws, losses and goals are clearly colour-coded.

Match Reports

The Match Report section contains reports, quotes, facts and stats from every Argyle match of the 2005/06 season.

Stats Order (Home and Away)
The order of the stats varies depending on whether a match was home or away: for home matches, Argyle stats are shown on the left, for away matches they're on the right:

Championship Totals	O Plymouth	Watford O
Championship Appearances	281	369
Team Appearances	271	232
Goals Scored	32	25
Assists	21	18
Clean Sheets (goalkeepers)	4	0
Yellow Cards	30	41
Red Cards	2	4
Full Internationals	2	2

Figure 3: For home matches, Plymouth stats appear on the left.

Championship Totals	o Reading	Plymouth o
Championship Appearances	389	278
Team Appearances	389	258
Goals Scored	34	27
Assists	26	25
Clean Sheets (goalkeepers)	19	4
Yellow Cards	30	31
Red Cards	0	2
Full Internationals	4	3

Figure 4: For away matches, Plymouth stats appear on the right.

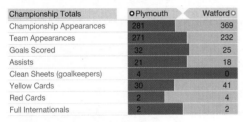

Figure 6: Major positions are shown in dark green; minor positions are shown in light green.

Form Coming into Fixture

Stats are from the previous seven league games. For the first few matches, these stats include games from the end of the previous season.

Team Statistics

Stats are for starters and playing subs. The "Championship Totals" chart measures performance within the Championship (with the exception of "Full Internationals").

Championship Totals	o Plymouth	Watford o
Championship Appearances	281	369
Team Appearances	271	232
Goals Scored	32	25
Assists	21	18
Clean Sheets (goalkeepers)	4	0
Yellow Cards	30	41
Red Cards	2	4
Full Internationals	2	2

Age/Height

Reading Age	Plymouth Argyle Age
▶ **25 yrs, 7 mo**	▶ **27 yrs, 4 mo**
Reading Height	Plymouth Argyle Height
▶ **5'11"**	▶ **5'11"**

Figure 5: Team statistics are for starters and playing subs.

Player Profiles

The Player Profile section provides season reviews and comprehensive stats for Argyle's players. The section is organised by position, starting with goalkeepers.

Pitch Diagram

The diagram shows all positions the player played during 2005/06. The main position is denoted by a dark green circle; alternative positions are denoted by light green circles:

Player Performance

All stats show league performance, with the exception of the "Cup Games" table. The "League Performance" chart provides an excellent overview of the player's performance over the course of the season. At a glance, you can see when and how much he played, and how he contributed to the team's overall performance at different stages of the season.

Career History

Due to the difficulties involved in obtaining reliable stats for international clubs, the "Clubs" table is incomplete for players who have played for non-English clubs. The names of all clubs have been included for the reader's interest, but international stats have been left blank.

The Opposition

The Opposition section shows how Argyle sizes up against the other 23 teams in the Championship.

Points / Position

The points / position chart is a snapshot of the last 10 years' league performance of Argyle and the opponent. For any season when the two teams met in the league, the results of their clashes are shown at the bottom of the chart.

Championship Head-to-Head

Stats are only for the two teams' meetings in the Championship.

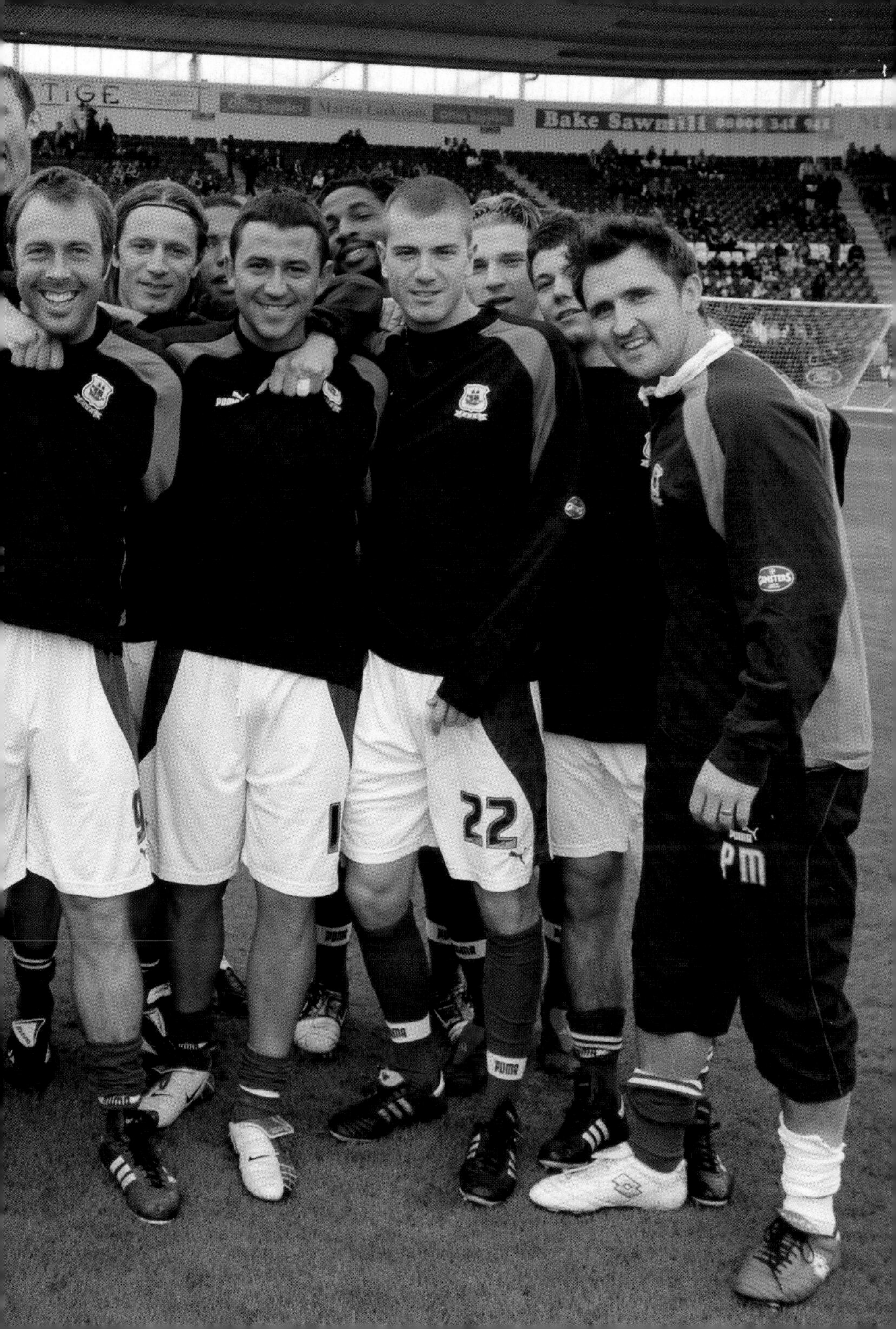
Bake Sawmill
PUMA
22
PM
GINSTERS

1-2 Reading ○
Plymouth Argyle ○

▶ Nick Chadwick celebrates his late winner

Event Line

12	○ ▪	Doyle
21	○ ⊕	Evans / LF / OP / IA
		Assist: Brevett
43	○ ▪	Little
Half time 0-1		
54	○ ⊕	Lita / H / IFK / IA
		Assist: Murty
76	○ ⇄	Kitson > Little
78	○ ⇄	Hunt > Convey
83	○ ▪	Wotton
85	○ ⇄	Chadwick > Evans
90	○ ⊕	Chadwick / RF / IFK / IA
		Assist: Wotton
90	○ ⇄	Djordjic > Buzsaky
Full time 1-2		

A dramatic injury-time winner from substitute Nick Chadwick saw Argyle begin the season in fine style with a smash and grab raid at the Madejski Stadium.

Chadwick, who has his doubters among the Green Army, was 100 per cent adored by the 4,000 footsoldiers who had made the trek to Berkshire when he netted in front of their massed ranks in the South Stand.

There were Argyle league debuts on both flanks of the defence, for Anthony Barness, on the right, and Rufus Brevett, on the left.

Micky Evans opened the scoring with a fine finish at the near post following a low cross from Brevett, before Reading equalized early in the second half.

A quickly taken free-kick caught the back-line on the back foot and Glen Little dinked in a little cross which Reading's new £3 million striker Leroy Lita headed past the hopelessly exposed Romain Larrieu.

Chadwick snatched the winner after diverting Paul Wotton's misdirected shot into the bottom left-hand corner of Marcus Hahnemann's net.

Player of the Match	Quote	Championship Milestone
11 Nick Chadwick	🔊 **Bobby Williamson**	▶ **Debut**
More man of the moment, really, but still the only player to score a winner against the champions at the Madejski.	I don't think we had a bad player. Everybody worked hard – it was certainly a team game. We were well organised, and defended well at times.	Both Anthony Barness and Bojan Djordjic made their Championship debuts.

Venue:	Madejski Stadium	Referee:	P.Taylor - 05/06	Reading
Attendance:	16,836	Matches:	0	Plymouth Argyle
Capacity:	24,200	Yellow Cards:	0	
Occupancy:	70%	Red Cards:	0	

Form Coming into Fixture

Position	Reading	vs	Plymouth Argyle

position in league table before match

Reading: 6 5 5 6 6 7 7
Plymouth Argyle: 18 16 15 15 16 18 18

Matches
- won
- drawn
- lost
- B home match

Reading matches:
02.04.05 vs Sheffield United
05.04.05 vs Millwall
09.04.05 vs Sunderland
16.04.05 vs Nottingham Forest
23.04.05 vs Cardiff City
30.04.05 vs Wolverhampton
08.05.05 vs Wigan Athletic

Plymouth Argyle matches:
08.05.05 vs Leicester City
30.04.05 vs Burnley
23.04.05 vs Coventry City
16.04.05 vs Stoke City
09.04.05 vs Nottingham Forest
05.04.05 vs Watford
02.04.05 vs Cardiff City

Goals
- scored
- conceded

Reading Goals scored: 0 2 2 1 0 1 1
Reading Goals conceded: 0 1 1 0 2 2 3

Plymouth Goals scored: 0 0 1 0 3 1 1
Plymouth Goals conceded: 0 2 1 2 0 0 1

Goal Statistics

Reading

by Half | by Situation

- first: 1 | set piece: 1
- second: 6 | open play: 6

Plymouth Argyle

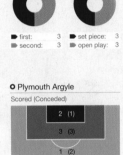

by Half | by Situation

- first: 3 | set piece: 3
- second: 3 | open play: 3

Goals by Area

Reading
Scored (Conceded)

3 (2)
4 (7)
0 (0)

Plymouth Argyle
Scored (Conceded)

2 (1)
3 (3)
1 (2)

Team Statistics

Starting Line-Ups

Reading:
Hahnemann
Shorey, Convey, Hunt
Ingimarsson, Harper
Doyle
Sonko, Sidwell
Lita
Murty, Little
Kitson

4/4/2

Unused Sub: Stack, Makin, Oster

Plymouth Argyle:
Larrieu
Norris, Barness
Gudjonsson
Doumbe
Evans Chadwick, Wotton
Aljofree
Buzsaky Djordjic
Capaldi, Brevett

4/5/1

Unused Sub: McCormick, Connolly, Taylor

Championship Totals

	Reading	Plymouth
Championship Appearances	389	278
Team Appearances	389	258
Goals Scored	34	27
Assists	26	25
Clean Sheets (goalkeepers)	19	4
Yellow Cards	30	31
Red Cards	0	2
Full Internationals	4	3

Age/Height

Reading Age

25 yrs, 7 mo

Plymouth Argyle Age

27 yrs, 4 mo

Reading Height

5'11"

Plymouth Argyle Height

5'11"

Match Statistics

League Table after Fixture

		Played	Won	Drawn	Lost	For	Against	Pts
1	Sheff Utd	1	1	0	0	4	1	3
2	Crewe	1	1	0	0	2	1	3
3	Luton	1	1	0	0	2	1	3
4	Plymouth	1	1	0	0	2	1	3
5	Preston	1	1	0	0	2	1	3
6	Ipswich	1	1	0	0	1	0	3
7	Brighton	1	0	1	0	1	1	1
...	...	...	...	...	...	...	...	...
21	Reading	1	0	0	1	1	2	0

Statistics

	Reading	Plymouth
Goals	1	2
Shots on Target	4	4
Shots off Target	5	5
Hit Woodwork	0	0
Possession %	51	49
Corners	4	5
Offsides	2	2
Fouls	20	22
Disciplinary Points	8	4

3-3

Plymouth Argyle ○
Watford ○

▶ Mathias Doumbe challenges Darius Henderson

Event Line

4 ○ ⊕	Evans / H / C / 6Y	
	Assist: Buzsaky	
12 ○ ⊕	Capaldi / LF / OP / OA	
	Assist: Evans	
22 ○ ▪	Bangura	
24 ○ ▪	Brevett	
35 ○ ⊕	King / RF / OP / IA	
	Assist: McNamee	
39 ○ ⇄	Stewart > Doyley	
43 ○ ▪	Foster	
43 ○ ⊕	Wotton / RF / IFK / IA	
	Assist: Aljofree	

Half time 3-1

46 ○ ⇄	Mahon > Bangura	
51 ○ ⇄	Devlin > McNamee	
52 ○ ⊕	Young / RF / DFK / OA	
	Assist: Henderson	
60 ○ ⇄	Taylor > Chadwick	
61 ○ ⊕	Young / RF / OP / OA	
	Assist: Henderson	
64 ○ ⇄	Djordjic > Capaldi	
86 ○ ▪	Devlin	
89 ○ ▪	Chambers	

Full time 3-3

Argyle twice squandered a two-goal lead to open their home Coca-Cola Championship campaign with an unsatisfactory draw.

Things looked rosy after 12 minutes, when Michael Evans and Tony Capaldi had given them a 2-0 lead and, even though Marlon King pulled one back before the break, the Pilgrims immediately restored their two-goal advantage through captain Paul Wotton.

However, Ashley Young struck twice in the early stages of the second period, after which the game seemed always beyond Argyle, and it was the visitors who came closest to taking all the points.

Evans opened the scoring with a close-range header following a delectable curling cross from Akos Buzsaky, and Capaldi doubled the score eight minutes later by firing a 20-yard left-foot shot into the bottom corner.

The best goal of the match was a Paul Wotton special. The Argyle skipper smashed the ball in off the bar from a difficult angle but it was not enough to overcome a resilient Watford side.

Player of the Match

9 Michael Evans

Opened the season's scoring at home and away, and was briefly the division's top marksman.

Quote

❝ **Bobby Williamson**

The way we were playing, I didn't think it was over at half-time. Second-half, we never played. Watford played all the football. Thankfully, we never conceded any more.

Championship Milestone

▶ **25**

Romain Larrieu made his 25th appearance in the Championship.

Venue:	Home Park	Referee:	L.Probert - 05/06		Plymouth Argyle
Attendance:	13,813	Matches:	1		Watford
Capacity:	20,922	Yellow Cards:	5		
Occupancy:	66%	Red Cards:	0		

Form Coming into Fixture

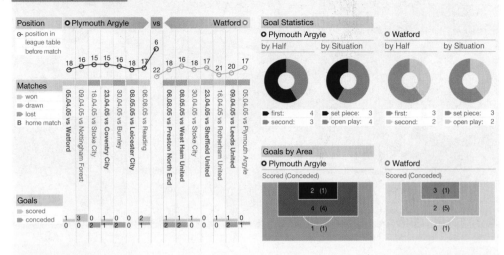

	Plymouth Argyle	vs	Watford

Position — position in league table before match

Matches: won, drawn, lost, B home match

Plymouth Argyle matches:
05.04.05 vs Watford, 09.04.05 vs Nottingham Forest, 16.04.05 vs Stoke City, 23.04.05 vs Coventry City, 30.04.05 vs Burnley, 08.05.05 vs Leicester City, 06.08.05 vs Reading

Watford matches:
06.08.05 vs Preston North End, 08.05.05 vs West Ham United, 30.04.05 vs Stoke City, 23.04.05 vs Sheffield United, 16.04.05 vs Rotherham United, 09.04.05 vs Leeds United, 05.04.05 vs Plymouth Argyle

Goals: scored, conceded

Plymouth: scored 1 3 0 1 0 0 2 / conceded 0 0 2 1 2 0 1
Watford: scored 1 1 1 0 1 1 0 / conceded 2 2 0 0 0 2 1

Goal Statistics

Plymouth Argyle

by Half — first: 4, second: 3
by Situation — set piece: 3, open play: 4

Watford

by Half — first: 3, second: 2
by Situation — set piece: 3, open play: 2

Goals by Area

Plymouth Argyle — Scored (Conceded)
2 (1)
4 (4)
1 (1)

Watford — Scored (Conceded)
3 (1)
2 (5)
0 (1)

Team Statistics

Starting Line-Ups

Plymouth Argyle (4/4/2):
Larrieu; Brevett, Capaldi, Djordjic, Aljofree, Buzsaky, Evans, King, Doumbe, Wotton, Chadwick, Taylor, Henderson, Barness, Norris

Watford (4/4/2):
Foster; Young, Doyley, Stewart, Bangura, Mahon, Carlisle, Blizzard, DeMerit, McNamee, Devlin, Chambers

Unused Sub: McCormick, Connolly, Gudjonsson

Unused Sub: Chamberlain, Bouazza

Championship Totals	Plymouth	Watford
Championship Appearances	281	369
Team Appearances	271	232
Goals Scored	32	25
Assists	21	18
Clean Sheets (goalkeepers)	4	0
Yellow Cards	30	41
Red Cards	2	4
Full Internationals	2	2

Age/Height

	Plymouth Argyle	Watford
Age	27 yrs, 6 mo	24 yrs, 1 mo
Height	5'11"	5'11"

Match Statistics

League Table after Fixture

		Played	Won	Drawn	Lost	For	Against	Pts
↑	1 Sheff Utd	2	2	0	0	6	2	6
↑	2 Luton	2	2	0	0	5	3	6
↑	3 Plymouth	2	1	1	0	5	4	4
↓	4 Crewe	2	1	1	0	3	2	4
↓	5 Preston	2	1	1	0	3	2	4
↑	6 QPR	2	1	1	0	2	1	4
↑	7 Wolverhampton	2	1	1	0	2	1	4
...	...	...	...	...	...	...	...	...
↑	18 Watford	2	0	1	1	4	5	1

Statistics	Plymouth	Watford
Goals	3	3
Shots on Target	4	8
Shots off Target	5	4
Hit Woodwork	0	0
Possession %	60	40
Corners	11	5
Offsides	6	5
Fouls	14	16
Disciplinary Points	4	16

0-2

Plymouth Argyle ○
Derby County ○

▶ Akos Buzsaky surges forward

Event Line

20 ○ ⊕	Rasiak / H / OP / IA
	Assist: Jackson
39 ○ ⊕	Bisgaard / H / OP / 6Y
	Assist: Rasiak
Half time 0-2	
60 ○ ⇄	Connolly > Brevett
72 ○ ▢	Johnson M
74 ○ ▢	Idiakez
79 ○ ▢	Edworthy
81 ○ ⇄	Tudgay > Smith
81 ○ ⇄	Norris > Djordjic
86 ○ ▢	Norris
Full time 0-2	

As they had done twice last season, the previous year's play-off semi-finalists again proved too good for Argyle, who were scintillating in the first 75 seconds and then ordinary for an hour, when Gregorz Rasiak and Morten Bisgaard scored the goals that secured the victory.

Only in the last half-hour did the Pilgrims, first match, then better, their opponents, leaving a frustrating feeling of what might have been.

Scott Taylor had a couple of long-range efforts for Argyle before Derby's Polish international striker Rasiak opened the scoring with a looping header, which evaded Romain Larrieu's despairing right hand and squeezed in off the far post.

The Rams doubled the lead six minutes before half-time when Rasiak nodded a deep cross from Tommy Smith into the path of Morten Bisgaard, who bundled the ball past Larrieu from two yards out.

Player of the Match

10 Scott Taylor

As busy as anyone out there.

Quote

🟢 **Bobby Williamson**

We'll be working hard to rectify the mistakes we made today and learn from them. It's a team effort to score goals and it's a team effort to defend them.

Venue:	Home Park	Referee:	P.Dowd - 05/06		Plymouth Argyle
Attendance:	14,279	Matches:	1		Derby County
Capacity:	20,922	Yellow Cards:	4		
Occupancy:	68%	Red Cards:	0		

Form Coming into Fixture

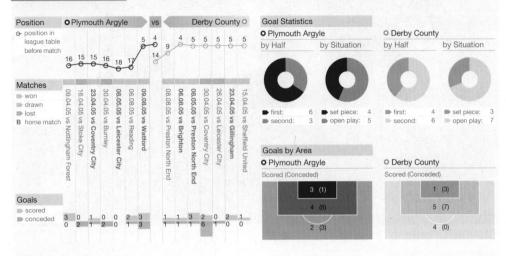

Position ● Plymouth Argyle vs Derby County ○
- position in league table before match

Plymouth Argyle: 16 15 15 16 18 17 5 4
Derby County: 9 14 4 5 5 5 5 5

Matches
- won
- drawn
- lost
- B home match

Plymouth Argyle matches: 09.04.05 vs Nottingham Forest, 16.04.05 vs Stoke City, 23.04.05 vs Coventry City, 30.04.05 vs Burnley, 08.05.05 vs Leicester City, 06.08.05 vs Reading, 09.08.05 vs Watford

Derby County matches: 08.08.05 vs Preston North End, 06.08.05 vs Brighton, 08.05.05 vs Preston North End, 30.04.05 vs Coventry City, 26.04.05 vs Leicester City, 23.04.05 vs Gillingham, 15.04.05 vs Sheffield United

Goals
- scored
- conceded

Plymouth scored: 3 0 1 0 0 2 3
Plymouth conceded: 0 2 1 2 0 1 3

Derby scored: 1 1 3 2 0 2 1
Derby conceded: 1 1 1 6 1 0 0

Goal Statistics

● Plymouth Argyle

by Half — first: 6, second: 3
by Situation — set piece: 4, open play: 5

○ Derby County

by Half — first: 4, second: 6
by Situation — set piece: 3, open play: 7

Goals by Area

● Plymouth Argyle — Scored (Conceded)
- 3 (1)
- 4 (5)
- 2 (3)

○ Derby County — Scored (Conceded)
- 1 (3)
- 5 (7)
- 4 (0)

Team Statistics

Starting Line-Ups

Plymouth Argyle: Connolly, Brevett, Djordjic, Norris, Aljofree, Buzsaky, Evans, Larrieu, Doumbe, Wotton, Taylor, Barness, Gudjonsson

Derby County: Bisgaard, Edworthy, Bolder, Davies, Rasiak, Idiakez, Camp, Johnson M, Thirlwell, Smith, Tudgay, Jackson

● 4/4/2   ○ 4/5/1

Unused Sub: McCormick, Mendes, Lasley

Unused Sub: Grant L, Mills, Konjic, Holmes

Championship Totals	● Plymouth	Derby ○
Championship Appearances	285	385
Team Appearances	265	346
Goals Scored	30	54
Assists	28	50
Clean Sheets (goalkeepers)	4	13
Yellow Cards	31	37
Red Cards	3	2
Full Internationals	2	3

Age/Height

Plymouth Argyle Age: ● **27 yrs, 8 mo**   Derby County Age: ● **26 yrs, 7 mo**

Plymouth Argyle Height: ● **5'11"**   Derby County Height: ● **5'11"**

Match Statistics

League Table after Fixture

		Played	Won	Drawn	Lost	For	Against	Pts
↑ 6	Derby	3	1	2	0	4	2	5
↓ 7	Crewe	3	1	2	0	5	4	5
↓ 8	Watford	3	1	1	1	7	6	4
↑ 9	Leeds	3	1	1	1	3	3	4
↑ 10	Southampton	3	1	1	1	3	3	4
● 11	Ipswich	3	1	1	1	2	2	4
● 12	Leicester	3	1	1	1	5	6	4
↓ 13	Plymouth	3	1	1	1	5	6	4
↑ 14	Stoke	3	1	1	1	3	4	4

Statistics	● Plymouth	Derby ○
Goals	0	2
Shots on Target	5	7
Shots off Target	8	2
Hit Woodwork	0	0
Possession %	50	50
Corners	8	4
Offsides	2	9
Fouls	17	15
Disciplinary Points	4	12

1-0

Crystal Palace ○
Plymouth Argyle ○

► A free-kick is won at Selhurst Park

Event Line

5 ○ ■	Djordjic	
45 ○ ■	Hall F	
Half time 0-0		
56 ○ ⇄	Gudjonsson > Aljofree	
59 ○ ⇄	Freedman > Andrews	
63 ○ ⊕	Ward / RF / IFK / 6Y	
63 ○ ■	Brevett	
66 ○ ■	McAnuff	
67 ○ ■	Norris	
73 ○ ■	Leigertwood	
79 ○ ⇄	Capaldi > Djordjic	
84 ○ ⇄	Taylor > Mendes	
89 ○ ⇄	Butterfield > Soares	
90 ○ ■	Ward	
90 ○ ⇄	Riihilahti > Watson	
Full time 1-0		

Concentration is apparently the watchword of Arsene Wenger, and, if it is good enough for the Arsenal manager, it ought to be good enough for Argyle.

One piece of dopiness, that perhaps lasted a fraction of second, allowed Palace centre-back Darren Ward the half-chance from which he scored the only goal of a closely-fought, otherwise even, encounter.

England international Andy Johnson had the two best openings of a tight opening period. Firstly, his near post flick could only find the side netting, before Romain Larrieu denied another effort with a low save to his left.

Palace opened the scoring just after the hour mark through Darren Ward, brother of a certain Elliott Ward, who would soon become a familiar face to the Green Army.

The big defender volleyed the ball home from a tight angle to break Argyle's dogged resistance, although he did appear to be in an offside position.

Player of the Match	Quote	Championship Milestone
32 Bojan Djordjic	🔵 **Bobby Williamson**	► **Debut**
Did not get many opportunities to shine last season, but it was he, more than any, who caught the eye at Selhurst Park.	I'm disappointed we never came away with anything, that's for sure. Palace never really caused us too many problems.	Nuno Mendes made his Championship debut.

Venue:	Selhurst Park	Referee:	P.Walton - 05/06	Crystal Palace
Attendance:	18,781	Matches:	1	Plymouth Argyle
Capacity:	26,309	Yellow Cards:	3	
Occupancy:	71%	Red Cards:	0	

Form Coming into Fixture

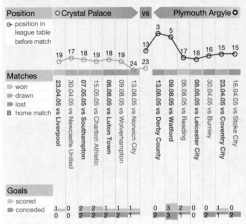

Position ○ Crystal Palace vs Plymouth Argyle ○
⊙ position in league table before match

19 17 18 19 18 19 24 23 / 13 3 5 17 18 16 15 15

Matches
▶ won
▶ drawn
▶ lost
B home match

Crystal Palace matches:
23.04.05 vs Liverpool
30.04.05 vs Newcastle United
07.05.05 vs Southampton
15.05.05 vs Charlton Athletic
06.08.05 vs Luton Town
09.08.05 vs Wolverhampton
13.08.05 vs Norwich City

Plymouth Argyle matches:
13.08.05 vs Derby County
09.08.05 vs Watford
06.08.05 vs Reading
08.05.05 vs Leicester City
30.04.05 vs Burnley
23.04.05 vs Coventry City
16.04.05 vs Stoke City

Goals
▶ scored   1 0 2 2 1 1 / 0 3 2 0 0 1 0
▶ conceded   0 0 2 2 2 2 1 / 2 3 1 0 2 1 2

Goal Statistics

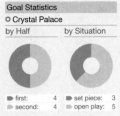

○ Crystal Palace

by Half		by Situation	
▶ first:	4	▶ set piece:	3
▶ second:	4	▶ open play:	5

● Plymouth Argyle

by Half		by Situation	
▶ first:	4	▶ set piece:	3
▶ second:	2	▶ open play:	3

Goals by Area

○ Crystal Palace
Scored (Conceded)
1 (5)
6 (4)
1 (0)

● Plymouth Argyle
Scored (Conceded)
1 (2)
4 (6)
1 (3)

Team Statistics

Starting Line-Ups

Crystal Palace: Kiraly; Borrowdale, McAnuff, Ward, Leigertwood, Hall F, Watson Riihilahti, Andrews Freedman, Johnson, Boyce, Soares Butterfield
4/4/2
Unused Sub: Speroni, Hughes

Plymouth Argyle: Larrieu; Norris, Barness, Wotton, Doumbe, Evans, Buzsaky, Aljofree Gudjonsson, Mendes Taylor, Djordjic Capaldi, Brevett
4/5/1
Unused Sub: McCormick, Connolly

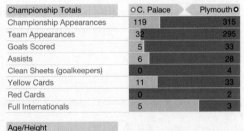

Championship Totals

Championship Totals	○ C. Palace	Plymouth ●
Championship Appearances	119	315
Team Appearances	32	295
Goals Scored	5	33
Assists	6	28
Clean Sheets (goalkeepers)	0	4
Yellow Cards	11	33
Red Cards	0	2
Full Internationals	5	3

Age/Height

Crystal Palace Age
▶ 25 yrs, 1 mo

Plymouth Argyle Age
▶ 27 yrs, 11 mo

Crystal Palace Height
▶ 6'

Plymouth Argyle Height
▶ 5'11"

Match Statistics

League Table after Fixture

		Played	Won	Drawn	Lost	For	Against	Pts
↑	16 Crystal Palace	4	1	1	2	4	5	4
↓	17 Plymouth	4	1	1	2	5	7	4
↓	18 Preston	4	1	1	2	4	7	4
↓	19 Burnley	4	1	0	3	7	7	3
↓	20 Norwich	4	0	3	1	3	4	3
↓	21 Cardiff	4	1	0	3	4	7	3
↓	22 Sheff Wed	4	0	2	2	2	4	2
↓	23 Brighton	4	0	2	2	3	7	2
●	24 Millwall	4	0	1	3	1	8	1

Statistics

Statistics	○ C. Palace	Plymouth ●
Goals	1	0
Shots on Target	10	2
Shots off Target	5	8
Hit Woodwork	0	0
Possession %	63	37
Corners	7	6
Offsides	5	2
Fouls	19	13
Disciplinary Points	16	12

2-1

Plymouth Argyle ○
Peterborough United ○

➡ Paul Wotton fires home from the spot

Event Line

20 ○ ⇄	Benjamin > Quinn	
22 ○ ⊕	Plummer / LF / C / IA	
	Assist: Arber	
35 ○ ⊕	Wotton / RF / P / IA	
	Assist: Norris	
38 ○ ⊕	Taylor / RF / C / IA	
	Assist: Buzsaky	

Half time 2-1

46 ○ ⇄	Logan > Farrell	
76 ○ ⇄	Capaldi > Evans	
83 ○ ⇄	Semple > Day	
83 ○ ⇄	Lasley > Buzsaky	
84 ○ ▯	Logan	

Full time 2-1

Anyone younger than a teenager will not have experienced what happened on a summer evening at Home Park – Argyle progressed to the second stage of the League Cup.

Five managers, countless players and a chairman have come and gone, two relegations have been suffered and two promotions gained, since Pilgrims' fans last had an interest in any draw other than the first round.

The League Two side scored the first goal with a thunderous left-foot volley from Chris Plummer after the ball had rebounded off the Argyle crossbar following a Mark Arber header.

The Pilgrims were behind for 13 minutes before David Norris was felled by a clumsy challenge from David Farrell. Paul Wotton fired the penalty into the bottom right corner to restore parity.

Three minutes later, and Argyle took the lead. Scott Taylor latched onto an ambitious effort from Akos Buzsaky to wander clear of the Posh defence, and slip the ball under the advancing Mark Tyler in the Peterborough goal.

Venue:	Home Park	Referee:	P.Melin - 05/06
Attendance:	5,974	Matches:	2
Capacity:	20,922	Yellow Cards:	6
Occupancy:	29%	Red Cards:	1

Plymouth Argyle
Peterborough United

▶ Mathias Doumbe takes no prisoners

Match Statistics

Starting Line-Ups

▶ **4/4/2**   ▶ **5/4/1**

Unused Sub: Debbage, Gudjonsson, Zebroski

Unused Sub: Harrison, Boucaud

Statistics	○ Plymouth	Peterborough ○
Goals	2	1
Shots on Target	7	2
Shots off Target	5	2
Hit Woodwork	0	1
Possession %	45	55
Corners	8	7
Offsides	7	6
Fouls	12	13
Disciplinary Points	0	4

Age/Height

Plymouth Argyle Age
▶ **26 yrs, 4 mo**

Peterborough United Age
▶ **26 yrs, 3 mo**

Plymouth Argyle Height
▶ **5'11"**

Peterborough United Height
▶ **6'**

Player of the Match

7 David Norris

Five matches into the campaign and the overwhelming eventual choice as player of the season makes his first impact.

Quote

❝ **Bobby Williamson**

I think we can play better than that. Lots of times we gave the ball away needlessly. We're pleased to be through, though.

0-1

Plymouth Argyle ○
Hull City ○

▶ Rufus Brevett demonstrates his defensive qualities

Event Line

25 ○ ◼	West	
29 ○ ◼	Brevett	
29 ○ ◼	Joseph	
	Violent Conduct	
42 ○ ◼	Evans	
Half time 0-0		
46 ○ ⇄	France > Barmby	
46 ○ ⇄	Welsh > Price	
51 ○ ◼	Fagan	
55 ○ ◼	Myhill	
58 ○ ⊕	Elliott / LF / OP / OA	
	Assist: Fagan	
63 ○ ⇄	Buzsaky > Evans	
63 ○ ⇄	Zebroski > Gudjonsson	
75 ○ ◼	Taylor	
80 ○ ⇄	McPhee > Fagan	
81 ○ ⇄	Connolly > Brevett	
Full time 0-1		

The return of Taribo West failed to inspire Argyle to a first home Championship victory of the season, despite the Pilgrims playing two-thirds of the game against opponents with only ten men.

Nigerian international West saw a brilliant individual goal by Northern Ireland international Stuart Elliott take the three points for Hull after the debutant had been stranded out of position upfield. Otherwise, it has to be said, he was the towering figure that many expected him to be.

After Elliott's 30-yard chip, Hull staged a magnificent rearguard action to preserve a victory achieved without defender Marc Joseph, who was sent off before the half-hour for clothes-lining Bojan Djordjic.

Argyle's lack of penetration was frustrating, not least of all to some sections of supporters, who raised their objections volubly in the time-honoured way.

Player of the Match

7 David Norris

Only the sun shone on an otherwise dull afternoon in which he just shaded the honours.

Quote

👋 **Bobby Williamson**

It's not good enough. It's very, very disappointing. This is the lowest I have felt for a long time, and I feel for the fans.

Championship Milestone

▶ **Debut**

Both Taribo West and Chris Zebroski made their Championship debuts.

Venue:	Home Park	Referee:	A.P.D'Urso - 05/06

Attendance: 12,329
Capacity: 20,922
Occupancy: 59%

Matches: 2
Yellow Cards: 2
Red Cards: 1

Plymouth Argyle
Hull City

Form Coming into Fixture

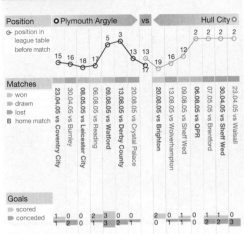

Position
G- position in league table before match

O Plymouth Argyle vs Hull City O

15 16 18 17 5 3 13 13 17 19 16 12 2 2 2 2

Matches
▶ won
▶ drawn
▶ lost
B home match

23.04.05 vs Coventry City
30.04.05 vs Burnley
08.05.05 vs Leicester City
06.08.05 vs Reading
09.08.05 vs Watford
13.08.05 vs Derby County
20.08.05 vs Crystal Palace
20.08.05 vs Brighton
13.08.05 vs Wolverhampton
09.08.05 vs Sheff Wed
06.08.05 vs QPR
07.05.05 vs Brentford
30.04.05 vs Sheff Wed
23.04.05 vs Walsall

Goals
▶ scored
▶ conceded

	scored												
	1	0	0	2	3	0	0		2	0	1	0	1	1	0
conceded	1	2	0	1	3	2	1	0	1	1	0	2	2	3

▶ There is no shortage of commitment on display at Home Park

Team Statistics

Starting Line-Ups

Brevett Djordjic
Connolly

Price
Welsh

Joseph

Larrieu

Doumbe Norris

Evans
Buzsaky

Barmby
France

Ashbee

Coles

Myhill

West Wotton

Taylor

Fagan
McPhee

Woodhouse

Delaney

Barness Gudjonsson
Zebroski

Elliott

Dawson

▶ **4/4/2**   ▶ 4/4/2

Unused Sub: McCormick, Mendes   Unused Sub: Leite, Green

Championship Totals	O Plymouth	Hull O
Championship Appearances	294	39
Team Appearances	274	39
Goals Scored	29	2
Assists	26	3
Clean Sheets (goalkeepers)	4	2
Yellow Cards	34	3
Red Cards	3	0
Full Internationals	3	2

Age/Height

Plymouth Argyle Age
▶ **27 yrs, 5 mo**

Hull City Age
▶ **25 yrs, 9 mo**

Plymouth Argyle Height
▶ **5'11"**

Hull City Height
▶ **5'11"**

Match Statistics

League Table after Fixture

	Played	Won	Drawn	Lost	For	Against	Pts
↑ 9 Hull	5	2	2	1	4	2	8
...	...	...	...	...	...	...	...
↑ 18 Burnley	5	1	1	3	9	9	4
↑ 19 Cardiff	5	1	1	3	6	9	4
↓ 20 Plymouth	5	1	1	3	5	8	4
↓ 21 Norwich	5	0	3	2	3	5	3
↓ 22 Sheff Wed	5	0	3	2	2	4	3
● 23 Brighton	5	0	3	2	3	7	3
● 24 Millwall	5	0	1	4	2	10	1

Statistics	O Plymouth	Hull O
Goals	0	1
Shots on Target	1	5
Shots off Target	13	5
Hit Woodwork	0	0
Possession %	58	42
Corners	6	2
Offsides	2	4
Fouls	21	16
Disciplinary Points	16	20

2-0

Brighton & Hove Albion ○
Plymouth Argyle ○

Championship
29.08.05

▶ Taribo West takes a watching brief

Event Line

11 ○ ⊕ Robinson / LF / OP / IA	
Assist: Knight	
Half time 1-0	
46 ○ ⊕ Carpenter / RF / OP / OA	
48 ○ ⇄ Taylor > Mendes	
75 ○ ▮ Robinson	
78 ○ ⇄ Gudjonsson > Djordjic	
78 ○ ⇄ Kazim-Richards > Jarrett	
79 ○ ⇄ Zebroski > Buzsaky	
86 ○ ▮ Wotton	
88 ○ ⇄ Cox > Robinson	
Full time 2-0	

Brighton on a sunny autumn Bank Holiday Monday afternoon is generally regarded as a pleasant place to be.

However, for Argyle manager Bobby Williamson, his underachieving team, and the 500 or so members of the Green Army that had forsaken the beaches of Cornwall and Devon, the visit to leafy Withdean was nothing short of torture.

Jake Robinson scored the first goal on 11 minutes after out-pacing Taribo West and slotting a low shot past the advancing Romain Larrieu into the far corner.

Mat Doumbe had Argyle's best chance of the first half, but he somehow headed over from five yards out, summing up a bleak day for the Pilgrims.

Richard Carpenter completed the misery at the start of the second half with a fantastic drive from 25 yards, which rocketed into the top left-hand corner.

Player of the Match

1 Romain Larrieu

If 'no-one' is not an option, then he at least kept the score down.

Quote

💬 **Bobby Williamson**

We've got to keep believing and trying hard; if we keep trying hard, we shouldn't be too far away. We are all in this together.

34

Venue:	Withdean Stadium	Referee:	D.J.Gallagher - 05/06		**Brighton & Hove Albion**
Attendance:	6,238	Matches:	5		**Plymouth Argyle**
Capacity:	7,999	Yellow Cards:	12		
Occupancy:	78%	Red Cards:	2		

Form Coming into Fixture

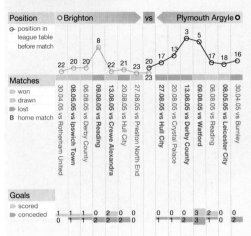

Position	○ Brighton	vs	Plymouth Argyle ●

position in league table before match

Matches
- won
- drawn
- lost
- B home match

Goals
- scored
- conceded

Goal Statistics

○ Brighton & Hove Albion

by Half | by Situation

- first: 4
- second: 1
- set piece: 3
- open play: 1
- own goals: 1

● Plymouth Argyle

by Half | by Situation

- first: 4
- second: 1
- set piece: 3
- open play: 2

Goals by Area

○ Brighton & Hove Albion

Scored (Conceded)

- 4 (2)
- 1 (4)
- 0 (2)

● Plymouth Argyle

Scored (Conceded)

- 1 (2)
- 3 (5)
- 1 (3)

Team Statistics

Starting Line-Ups

Reid — Jarrett (Kazim-Richards) — Buzsaky (Zebroski) — Barness — Wotton — Butters — Hammond — Knight — Doumbe — Henderson — Evans — Norris — Larrieu — Robinson (Cox) — McShane — Carpenter — West — Hart — Carole — Djordjic (Gudjonsson) — Brevett — Mendes (Taylor)

4/4/2 | **4/5/1**

Unused Sub: Chaigneau, Oatway, Nicolas

Unused Sub: McCormick, Connolly

Championship Totals	○ Brighton	Plymouth ●
Championship Appearances	271	288
Team Appearances	271	268
Goals Scored	22	29
Assists	19	23
Clean Sheets (goalkeepers)	1	4
Yellow Cards	27	34
Red Cards	2	2
Full Internationals	0	3

Age/Height

Brighton & Hove Albion Age: **23 yrs, 11 mo**

Plymouth Argyle Age: **27 yrs, 11 mo**

Brighton & Hove Albion Height: **5'10"**

Plymouth Argyle Height: **5'11"**

Match Statistics

League Table after Fixture

		Played	Won	Drawn	Lost	For	Against	Pts
↑	16 Brighton	6	1	3	2	5	7	6
↓	17 Crewe	6	1	3	2	8	11	6
↓	18 Leicester	6	1	3	2	8	11	6
↓	19 Burnley	6	1	1	4	10	11	4
↓	20 Cardiff	5	1	1	3	6	9	4
↓	21 Plymouth	6	1	1	4	5	10	4
●	22 Sheff Wed	5	0	3	2	2	4	3
↓	23 Norwich	6	0	3	3	4	8	3
●	24 Millwall	6	0	1	5	3	12	1

Statistics	○ Brighton	Plymouth ●
Goals	2	0
Shots on Target	10	5
Shots off Target	7	7
Hit Woodwork	0	0
Possession %	54	46
Corners	10	3
Offsides	11	2
Fouls	17	14
Disciplinary Points	4	4

2-0

Norwich City ○
Plymouth Argyle ○

▶ Nick Chadwick rises highest

Event Line

20 ○ ⊕	Doumbe / LF / OG / 6Y
	Assist: McVeigh
37 ○ ⊕	Ashton / RF / OP / 6Y
	Assist: Colin
45 ○ ■	Colin
45 ○ ■	Evans
Half time 2-0	
73 ○ ⇄	Lisbie > McVeigh
74 ○ ⇄	Derbyshire > Chadwick
76 ○ ⇄	Capaldi > Brevett
83 ○ ⇄	Henderson > Marney
83 ○ ⇄	Buzsaky > Djordjic
Full time 2-0	

Argyle's first post-Bobby Williamson outing was decided by an unfortunate own goal by Mathias Kouo-Doumbe and a strike from Dean Ashton, who appeared to come from an offside position.

There was much to admire in a battling performance from a team in a different financial league to Norwich and, up until a few games ago, in a different league altogether.

The first goal came after Paul McVeigh made a surging run down the right-wing and hit a low shot that was half-blocked by Romain Larrieu, and the ball bounced into the path of Kouo-Doumbe, who appeared to try to take the pace off it as a precursor to clearing, but succeeded only in helping it into the goal.

Dean Ashton got the decisive second goal on 37 minutes with a close-range volley after a deep cross from the right by Jurgen Colin, although his muted celebrations suggested that even Ashton knew it should not have counted.

Player of the Match	Quote	Championship Milestone
32 Bojan Djordjic	❝ **Jocky Scott**	▶ **Debut**
He kept Tony Capaldi on the bench at the end of a week in which the Northern Irish international had helped his country beat England.	Two bad errors have cost us the game. You just shouldn't concede goals like that at this level.	Matt Derbyshire made his Championship debut.

Venue:	Carrow Road	Referee:	B.Knight - 05/06	Norwich City
Attendance:	23,981	Matches:	3	Plymouth Argyle
Capacity:	27,470	Yellow Cards:	8	
Occupancy:	87%	Red Cards:	1	

Form Coming into Fixture

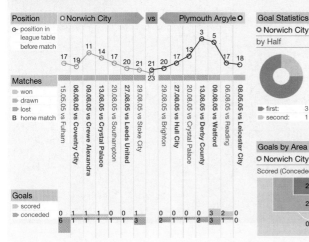

Position ○ Norwich City vs Plymouth Argyle ○

- ○ position in league table before match

Norwich City: 17, 19, 11, 14, 17, 20, 21, 21, 23, 20
Plymouth Argyle: 17, 13, 3, 5, 17, 18

Matches
- won
- drawn
- lost
- B home match

15.05.05 vs Fulham
06.08.05 vs Coventry City
09.08.05 vs Crewe Alexandra
13.08.05 vs Crystal Palace
20.08.05 vs Southampton
27.08.05 vs Leeds United
29.08.05 vs Stoke City
29.08.05 vs Brighton
27.08.05 vs Hull City
20.08.05 vs Crystal Palace
13.08.05 vs Derby County
09.08.05 vs Watford
06.08.05 vs Reading
08.05.05 vs Leicester City

Goals
- scored
- conceded

| 0 | 1 | 1 | 0 | 0 | 1 | | 0 | 0 | 0 | 3 | 2 | 0 |
| 6 | 1 | 1 | 1 | 1 | 3 | | 2 | 1 | 2 | 3 | 1 | 0 |

Goal Statistics

○ **Norwich City**

by Half	by Situation
first: 3	set piece: 1
second: 1	open play: 3

○ **Plymouth Argyle**

by Half	by Situation
first: 4	set piece: 3
second: 1	open play: 2

Goals by Area

○ **Norwich City**
Scored (Conceded)

| 2 (3) |
| 2 (9) |
| 0 (2) |

○ **Plymouth Argyle**
Scored (Conceded)

| 1 (2) |
| 3 (4) |
| 1 (4) |

Team Statistics

Starting Line-Ups

Norwich City:
Green
Drury, Brennan
Shackell, Hughes
Ashton, Chadwick Derbyshire
McVeigh Lisbie, Evans
Fleming, Safri
Colin, Marney Henderson

Plymouth Argyle:
Larrieu
Barness
Norris, Doumbe
Wotton, West
Djordjic Buzsaky
Brevett Capaldi
Aljofree

▶ **4/4/2**   ▶ **5/3/2**

Unused Sub: Gallacher, Doherty, Jarrett

Unused Sub: McCormick, Gudjonsson

Championship Totals	○ Norwich	Plymouth ○
Championship Appearances	118	318
Team Appearances	50	308
Goals Scored	21	32
Assists	16	24
Clean Sheets (goalkeepers)	0	4
Yellow Cards	7	39
Red Cards	0	2
Full Internationals	5	4

Age/Height

Norwich City Age	Plymouth Argyle Age
▶ **25 yrs, 11 mo**	▶ **27 yrs, 2 mo**
Norwich City Height	Plymouth Argyle Height
▶ **5'11"**	▶ **5'11"**

Match Statistics

League Table after Fixture

	Played	Won	Drawn	Lost	For	Against	Pts
● 16 Brighton	7	1	4	2	8	10	7
↓ 17 Coventry	7	1	4	2	7	9	7
↑ 18 Norwich	7	1	3	3	6	8	6
↓ 19 Crewe	6	1	3	2	8	11	6
↓ 20 Burnley	7	1	2	4	13	14	5
↓ 21 Cardiff	6	1	2	3	9	12	5
↓ 22 Plymouth	7	1	1	5	5	12	4
↓ 23 Sheff Wed	6	1	0	3	3	6	3
● 24 Millwall	7	0	1	6	4	14	1

Statistics	○ Norwich	Plymouth ○
Goals	2	0
Shots on Target	7	4
Shots off Target	5	6
Hit Woodwork	0	1
Possession %	57	43
Corners	9	7
Offsides	5	0
Fouls	20	17
Disciplinary Points	4	4

1-1

Plymouth Argyle ○
Crewe Alexandra ○

▶ Matt Derbyshire takes on Stephen Foster

Event Line

8 ○ ⊕	Johnson / LF / C / IA
	Assist: Foster
12 ○ ⊕	Taylor / RF / OP / 6Y
	Assist: Derbyshire
34 ○ ⇄	Buzsaky > Barness
39 ○ ⇄	Higdon > Johnson
Half time 1-1	
63 ○	Buzsaky
67 ○	Higdon
74 ○ ⇄	Roberts G > Rivers
76 ○ ⇄	Evans > Chadwick
83 ○	Jones B
89 ○	Brevett
Full time 1-1	

Managerless Argyle ended their five-game goalless streak but were still unable to more than double the single point they had previously earned in three other Championship games at Home Park.

They bounced back immediately after conceding a soft goal to Eddie Johnson in the opening ten minutes, Scott Taylor netting for the second home game in succession.

Johnson gave Crewe the perfect start when he slotted the ball into an unguarded net after a goalmouth scramble had left Romian Larrieu hopelessly out of position.

The Argyle response was immediate, with Taylor's neat volley into the bottom right corner following a weaving run and cross from loan striker Matt Derbyshire.

Hasney Aljofree almost stole a victory for Argyle, but Ross Turnbull, in the Crewe goal, did well to beat away his powerful drive, and a draw was probably a fair result.

Player of the Match	Quote	Championship Milestone
16 Hasney Aljofree	66 **Jocky Scott**	▶ **50**
He defended well, hit the crossbar with a header and had a decent shot blocked by the goalkeeper.	I think we did everything except win the game. The players' commitment was brilliant, their application, their desire to get a result, was brilliant.	Micky Evans made his 50th appearance in the Championship.

Venue:	Home Park	Referee:	S.Tanner - 05/06	Plymouth Argyle
Attendance:	10,460	Matches:	5	Crewe Alexandra
Capacity:	20,922	Yellow Cards:	23	
Occupancy:	50%	Red Cards:	1	

Form Coming into Fixture

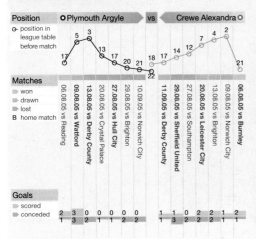

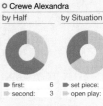

Goal Statistics

O Plymouth Argyle

by Half — first: 4, second: 1
by Situation — set piece: 3, open play: 2

O Crewe Alexandra

by Half — first: 6, second: 3
by Situation — set piece: 3, open play: 6

Goals by Area

O Plymouth Argyle
Scored (Conceded)

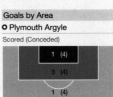

O Crewe Alexandra
Scored (Conceded)

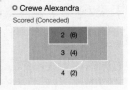

Team Statistics

Starting Line-Ups

▶ 4/3/3   ▶ 4/3/3

Unused Sub: McCormick, Capaldi, Gudjonsson

Unused Sub: Williams B, Walker, Jones S

Championship Totals	O Plymouth	Crewe O
Championship Appearances	311	383
Team Appearances	301	357
Goals Scored	32	40
Assists	21	43
Clean Sheets (goalkeepers)	4	0
Yellow Cards	36	22
Red Cards	2	1
Full Internationals	2	1

Age/Height

Plymouth Argyle Age
▶ **27 yrs, 3 mo**

Crewe Alexandra Age
▶ **23 yrs, 2 mo**

Plymouth Argyle Height
▶ **5'11"**

Crewe Alexandra Height
▶ **5'11"**

Match Statistics

League Table after Fixture

		Played	Won	Drawn	Lost	For	Against	Pts
↑	16 Cardiff	7	2	2	3	10	12	8
↑	17 Crewe	8	1	5	2	10	13	8
↓	18 Coventry	7	1	4	2	7	9	7
↓	19 Brighton	8	1	4	3	8	11	7
●	20 Burnley	8	1	3	4	13	14	6
↓	21 Norwich	8	1	3	4	7	10	6
●	22 Sheff Wed	7	1	3	3	6	6	6
↓	23 Plymouth	8	1	2	5	6	13	5
●	24 Millwall	8	1	1	6	6	15	4

Statistics	O Plymouth	Crewe O
Goals	1	1
Shots on Target	4	3
Shots off Target	13	3
Hit Woodwork	1	0
Possession %	53	47
Corners	10	4
Offsides	3	8
Fouls	13	15
Disciplinary Points	8	8

1-0

Plymouth Argyle ○
Burnley ○

▶ David Norris holds off James O'Connor

Event Line	
31 ○ ■	Doumbe
Half time 0-0	
46 ○ ⊕	Evans / LF / OP / IA
50 ○ ■	Djordjic
51 ○ ■	Brevett
56 ○ ■	Harley
57 ○ ⇄	Branch > Elliott
71 ○ ⇄	Chadwick > Derbyshire
74 ○ ⇄	Barness > Brevett
80 ○ ■	Duff
82 ○ ■	Barness
82 ○ ■	Norris
87 ○ ⇄	Capaldi > Djordjic
Full time 1-0	

A first league win at Home Park since last season; a first Coca-Cola Championship victory since the opening day of the campaign; a first triumph for the man in temporary charge of Argyle's first team – the light at the end of the tunnel was not an oncoming train after all.

Michael Evans' third goal of the season, less than a minute after the start of the second half, divided two teams high on effort and anxiety as the Pilgrims swapped places with their visitors in the Championship relegation zone.

Argyle created the better chances in the opening period, but their reward did not arrive until the first minute of the second half, when Evans unleashed a left-foot half volley into the bottom right corner from the edge of the penalty area.

Player of the Match

4 Taribo West

He will be remembered for much during his short time at Home Park, not all of it on the pitch, but this was his finest hour and a half.

Quote

● Jocky Scott

I told Micky last Monday that he wouldn't be playing against Crewe on Tuesday, that I was saving him for today. He scored the winning goal, which is great.

Venue:	Home Park	Referee:	K.Stroud - 05/06	Plymouth Argyle
Attendance:	11,829	Matches:	7	Burnley
Capacity:	20,922	Yellow Cards:	34	
Occupancy:	57%	Red Cards:	2	

Form Coming into Fixture

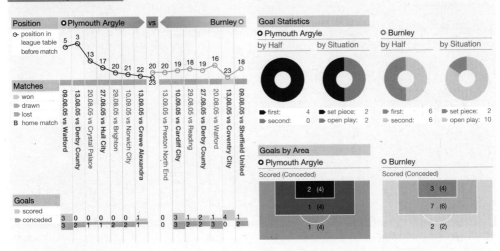

Position

⊖ position in league table before match

Plymouth Argyle vs **Burnley**

5, 3, 13, 17, 20, 21, 22, 20, 20, 19, 18, 19, 16, 23, 18, 23

Matches
- won
- drawn
- lost
- B home match

09.08.05 vs Watford
13.08.05 vs Derby County
20.08.05 vs Crystal Palace
27.08.05 vs Hull City
29.08.05 vs Brighton
10.09.05 vs Norwich City
13.09.05 vs Crewe Alexandra
13.09.05 vs Preston North End
10.09.05 vs Cardiff City
29.08.05 vs Reading
27.08.05 vs Derby County
20.08.05 vs Watford
13.08.05 vs Coventry City
09.08.05 vs Sheffield United

Goals
- scored
- conceded

3	0	0	0	0	0	1		0	3	1	2	1	4	1	
3	2	1	1	2	2	1		0	2	1	2	3	0	2	

Goal Statistics

Plymouth Argyle

by Half
- first: 4
- second: 0

by Situation
- set piece: 2
- open play: 2

Burnley

by Half
- first: 6
- second: 6

by Situation
- set piece: 2
- open play: 10

Goals by Area

Plymouth Argyle
Scored (Conceded)

2 (4)
1 (4)
1 (4)

Burnley
Scored (Conceded)

3 (4)
7 (6)
2 (2)

Team Statistics

Starting Line-Ups

Plymouth Argyle (4/3/3)

Brevett / Barness, Taylor, Djordjic / Capaldi, Aljofree, Larrieu, Akinbiyi, Wotton, Evans, West, Noel-Williams, Norris, Doumbe, Derbyshire / Chadwick

Unused Sub: Buzsaky, Gudjonsson

Burnley (4/4/2)

Elliott / Branch, Duff, O'Connor J, Lowe, Coyne, Hyde, McGreal, Spicer, Harley

Unused Sub: Jensen, Courtney, McCann, Bermingham

Championship Totals	Plymouth	Burnley
Championship Appearances	343	422
Team Appearances	333	288
Goals Scored	35	43
Assists	24	34
Clean Sheets (goalkeepers)	4	9
Yellow Cards	40	52
Red Cards	2	5
Full Internationals	3	4

Age/Height

	Plymouth Argyle	Burnley
Age	27 yrs, 8 mo	27 yrs, 10 mo
Height	5'11"	6'

Match Statistics

League Table after Fixture

		Played	Won	Drawn	Lost	For	Against	Pts
↓	14 Crystal Palace	8	3	1	4	10	9	10
•	15 Leicester	9	2	4	3	10	12	10
↑	16 Coventry	9	1	6	2	10	12	9
↓	17 Hull	9	2	3	4	5	7	9
↑	18 Brighton	9	1	5	3	10	13	8
↓	19 Crewe	9	1	5	3	10	14	8
↑	20 Plymouth	9	2	2	5	7	13	8
↑	21 Millwall	9	2	1	6	8	16	7
↓	22 Burnley	9	1	3	5	13	15	6

Statistics	Plymouth	Burnley
Goals	1	0
Shots on Target	6	8
Shots off Target	4	7
Hit Woodwork	0	0
Possession %	40	60
Corners	6	9
Offsides		12
Fouls	17	18
Disciplinary Points	20	8

2-1

Barnet ○
Plymouth Argyle ○

▶ Keith Lasley tries to make progress

Event Line

12 ○ ⊕ King / LF / C / IA	
19 ○ ⊕ Buzsaky / RF / DFK / OA	
19 ○ ▪ Bailey	
Half time 1-1	
46 ○ ⊕ Grazioli / RF / OP / OA	
Assist: Sinclair	
69 ○ ⇄ Djordjic > Taylor	
78 ○ ⇄ Bowditch > Soares	
81 ○ ⇄ Summerfield > Lasley	
90 ○ ⇄ Norville > Grazioli	
Full time 2-1	

Whoever the new manager was going to be, he could chalk off the Carling Cup from what was probably a longish list of things to worry about.

A switch-off goal by Giuliano Grazioli 21 seconds into the second half, the like of which has blighted the Pilgrims all season, proved the difference between two teams who had swapped stunning first-half strikes – Simon King for the home side and Akos Buzsaky for Argyle.

King opened the scoring with an unstoppable volley from 18 yards out that flew past Argyle goalkeeper Luke McCormick and into the top corner.

Buzsaky's equalizer was equally brilliant. The Hungarian midfielder curled a delicious free-kick into the top corner from 25 yards.

The winner was another exquisite finish, with Grazioli lobbing McCormick after bursting through the middle of an Argyle defence that was, mentally, still in the dressing-room.

The Pilgrims were watched by future manager Tony Pulis, who will have soon realized the size of the task ahead.

▶ Matt Derbyshire is brought crashing to the ground

Match Statistics

Starting Line-Ups

▶ 4/4/2   ▶ 4/3/3

Unused Sub: Flitney, Gross, Roache   Unused Sub: Larrieu, Mendes, Martin

Statistics	○ Barnet	Plymouth ○
Goals	2	1
Shots on Target	5	4
Shots off Target	7	9
Hit Woodwork	0	1
Possession %	50	50
Corners	7	1
Offsides	6	6
Fouls	16	14
Disciplinary Points	4	0

Age/Height

Barnet Age	Plymouth Argyle Age
▶ 24 yrs	▶ 25 yrs
Barnet Height	Plymouth Argyle Height
▶ 5'11"	▶ 5'11"

Player of the Match

8 Akos Buzsaky

The season's nadir had little to redeem it apart from his stunning goal.

Quote

🔵 Jocky Scott

Barnet wanted to win the game more than we did, which is a bad thing to say, but it's true.

43

0-0

Southampton ○
Plymouth Argyle ○

▶ Tony Capaldi shrugs off a challenge

Event Line

24 ○ ▪	Wotton	
Half time 0-0		
59 ○ ▪	Capaldi	
68 ○ ⇄	Jones > Hajto	
68 ○ ⇄	Walcott > Ormerod	
73 ○ ⇄	Taylor > Djordjic	
80 ○ ▪	Gudjonsson	
85 ○ ⇄	Derbyshire > Gudjonsson	
86 ○ ⇄	Cranie > Oakley	
86 ○ ⇄	Buzsaky > Chadwick	
90 ○ ▪	Powell	
Full time 0-0		

Tony Pulis had not had time to add much to Argyle since his appointment the previous Friday morning – a touch of discipline, a tad of organisation, a pinch of self-belief, a modicum of commitment, maybe – but it was enough to inspire Argyle to an unlikely point on their first visit to Southampton for 28 years.

The Pilgrims' players – and their fantastic supporters – deserved nothing less for a whole-hearted performance in which the dreaded long ball was nowhere to be seen.

A goalless draw might not seem the best way to start a new era, but, given the events of the season and the week, it was a momentous point.

Argyle's Green Army were in magnificent voice from the off, reminding Saints' chairman Rupert Lowe that Janners are loyal and have long memories with an early chorus of – no offence, Tony – 'There's Only One Paul Sturrock', which was applauded by Saints' fans, by the way.

Player of the Match	Quote	Championship Milestone
1 Romain Larrieu	🗨 **Tony Pulis**	▶ **50**
In a game of few chances, his save to deny Kamil Kosowski did as much as anything to earn the Pilgrims a point.	I could have avoided this week, and taken over after the week was over, where there's 12 or 13 days left to prepare for the next game, but I wanted to get in the mix straight away.	Paul Wotton made his 50th appearance in the Championship.

Venue:	Friends Provident St	Referee:	A.R.Leake - 05/06	Southampton
Attendance:	26,331	Matches:	9	Plymouth Argyle
Capacity:	32,251	Yellow Cards:	23	
Occupancy:	82%	Red Cards:	2	

Form Coming into Fixture

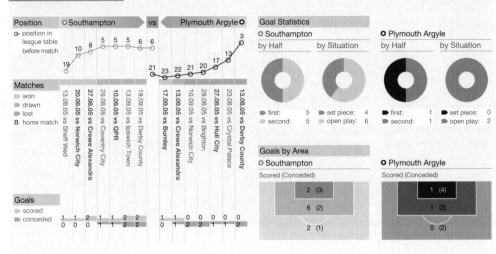

Position ○ Southampton vs Plymouth Argyle ○

position in league table before match

Matches
- won
- drawn
- lost
- B home match

Southampton: 13.08.05 vs Sheff Wed, 20.08.05 vs Norwich City, 27.08.05 vs Crewe Alexandra, 29.08.05 vs Coventry City, 10.09.05 vs QPR, 13.09.05 vs Ipswich Town, 18.09.05 vs Derby County

Plymouth Argyle: 17.09.05 vs Burnley, 13.08.05 vs Crewe Alexandra, 10.09.05 vs Norwich City, 29.08.05 vs Brighton, 27.08.05 vs Hull City, 20.08.05 vs Crystal Palace, 13.08.05 vs Derby County

Goals
- scored
- conceded

Southampton scored: 1 1 2 1 1 2 2
Southampton conceded: 0 0 0 1 1 2 2

Plymouth scored: 1 1 0 0 0 0 0
Plymouth conceded: 0 1 2 2 1 1 2

Goal Statistics

○ Southampton
by Half / by Situation
- first: 5
- second: 5
- set piece: 4
- open play: 6

○ Plymouth Argyle
by Half / by Situation
- first: 1
- second: 1
- set piece: 0
- open play: 2

Goals by Area

○ Southampton — Scored (Conceded)
- 2 (3)
- 6 (2)
- 2 (1)

○ Plymouth Argyle — Scored (Conceded)
- 1 (4)
- 1 (3)
- 0 (2)

Team Statistics

Starting Line-Ups

Southampton: Higginbotham, Kosowski, Powell, Quashie, Ormerod (Walcott), Chadwick (Buzsaky), Niemi, Lundekvam, Wise, Fuller, Evans, Hajto (Jones), Oakley (Cranie)

Plymouth Argyle: Gudjonsson (Derbyshire), Barness, Norris, Doumbe, Larrieu, Wotton, Aljofree, Djordjic (Taylor), Capaldi

Southampton ▶ 4/4/2
Plymouth ▶ 4/4/2

Unused Sub: Smith, Delap
Unused Sub: McCormick, Lasley

Championship Totals	○ Southampton	Plymouth ○
Championship Appearances	153	387
Team Appearances	96	377
Goals Scored	21	36
Assists	13	30
Clean Sheets (goalkeepers)	4	5
Yellow Cards	28	42
Red Cards	2	1
Full Internationals	8	4

Age/Height

Southampton Age ▶ **27 yrs, 9 mo**
Plymouth Argyle Age ▶ **26 yrs, 5 mo**
Southampton Height ▶ **6'**
Plymouth Argyle Height ▶ **5'11"**

Match Statistics

League Table after Fixture

		Played	Won	Drawn	Lost	For	Against	Pts
↓	7 Southampton	10	3	6	1	12	9	15
...	...	...	...	...	...	...	...	...
↓	18 Norwich	10	2	3	5	8	11	9
↓	19 Coventry	10	1	6	3	10	14	9
●	20 Crewe	10	1	6	3	10	14	9
●	21 Plymouth	10	2	3	5	7	13	9
↑	22 Millwall	10	2	2	6	8	16	8
↑	23 Burnley	10	1	4	5	14	16	7
↓	24 Sheff Wed	9	1	4	4	6	10	7

Statistics	○ Southampton	Plymouth ○
Goals	0	0
Shots on Target	2	6
Shots off Target	9	7
Hit Woodwork	0	0
Possession %	52	48
Corners	6	4
Offsides	2	0
Fouls	14	17
Disciplinary Points	4	12

2-0

Sheffield United ○
Plymouth Argyle ○

▶ David Norris is felled by Nick Montgomery

Event Line

10 ○ ⊕	Shipperley / H / OP / IA
	Assist: Ifill
18 ○ ▨	Montgomery
20 ○ ▨	Wotton
30 ○ ▨	Barness
31 ○ ⊕	Quinn A / RF / DFK / OA
	Assist: Quinn A
45 ○ ▨	Shipperley
Half time 2-0	
56 ○ ⇄	Djordjic > Brevett
57 ○ ⇄	Taylor > Chadwick
57 ○ ⇄	Buzsaky > Gudjonsson
64 ○ ⇄	Pericard > Shipperley
69 ○ ⇄	Gillespie > Ifill
73 ○ ▨	Kozluk
78 ○ ⇄	Webber > Kabba
Full time 2-0	

The gap in league position between Neil Warnock's current side and the previous one for which, he admitted in his programme notes, he still has a soft spot proved to represent the gulf in class we all feared it might.

While Argyle could not be faulted for effort, hard work, organisation and sundry other admirable disciplines, they were clearly second best to the then runaway Coca-Cola Championship leaders who registered a tenth win from 11 games with several degrees of comfort.

Shipperley scored the opener on 10 minutes. Romain Larrieu initially blocked his close-range header but the ball bounced down on to the unfortunate Frenchman's foot and squeezed, agonizingly, in to the corner of the net.

Paul Wotton hit the Blades' post, before Anthony Barness clipped the heels of Quinn in such a position to be relieved when referee Graham Laws showed him merely a yellow card, but one which offered Quinn the chance to exact maximum revenge with a right-footed grubber free-kick that left Larrieu with no chance.

Player of the Match	Quote	Championship Milestone
15 Paul Wotton	🗨 **Tony Pulis**	▶ **25**
Playing against his former manager, the captain's blood and guts performance must have impressed his new one.	There's a lot of work to be done – I knew that when I took the job. But there were encouraging signs.	Both Akos Buzsaky and Scott Taylor made their 25th appearances in the Championship.

Venue:	Bramall Lane	Referee:	G.Laws - 05/06	**Sheffield United**
Attendance:	20,111	Matches:	7	**Plymouth Argyle**
Capacity:	30,558	Yellow Cards:	27	
Occupancy:	66%	Red Cards:	1	

Form Coming into Fixture

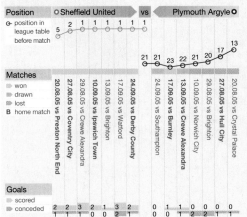

Position

position in league table before match

Sheffield United vs **Plymouth Argyle**

5 2 1 1 1 1 1 1

21 21 23 22 21 20 17 13

Matches
- won
- drawn
- lost
- B home match

Sheffield United matches:
20.08.05 vs Preston North End
27.08.05 vs Coventry City
29.08.05 vs Crewe Alexandra
10.09.05 vs Ipswich Town
13.09.05 vs Brighton
17.09.05 vs Watford
24.09.05 vs Derby County

Plymouth Argyle matches:
24.09.05 vs Southampton
17.09.05 vs Burnley
13.09.05 vs Crewe Alexandra
10.09.05 vs Norwich City
29.08.05 vs Brighton
27.08.05 vs Hull City
20.08.05 vs Crystal Palace

Goals
- scored
- conceded

Sheffield United: 2/1 2/1 3/1 2/0 1/0 3/2 2/1
Plymouth Argyle: 0/0 1/0 1/1 0/2 0/2 0/1 0/1

Goal Statistics

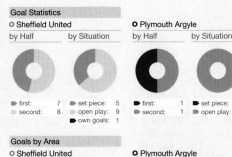

Sheffield United

by Half		by Situation	
first:	7	set piece:	5
second:	8	open play:	9
		own goals:	1

Plymouth Argyle

by Half		by Situation	
first:	1	set piece:	0
second:	1	open play:	2

Goals by Area

Sheffield United

Scored (Conceded)
4 (2)
9 (3)
2 (1)

Plymouth Argyle

Scored (Conceded)
1 (3)
1 (2)
0 (2)

Team Statistics

Starting Line-Ups

Sheffield United:
Unsworth, Quinn A
Morgan, Jagielka, Shipperley (Pericard), Chadwick (Taylor)
Kabba (Webber), Evans
Bromby, Montgomery
Kozluk, Ifill (Gillespie)
Kenny

4/4/2

Unused Sub: Geary, Tonge

Plymouth Argyle:
Gudjonsson, Barness (Buzsaky)
Wotton, Doumbe
Norris, Aljofree
Capaldi, Brevett (Djordjic)
Larrieu

4/4/2

Unused Sub: McCormick, West

Championship Totals

	Sheff Utd	Plymouth
Championship Appearances	476	416
Team Appearances	383	396
Goals Scored	59	37
Assists	45	30
Clean Sheets (goalkeepers)	14	6
Yellow Cards	41	51
Red Cards	5	2
Full Internationals	5	4

Age/Height

Sheffield United Age: **26 yrs, 7 mo**
Plymouth Argyle Age: **27 yrs, 7 mo**
Sheffield United Height: **5'11"**
Plymouth Argyle Height: **5'11"**

Match Statistics

League Table after Fixture

		Played	Won	Drawn	Lost	For	Against	Pts
● 1	Sheff Utd	11	10	0	1	24	10	30
...		...	...	...	...	...	...	...
↑ 18	Burnley	11	2	4	5	17	16	10
↓ 19	Brighton	11	1	7	3	11	14	10
↓ 20	Coventry	10	1	6	3	10	14	9
↓ 21	Crewe	11	1	6	4	10	18	9
● 22	Millwall	11	2	3	6	9	17	9
↓ 23	Plymouth	11	2	3	6	7	15	9
● 24	Sheff Wed	10	1	4	5	6	12	7

Statistics

	Sheff Utd	Plymouth
Goals	2	0
Shots on Target	6	8
Shots off Target	7	3
Hit Woodwork	0	0
Possession %	60	40
Corners	1	5
Offsides	1	1
Fouls	5	11
Disciplinary Points	12	8

2-1

Plymouth Argyle ○
Stoke City ○

▶ The ball hits the back of the Stoke net

Event Line
Half time 0-0
46 ○ ⇄ Sigurdsson > Kolar
47 ○ ⊕ Chadwick / RF / OP / 6Y
Assist: Gallagher
50 ○ ⊕ Russell / LF / OG / 6Y
Assist: Capaldi
53 ○ ⇄ Taylor > Chadwick
53 ○ ⇄ Buzsaky > Gudjonsson
70 ○ ▮ Gallagher
71 ○ ⇄ Dyer > Sidibe
76 ○ ▮ Buxton
77 ○ ⊕ Buzsaky / LF / IFK / IA
86 ○ ⇄ Henry > Chadwick
Full time 2-1

Much has been made of Tony Pulis's attitude towards foreign players.

He was sacked by Stoke last summer for "failing to exploit foreign markets" and even on the eve of his home bow as Argyle manager, ITV's 'The Championship' presenter Gabriel Clarke was questioning him on the subject.

The irony, then, that Argyle's late winner came from Hungarian international Akos Buzsaky, a second-half substitute for former Potter Bjarni Gudjonsson, from Iceland. It was created by a Frenchman, too.

Paul Gallagher had hit the post for Stoke before setting up Luke Chadwick for the first goal. The former Manchester United winger skipped past Larrieu and slotted the ball into the empty net.

The Argyle response was immediate with Darel Russell turning the ball into his own net after an excellent run and cross from Capaldi.

The winner was not too pretty, either. Akos Buzsaky's bobbling left-foot shot somehow trundled through a huge crowd of players to give Pulis his first victory as Argyle manager.

Player of the Match

14 Tony Capaldi

Making only his second home start of the campaign, he turned in the sort of display that ensured his place in the side for the remainder.

Quote

❝ Tony Pulis

We have got to make this place a fortress, but we will need their support. If I've come away with anything from the game, it was that those supporters really stuck behind us.

Venue:	Home Park	Referee:	M.Russell - 05/06		Plymouth Argyle
Attendance:	12,604	Matches:	9		Stoke City
Capacity:	20,922	Yellow Cards:	16		
Occupancy:	60%	Red Cards:	1		

Form Coming into Fixture

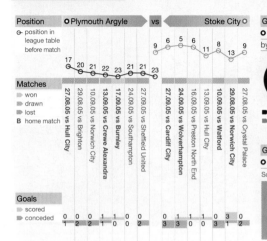

Position

O Plymouth Argyle vs Stoke City O

ϙ- position in league table before match

Stoke City positions: 9, 6, 5, 6, 11, 8, 13, 9
Plymouth positions: 17, 20, 21, 22, 23, 21, 21, 23

Matches
- won
- drawn
- lost
- B home match

Plymouth matches:
27.08.05 vs Hull City
29.08.05 vs Brighton
10.09.05 vs Norwich City
13.09.05 vs Crewe Alexandra
17.09.05 vs Burnley
24.09.05 vs Southampton
27.09.05 vs Sheffield United

Stoke matches:
27.09.05 vs Cardiff City
24.09.05 vs Wolverhampton
16.09.05 vs Preston North End
13.09.05 vs Hull City
10.09.05 vs Watford
29.08.05 vs Norwich City
27.08.05 vs Crystal Palace

Goals
	scored	conceded
Plymouth	0 0 0 1 1 0 0	1 2 2 1 0 0 2
Stoke	0 1 1 1 0 3 0	3 3 0 0 3 1 2

Goal Statistics

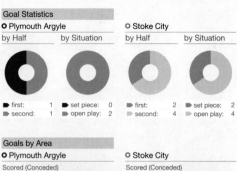

O Plymouth Argyle

by Half / by Situation
- first: 1
- second: 1
- set piece: 0
- open play: 2

O Stoke City

by Half / by Situation
- first: 2
- second: 4
- set piece: 2
- open play: 4

Goals by Area

O Plymouth Argyle
Scored (Conceded)
1 (2)
1 (3)
0 (3)

O Stoke City
Scored (Conceded)
1 (2)
5 (5)
0 (5)

Team Statistics

Starting Line-Ups

Plymouth Argyle:
Larrieu
Brevett, Capaldi
Aljofree, Norris
Evans
Chadwick Taylor, Doumbe, Wotton
Sidibe Dyer
Barness, Gudjonsson Buzsaky

4/4/2

Unused Sub: McCormick, Connolly, Djordjic

Stoke City:
Simonsen
Chadwick Henry, Buxton
Russell, Hoefkens
Gallagher
Junior, Duberry
Kolar Sigurdsson, Broomes

4/4/1/1

Unused Sub: de Goey, Taggart

Championship Totals

	O Plymouth	Stoke O
Championship Appearances	419	386
Team Appearances	399	268
Goals Scored	37	21
Assists	30	26
Clean Sheets (goalkeepers)	6	17
Yellow Cards	51	40
Red Cards	2	4
Full Internationals	4	4

Age/Height

Plymouth Argyle Age	Stoke City Age
27 yrs, 11 mo	**25 yrs, 1 mo**
Plymouth Argyle Height	Stoke City Height
5'11"	**6'**

Match Statistics

League Table after Fixture

	Played	Won	Drawn	Lost	For	Against	Pts
↓ 10 Stoke	12	5	1	6	12	19	16
...	...	...	...	...	...	...	...
↓ 18 Coventry	12	2	6	4	15	18	12
• 19 Leicester	12	2	6	4	12	15	12
↑ 20 Plymouth	12	3	3	6	9	16	12
↓ 21 Brighton	12	1	7	4	12	17	10
↑ 22 Sheff Wed	11	2	4	5	9	14	10
↓ 23 Millwall	12	2	4	6	10	18	10
↓ 24 Crewe	12	1	6	5	11	20	9

Statistics

	O Plymouth	Stoke O
Goals	2	1
Shots on Target	4	4
Shots off Target	4	8
Hit Woodwork	0	0
Possession %	59	41
Corners	1	3
Offsides	2	1
Fouls	8	17
Disciplinary Points	0	8

1-1

Plymouth Argyle ○
Sheffield Wednesday ○

Championship
15.10.05

▶ Paul Wotton keeps Craig Rocastle at bay

Event Line

18 ○ ▇	Connolly	
24 ○ ⊕	Buzsaky / H / OG / IA	
	Assist: Peacock	
25 ○ ▇	Coughlan	
33 ○ ▇	Rocastle	
43 ○ ▇	Whelan	
45 ○ ▇	Hills	

Half time 0-1

46 ○ ⇄	O'Brien > Whelan	
57 ○ ⇄	Djordjic > Brevett	
59 ○ ▇	Djordjic	
63 ○ ⇄	Taylor > Chadwick	
67 ○ ⇄	Bullen > Graham	
75 ○ ▇	Lee	
79 ○ ⊕	Wotton / RF / P / IA	
	Assist: Norris	
80 ○ ⇄	Gudjonsson > Buzsaky	
84 ○ ⇄	Wood > Brunt	

Full time 1-1

Paul Wotton, the man who admitted in his autobiography that he owes his career to Paul Sturrock, bit his mentor in the bum, as the man himself would have said, by firing home the penalty that won the Pilgrims a deserved point.

Wotton converted ten minutes from the end of a sometimes emotional, often frustrating game in which both sides struggled to give an impression that they will finish this season too far clear of the danger area.

Sturrock's current side took the lead in remarkable fashion midway through the first half when Hungarian midfielder Akos Buzsaky headed Lee Peacock's cross into his own net under no pressure whatsoever.

It was a truly bizarre goal, and the Hungarian will have been very grateful when his skipper came to the, belated, rescue.

Buzsaky hit the post and Chadwick hit the bar for the Pilgrims, before Wotton smashed home the equalizer from the penalty spot after Norris had been felled by Frankie Simek.

Player of the Match

14 Tony Capaldi

It would have been Buzsaky, if not for the oggie – instead, Tony Capaldi again grabbed the attention.

Quote

❝ Tony Pulis

We are fighting and scrapping and they are fighting and scrapping so it was never going to be a pretty game, but we are disappointed we didn't win it.

Venue:	Home Park	Referee:	I.Williamson - 05/06		Plymouth Argyle
Attendance:	16,534	Matches:	11		Sheffield Wednesday
Capacity:	20,922	Yellow Cards:	36		
Occupancy:	79%	Red Cards:	3		

Form Coming into Fixture

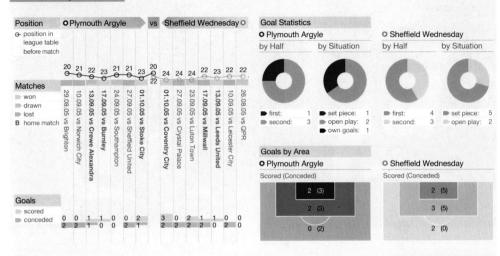

Goal Statistics

Plymouth Argyle

by Half — first: 1, second: 3

by Situation — set piece: 1, open play: 2, own goals: 1

Sheffield Wednesday

by Half — first: 4, second: 3

by Situation — set piece: 5, open play: 2

Goals by Area

Plymouth Argyle — Scored (Conceded)

2 (3) / 2 (3) / 0 (2)

Sheffield Wednesday — Scored (Conceded)

2 (5) / 3 (5) / 2 (0)

Team Statistics

Starting Line-Ups

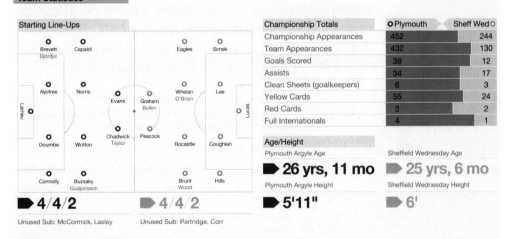

Unused Sub: McCormick, Lasley

Unused Sub: Partridge, Corr

4/4/2   4/4/2

Championship Totals	Plymouth	Sheff Wed
Championship Appearances	452	244
Team Appearances	432	130
Goals Scored	38	12
Assists	34	17
Clean Sheets (goalkeepers)	6	3
Yellow Cards	55	24
Red Cards	3	2
Full Internationals	4	1

Age/Height

Plymouth Argyle Age: **26 yrs, 11 mo**

Sheffield Wednesday Age: **25 yrs, 6 mo**

Plymouth Argyle Height: **5'11"**

Sheffield Wednesday Height: **6'**

Match Statistics

League Table after Fixture

	Played	Won	Drawn	Lost	For	Against	Pts
↓ 14 Stoke	13	5	1	7	13	21	16
↑ 15 Leicester	13	3	6	4	14	16	15
↓ 16 Preston	13	3	6	4	13	15	15
● 17 Hull	13	3	5	5	10	11	14
↓ 18 Burnley	13	3	4	6	19	18	13
↑ 19 Plymouth	13	3	4	6	10	17	13
↓ 20 Coventry	13	2	6	5	16	22	12
↑ 21 Crewe	13	2	6	5	14	21	12
● 22 Sheff Wed	12	2	5	5	10	15	11

Statistics	Plymouth	Sheff Wed
Goals	1	1
Shots on Target	8	4
Shots off Target	4	6
Hit Woodwork	1	0
Possession %	57	43
Corners	6	4
Offsides	2	4
Fouls	11	28
Disciplinary Points	8	20

1-1

Queens Park Rangers o
Plymouth Argyle o

▶ Akos Buzsaky celebrates opening the scoring

Event Line

22 ○ ■	Doherty
39 ○ ⊕	Buzsaky / RF / OP / OA
	Assist: Wotton
Half time 0-1	
56 ○ ■	Furlong
63 ○ ⇄	Ainsworth > Doherty
68 ○ ■	Taylor
69 ○ ⊕	Gallen / RF / P / IA
69 ○ ⇄	Chadwick > Djordjic
80 ○ ⇄	Sturridge > Furlong
80 ○ ⇄	Gudjonsson > Taylor
86 ○ ⇄	Brevett > Buzsaky
90 ○ ⇄	Santos > Cook
Full time 1-1	

Argyle's improved away form under Tony Pulis continued down at Shepherd's Bush on Tuesday night as a thoroughly disciplined defensive display yielded a point at one of the Pilgrims' historically least happy hunting-grounds.

A ripper of a 30-yard shot from magnificent Magyar Akos Buzsaky six minutes from half-time gave Argyle an ascendancy against familiar rivals which was cancelled out by Rangers' captain Kevin Gallen's penalty midway through the second half.

Paul Wotton fed Buzsaky in midfield and the Hungarian unleashed a stunning 30-yard strike beyond the reach of QPR goalkeeper Simon Royce, and into the far corner of the net – a serious favourite for goal of the season.

An unfortunate handball by Scott Taylor enabled Kevin Gallen to smash home the equalizer from the penalty spot and earn the London side a point.

Player of the Match

8 Akos Buzsaky

No oggie, so nothing to detract from a splendid performance and goal.

Quote

🎙 Tony Pulis

We got the goal – a smashing goal – and I thought, in the second half, we got more nervous about the position we were in and dropped deeper and deeper.

Championship Milestone

▶ 25

Bjarni Gudjonsson made his 25th appearance in the Championship for Plymouth.

Venue:	Loftus Road	Referee:	M.D.Messias - 05/06	Queens Park Rangers
Attendance:	11,741	Matches:	5	Plymouth Argyle
Capacity:	18,500	Yellow Cards:	27	
Occupancy:	63%	Red Cards:	2	

Form Coming into Fixture

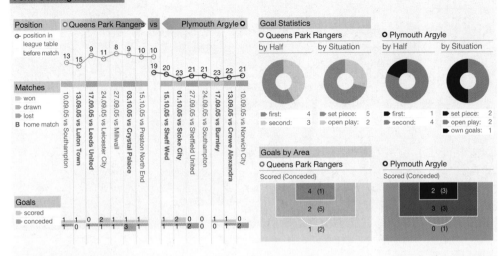

Position ○ Queens Park Rangers vs Plymouth Argyle ○

⊙ position in league table before match

Queens Park Rangers: 13 15 9 11 8 9 10 10

Plymouth Argyle: 19 20 23 21 21 23 22 21

Matches
- ▶ won
- ▶ drawn
- ▶ lost
- B home match

Queens Park Rangers fixtures:
- 10.09.05 vs Southampton
- 13.09.05 vs Luton Town
- 17.09.05 vs Leeds United
- 24.09.05 vs Leicester City
- 27.09.05 vs Millwall
- 03.10.05 vs Crystal Palace
- 15.10.05 vs Preston North End

Plymouth Argyle fixtures:
- 15.10.05 vs Sheff Wed
- 01.10.05 vs Stoke City
- 27.09.05 vs Sheffield United
- 24.09.05 vs Southampton
- 17.09.05 vs Burnley
- 13.09.05 vs Crewe Alexandra
- 10.09.05 vs Norwich City

Goals
- ▶ scored
- ▶ conceded

QPR scored: 1 1 0 2 1 1 1
QPR conceded: 1 0 1 1 3 1

Plymouth scored: 1 2 0 0 1 0
Plymouth conceded: 1 1 2 0 1 2

Goal Statistics

○ Queens Park Rangers

by Half | by Situation
- ▶ first: 4
- ▶ second: 3
- ▶ set piece: 5
- ▶ open play: 2

○ Plymouth Argyle

by Half | by Situation
- ▶ first: 1
- ▶ second: 4
- ▶ set piece: 2
- ▶ open play: 2
- ▶ own goals: 1

Goals by Area

○ Queens Park Rangers

Scored (Conceded)
- 4 (1)
- 2 (5)
- 1 (2)

○ Plymouth Argyle

Scored (Conceded)
- 2 (3)
- 3 (3)
- 0 (1)

Team Statistics

Starting Line-Ups

Queens Park Rangers:
- Royce
- Dyer, Cook Santos, Evatt, Doherty Ainsworth
- Furlong Sturridge, Taylor Gudjonsson, Nygaard, Evans
- Shittu, Bircham
- Bignot, Gallen

▶ 4 / 4 / 2

Unused Sub: Langley, Moore

Plymouth Argyle:
- Larrieu
- Buzsaky Brevett, Connolly, Wotton, Doumbe
- Norris, Aljofree
- Djordjic Chadwick, Capaldi

▶ 4 / 4 / 2

Unused Sub: McCormick, Derbyshire

Championship Totals	○QPR	Plymouth○
Championship Appearances	465	466
Team Appearances	448	446
Goals Scored	53	39
Assists	46	35
Clean Sheets (goalkeepers)	9	6
Yellow Cards	71	57
Red Cards	5	3
Full Internationals	5	4

Age/Height

Queens Park Rangers Age
▶ 29 yrs, 4 mo

Plymouth Argyle Age
▶ 26 yrs, 11 mo

Queens Park Rangers Height
▶ 6'

Plymouth Argyle Height
▶ 5'11"

Match Statistics

League Table after Fixture

	Played	Won	Drawn	Lost	For	Against	Pts
↓ 11 QPR	14	4	6	4	13	17	18
↓ 12 Ipswich	14	5	3	6	14	21	18
↓ 13 Derby	14	3	8	3	19	19	17
↑ 14 Burnley	14	4	4	6	20	18	16
↓ 15 Norwich	14	4	4	6	16	18	16
● 16 Preston	14	3	7	4	15	17	16
● 17 Hull	14	3	6	5	11	12	15
↓ 18 Leicester	14	3	6	5	14	17	15
● 19 Plymouth	14	3	5	6	11	18	14

Statistics	○QPR	Plymouth○
Goals	1	1
Shots on Target	4	3
Shots off Target	5	0
Hit Woodwork	0	0
Possession %	52	48
Corners	11	2
Offsides	3	2
Fouls	18	13
Disciplinary Points	8	4

1-1 Luton Town ○
Plymouth Argyle ○

▶ Bojan Djordjic pops up with a late leveller

Event Line
Half time 0-0

55 ○ ⇄	Foley > Morgan	
57 ○	Connolly	
58 ○ ⇄	Chadwick > Taylor	
62 ○ ⇄	Showunmi > Brkovic	
64 ○ ⊕	Feeney / H / OP / IA	
	Assist: Edwards	
77 ○ ⇄	Djordjic > Buzsaky	
83 ○ ⇄	Derbyshire > Evans	
88 ○	Doumbe	
90 ○	Capaldi	
90 ○ ⊕	Djordjic / H / OP / 6Y	
	Assist: Derbyshire	

Full time 1-1

It took Bojan Djordjic a while to announce his arrival at Home Park, but he did it with some style at Kenilworth Road, coming off the substitutes' bench to head home an injury-time equaliser to extend Tony Pulis's unbeaten run to four games.

Any Pilgrims' hopes that rampant Luton had used up their quota of goals for the week in Tuesday's four-goal drubbing of Norwich proved unfounded as the Hatters so nearly topped another admirably stodgy Argyle display.

Northern Ireland international Warren Feeney scored the first goal on 64 minutes with a towering header from a pin-point cross by Carlos Edwards.

The Pilgrims had to wait until injury time for the equalizer from Serbia-born-Swede Djordjic.

A deep cross from fellow substitute Matt Derbyshire found Djordjic powering in at the back post to out-jump his marker and force his header past Marlon Beresford in the Luton goal.

Player of the Match	Quote	Championship Milestone
8 Akos Buzsaky	🔊 **Tony Pulis**	▶ **First Goal**
Djordjic might have grabbed the headlines, but his fellow European tyro took the plaudits.	Luton got loads of crosses in today; we haven't done the same. That's something we'll talk about and we'll work on.	Bojan Djordjic netted his first goal in the Championship.

Venue:	Kenilworth Road	Referee:	B.Curson - 05/06	**Luton Town**
Attendance:	8,714	Matches:	10	**Plymouth Argyle**
Capacity:	10,300	Yellow Cards:	23	
Occupancy:	85%	Red Cards:	1	

Form Coming into Fixture

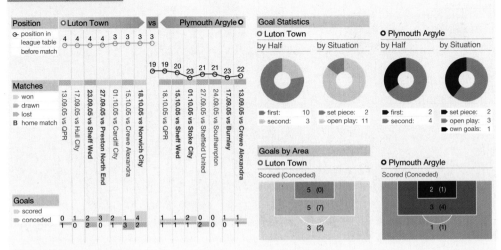

Goal Statistics

○ Luton Town

by Half | by Situation

■ first: 10 ■ set piece: 2
■ second: 3 ■ open play: 11

● Plymouth Argyle

by Half | by Situation

■ first: 2 ■ set piece: 2
■ second: 4 ■ open play: 3
             ■ own goals: 1

Goals by Area

○ Luton Town

Scored (Conceded)

5 (0)
5 (7)
3 (2)

● Plymouth Argyle

Scored (Conceded)

2 (1)
3 (4)
1 (1)

Team Statistics

Starting Line-Ups

Davis, Morgan / Foley, Heikkinen, Holmes, Howard, Taylor / Chadwick, Beresford, Coyne, Nicholls, Feeney, Evans / Derbyshire, Edwards, Brkovic / Showunmi

Buzsaky, Connolly / Djordjic, Wotton, Doumbe, Larrieu, Norris, Aljofree, Capaldi, Barness

➤ 4/4/2   ➤ 4/4/2

Unused Sub: Brill, Perrett, Robinson
Unused Sub: McCormick, Lasley

Championship Totals	○ Luton	Plymouth ●
Championship Appearances	167	438
Team Appearances	149	438
Goals Scored	25	39
Assists	23	30
Clean Sheets (goalkeepers)	3	6
Yellow Cards	16	50
Red Cards	1	2
Full Internationals	4	3

Age/Height

Luton Town Age	Plymouth Argyle Age
➤ **26 yrs, 8 mo**	➤ **26 yrs, 2 mo**
Luton Town Height	Plymouth Argyle Height
➤ **6'**	➤ **5'11"**

Match Statistics

League Table after Fixture

		Played	Won	Drawn	Lost	For	Against	Pts
● 3	Luton	15	8	4	3	25	17	28
...	...	...	...	...	...	...	...	...
● 18	Leicester	14	3	6	5	14	17	15
● 19	Plymouth	15	3	6	6	12	19	15
● 20	Brighton	14	2	7	5	14	19	13
● 21	Coventry	14	2	7	5	18	24	13
● 22	Sheff Wed	13	2	6	5	11	16	12
● 23	Crewe	15	2	6	7	15	29	12
● 24	Millwall	15	2	5	8	11	25	11

Statistics	○ Luton	Plymouth ●
Goals	1	1
Shots on Target	4	2
Shots off Target	11	4
Hit Woodwork	0	0
Possession %	53	47
Corners	4	3
Offsides	12	6
Fouls	10	13
Disciplinary Points	0	12

0-0

Plymouth Argyle ○
Millwall ○

► Tony Capaldi attempts to make progress

Event Line

Half time 0-0

59 ○ ⇄	May > Asaba
62 ○ ⇄	Djordjic > Barness
62 ○ ⇄	Derbyshire > Taylor
70 ○ ⇄	Elliott > Dunne
70 ○ ⇄	Craig > Williams
82 ○ ⇄	Chadwick > Evans
87 ○	Ifil

Full time 0-0

A fifth draw from the seven games in which he has been in charge these last five weeks did little to cheer Argyle manager Tony Pulis and will not have wowed Sky's television audience.

Victory over bottom-placed Millwall would have seen the Pilgrims climb five places further up the Coca-Cola Championship table, but victories – and goals – are difficult to come by for the Pilgrims at the moment.

Seven goals from their last nine games – including an own goal and a penalty – adequately tells the story of Argyle's plight. It has been eight games since a forward found the target.

Player of the Match

1 Romain Larrieu

He made three outstanding saves towards the end of a game which failed to impress Sky's cameras.

Quote

❝ Tony Pulis

The big disappointment for me today was that, for a majority of the game, I thought we were better than Millwall – we created the better chances, had the better opportunities.

Championship Milestone

➡ 25

Paul Connolly made his 25th appearance in the Championship.

Venue:	Home Park	Referee:	C.Penton - 05/06	**Plymouth Argyle**
Attendance:	11,764	Matches:	13	**Millwall**
Capacity:	20,922	Yellow Cards:	45	
Occupancy:	56%	Red Cards:	3	

Form Coming into Fixture

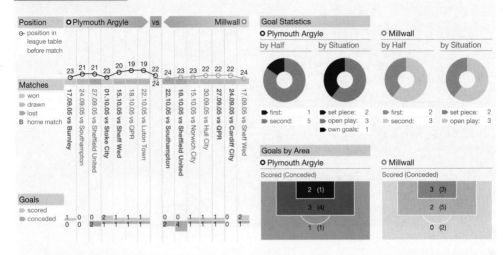

Position

⊙ position in league table before match

○ Plymouth Argyle vs Millwall

Matches
- won
- drawn
- lost
- B home match

Goals
- scored
- conceded

Goal Statistics

○ Plymouth Argyle

by Half
- first: 1
- second: 5

by Situation
- set piece: 2
- open play: 3
- own goals: 1

○ Millwall

by Half
- first: 2
- second: 3

by Situation
- set piece: 2
- open play: 2

Goals by Area

○ Plymouth Argyle — Scored (Conceded)
- 2 (1)
- 3 (4)
- 1 (1)

○ Millwall — Scored (Conceded)
- 3 (3)
- 2 (5)
- 0 (2)

Team Statistics

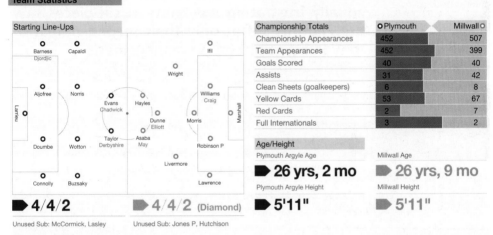

Starting Line-Ups

Plymouth Argyle: Larrieu; Barness, Capaldi (Djordjic), Aljofree, Norris, Doumbe, Wotton, Taylor (Derbyshire), Evans (Chadwick), Hayles, Connolly, Buzsaky

4/4/2

Unused Sub: McCormick, Lasley

Millwall: Marshall; Ifil, Wright, Williams (Craig), Morris, Dunne (Elliott), Asaba (May), Robinson P, Livermore, Lawrence

4/4/2 (Diamond)

Unused Sub: Jones P, Hutchison

Championship Totals	○ Plymouth	Millwall ○
Championship Appearances	452	507
Team Appearances	452	399
Goals Scored	40	40
Assists	31	42
Clean Sheets (goalkeepers)	6	8
Yellow Cards	53	67
Red Cards	2	7
Full Internationals	3	2

Age/Height

Plymouth Argyle Age: 26 yrs, 2 mo

Millwall Age: 26 yrs, 9 mo

Plymouth Argyle Height: 5'11"

Millwall Height: 5'11"

Match Statistics

League Table after Fixture

		Played	Won	Drawn	Lost	For	Against	Pts
●	16 Preston	16	3	9	4	16	18	18
●	17 Derby	16	3	8	5	21	23	17
●	18 Sheff Wed	15	3	7	5	13	17	16
●	19 Coventry	16	3	7	6	20	26	16
●	20 Norwich	16	4	4	8	16	22	16
↑	21 Plymouth	16	3	7	6	12	19	16
↓	22 Brighton	16	2	9	5	16	21	15
●	23 Crewe	16	2	7	7	17	31	13
●	24 Millwall	16	2	6	8	11	25	12

Statistics	○ Plymouth	Millwall ○
Goals	0	0
Shots on Target	5	7
Shots off Target	7	0
Hit Woodwork	0	0
Possession %	49	51
Corners	3	7
Offsides	1	9
Fouls	17	18
Disciplinary Points	0	4

3-1

Ipswich Town ○
Plymouth Argyle ○

▶ Jason De Vos gets to grips with Nick Chadwick

Event Line

23 ○ ⊕ McEveley / LF / C / OA	
31 ○ ⊕ Juan / H / C / 6Y	
Assist: De Vos	
Half time 2-0	
51 ○ ⊕ Buzsaky / RF / DFK / OA	
Assist: Norris	
55 ○ Connolly	
56 ○ ⊕ Richards / LF / P / IA	
Assist: Forster	
60 ○ ⇄ Bowditch > Forster	
72 ○ Parkin	
76 ○ ⇄ Westlake > Richards	
79 ○ Horlock	
Full time 3-1	

A familiar failure to finish off chances and an equally frustrating weakness at set-pieces saw the Pilgrims suffer only their second defeat in Tony Pulis's eight-game management.

The first goal came after Argyle only half-cleared a Darren Currie corner from the left and the ball fell to James McEveley on the edge of the box, and he fired a sweet half-volley through the crowd and under the despairing dive of Romain Larrieu.

It was 2-0 eight minutes later when Jason de Vos flicked on another Currie corner, and Jimmy Juan stooped to head the ball home at the far post.

The Pilgrims deservedly clawed their way back into the game with another wonderful goal from the right boot of Akos Buzsaky. This time, the Hungarian magician curled a glorious shot into the top corner from 25 yards to add to the peaches he scored at Barnet and QPR.

Five minutes later, however, and the Tractor Boys were awarded a soft penalty when Nicky Forster clearly dived over the advancing Larrieu, and Matt Richards duly converted from the spot.

Player of the Match	Quote
8 Akos Buzsaky	🟠 **Tony Pulis**
Another sublime free-kick in another away defeat helped make Akos Buzsaky the pick of the Pilgrims.	I don't think there was a lot between the teams. It was just that Ipswich got the breaks, and we didn't defend properly.

Venue:	Portman Road	Referee:	M.Atkinson - 05/06		**Ipswich Town**
Attendance:	23,083	Matches:	12		**Plymouth Argyle**
Capacity:	30,300	Yellow Cards:	24		
Occupancy:	76%	Red Cards:	1		

Form Coming into Fixture

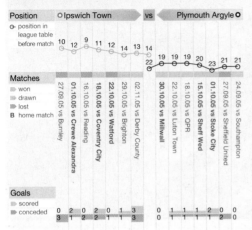

Goal Statistics

Ipswich Town

by Half / by Situation

- first: 5
- second: 3
- set piece: 5
- open play: 3

Plymouth Argyle

by Half / by Situation

- first: 1
- second: 4
- set piece: 2
- open play: 2
- own goals: 1

Goals by Area

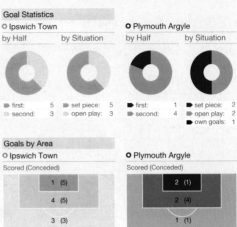

Ipswich Town

Scored (Conceded)

| 1 (5) |
| 4 (5) |
| 3 (3) |

Plymouth Argyle

Scored (Conceded)

| 2 (1) |
| 2 (4) |
| 1 (1) |

Team Statistics

Starting Line-Ups

McEveley, Richards, Westlake, Buzsaky, Connolly
De Vos, Horlock, Parkin, Chadwick, Wotton, Doumbe
Price / Larrieu
Naylor, Juan, Forster, Bowditch, Evans, Norris, Aljofree
Sito, Currie, Capaldi, Barness

4/4/2 4/4/2

Unused Sub: Supple, Magilton, Proudlock

Unused Sub: McCormick, Djordjic, Lasley, Derbyshire, Taylor

Championship Totals

	Ipswich	Plymouth
Championship Appearances	490	415
Team Appearances	418	415
Goals Scored	50	35
Assists	54	29
Clean Sheets (goalkeepers)	3	7
Yellow Cards	51	48
Red Cards	3	2
Full Internationals	2	3

Age/Height

Ipswich Town Age: **25 yrs, 8 mo**

Plymouth Argyle Age: **26 yrs, 9 mo**

Ipswich Town Height: **6'**

Plymouth Argyle Height: **5'11"**

Match Statistics

League Table after Fixture

	Played	Won	Drawn	Lost	For	Against	Pts
↑ 13 Ipswich	18	6	5	7	21	27	23
...	...	...	...	...	...	...	...
↑ 18 Crewe	18	4	7	7	21	32	19
↓ 19 Derby	18	3	9	6	25	28	18
↓ 20 Hull	18	4	6	8	14	19	18
● 21 Coventry	17	3	7	7	21	28	16
↓ 22 Brighton	18	2	10	6	17	25	16
↓ 23 Plymouth	17	3	7	7	13	22	16
● 24 Millwall	18	2	6	10	13	30	12

Statistics

	Ipswich	Plymouth
Goals	3	1
Shots on Target	6	6
Shots off Target	4	6
Hit Woodwork	0	0
Possession %	52	48
Corners	7	5
Offsides	8	4
Fouls	14	12
Disciplinary Points	8	4

3-1

Plymouth Argyle ○
Queens Park Rangers ○

▶ Both Romain Larrieu and Anthony Barness outjump Gareth Ainsworth

Event Line

5 ○ ■	Royce	
7 ○ ⊕	Wotton / RF / P / IA	
	Assist: Norris	
8 ○ ■	Santos	
37 ○ ⊕	Doumbe / RF / C / IA	
	Assist: Wotton	
40 ○ ■	Gallen	
45 ○ ■	Cook	
45 ○ ■	Dyer	
45 ○ ■	Norris	
Half time 2-0		
49 ○ ⇄	Rowlands > Doherty	
51 ○ ⊕	Chadwick / H / IFK / IA	
	Assist: Buzsaky	
53 ○ ■	Chadwick	
54 ○ ⇄	Lasley > Buzsaky	
56 ○ ■	Ainsworth	
57 ○ ⇄	Baidoo > Langley	
57 ○ ⇄	Bean > Santos	
61 ○ ⊕	Baidoo / RF / C / 6Y	
	Assist: Evatt	
62 ○ ■	Connolly	
63 ○ ■	Baidoo	
80 ○ ⇄	Taylor > Chadwick	
90 ○ ■	Bean	
90 ○ ■	Shittu	
90 ○ ■	Wotton	
90 ○ ⇄	Derbyshire > Evans	
Full time 3-1		

This was just the tonic Tony Pulis and his hard-working players needed following the two-week international break.

Argyle produced a pulsating performance to help them soar six places upwards in the Championship to 17th.

The frustration of their previous Home Park performance – a 1-0 advantage against Leicester before the half-time wash-out – was swept aside within minutes as man of the match David Norris skipped through the Rangers back four and was felled by Hoops keeper Simon Royce.

A fairly regular name on the score-sheet, Paul Wotton, smacked the penalty past Royce, but the second goal came from a more unlikely source.

French defender Matt Doumbe hooked a slightly mis-hit volley past Royce to double the lead, and Nick Chadwick made it three just after half-time, with a glancing header from a wickedly curling free-kick by Akos Buzsaky.

The consolation for QPR was particularly messy – Shabazz Baidoo turning the ball in with his knee after a header from Ian Evatt.

Player of the Match

7 David Norris

Like the man said – David Norris, who never stopped chasing all game. All season, in fact.

Quote

💬 **Tony Pulis**

It was important that we got a win on the board, moved up the table. We needed the three points and I thought that the players showed just how much they wanted them.

Championship Milestone

▶ **25**

Keith Lasley made his 25th appearance in the Championship.

Venue:	Home Park	
Attendance:	13,213	
Capacity:	20,922	
Occupancy:	63%	

Referee:	S.Tanner - 05/06
Matches:	14
Yellow Cards:	51
Red Cards:	6

**Plymouth Argyle
Queens Park Rangers**

Form Coming into Fixture

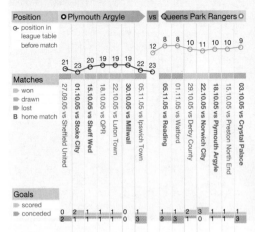

Goal Statistics

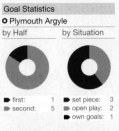

○ Plymouth Argyle

by Half — by Situation

- first: 1
- second: 5
- set piece: 3
- open play: 2
- own goals: 1

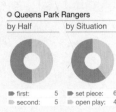

○ Queens Park Rangers

by Half — by Situation

- first: 5
- second: 5
- set piece: 6
- open play: 4

Goals by Area

○ Plymouth Argyle

Scored (Conceded)

| 2 (2) |
| 2 (5) |
| 2 (2) |

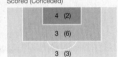

○ Queens Park Rangers

Scored (Conceded)

| 4 (2) |
| 3 (6) |
| 3 (3) |

Team Statistics

Starting Line-Ups

▶ **4/4/2**   ▶ 4/4/2

Unused Sub: McCormick, Djordjic

Unused Sub: Milanese, Moore

Championship Totals

	○Plymouth	QPR○
Championship Appearances	486	492
Team Appearances	486	461
Goals Scored	40	42
Assists	33	54
Clean Sheets (goalkeepers)	7	10
Yellow Cards	52	59
Red Cards	2	3
Full Internationals	3	5

Age/Height

Plymouth Argyle Age

▶ **26 yrs, 5 mo**

Queens Park Rangers Age

▶ **26 yrs, 11 mo**

Plymouth Argyle Height

▶ **5'11"**

Queens Park Rangers Height

▶ **5'11"**

Match Statistics

League Table after Fixture

	Played	Won	Drawn	Lost	For	Against	Pts
↓ 13 QPR	19	6	6	7	21	26	24
↓ 14 Ipswich	19	6	6	7	22	28	24
↑ 15 Norwich	19	6	4	9	19	24	22
↓ 16 Leicester	18	4	8	6	16	20	20
↑ 17 Plymouth	18	4	7	7	16	23	19
↓ 18 Sheff Wed	19	4	7	8	17	25	19
↓ 19 Crewe	19	4	7	8	22	34	19
● 20 Derby	19	3	9	7	25	31	18
● 21 Coventry	19	3	9	7	22	29	18

Statistics

	○Plymouth	QPR○
Goals	3	1
Shots on Target	7	5
Shots off Target	2	3
Hit Woodwork	0	0
Possession %	52	48
Corners	5	8
Offsides	1	4
Fouls	14	14
Disciplinary Points	16	36

0-0

Sheffield Wednesday ○
Plymouth Argyle ○

▶ Tony Capaldi is a picture of concentration

Event Line

Half time 0-0

60 ○ ⇄ Graham > Agbonlahor
60 ○ ⇄ Corr > Lee
75 ○ ⇄ Partridge > Eagles
84 ○ ⇄ Lasley > Buzsaky
84 ○ ⇄ Djordjic > Chadwick
90 ○ ⇄ Ward > Connolly

Full time 0-0

For the second time of asking, honours ended even between Argyle and the side managed by their most recent favourite son.

In a reversal of fortunes from their October Home Park encounter, Argyle will gain the greater satisfaction from the point earned, having restricted Paul Sturrock's Wednesday to just two shots on target.

For their own part, the Pilgrims failed to make the most of the relatively few clear-cut chances they hewed out of the rock of the home side's somewhat familiar resoluteness.

Nevertheless, Argyle's own determination and discipline in front of a fiercely partisan crowd will have won an approving nod of recognition from the man who, in no small part, took them to the level at which they are now competing.

Player of the Match

2 Anthony Barness

No goals, so that puts a defender in the frame, and his attacking play was better than any.

Quote

 Tony Pulis

Overall, I think we deserved it – up until the last 20 minutes, we were the team that was going to create the better chances.

Championship Milestone

▶ **50**

Tony Capaldi made his 50th appearance in the Championship.

Venue:	Hillsborough	Referee:	C.H.Webster - 05/06		Sheffield Wednesday
Attendance:	20,244	Matches:	17		Plymouth Argyle
Capacity:	39,859	Yellow Cards:	66		
Occupancy:	51%	Red Cards:	7		

Form Coming into Fixture

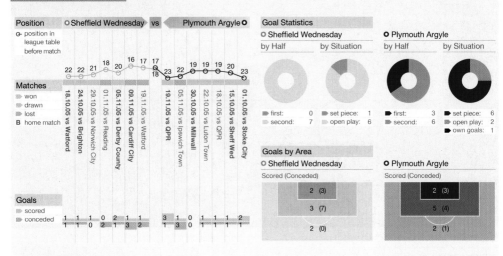

Team Statistics

Starting Line-Ups

Unused Sub: Adamson, Rocastle

Unused Sub: McCormick, Derbyshire

Championship Totals	○ Sheff Wed	Plymouth ○
Championship Appearances	240	488
Team Appearances	164	477
Goals Scored	13	40
Assists	14	36
Clean Sheets (goalkeepers)	0	7
Yellow Cards	20	60
Red Cards	0	2
Full Internationals	2	3

Age/Height

Sheffield Wednesday Age	Plymouth Argyle Age
24 yrs	26 yrs, 1 mo
Sheffield Wednesday Height	Plymouth Argyle Height
6'	5'11"

Match Statistics

League Table after Fixture

	Played	Won	Drawn	Lost	For	Against	Pts
↓ 11 Stoke	20	9	1	10	23	28	28
↓ 12 Southampton	19	5	11	3	23	18	26
● 13 QPR	20	6	6	8	21	28	24
● 14 Ipswich	20	6	6	8	22	31	24
● 15 Norwich	20	6	4	10	19	25	22
● 16 Leicester	19	4	9	6	18	21	21
↑ 17 Derby	20	4	9	7	27	32	21
↓ 18 Plymouth	19	4	8	7	16	23	20
↓ 19 Sheff Wed	20	4	8	8	17	25	20

Statistics	○ Sheff Wed	Plymouth ○
Goals	0	0
Shots on Target	2	1
Shots off Target	5	6
Hit Woodwork	0	0
Possession %	53	47
Corners	4	2
Offsides	2	2
Fouls	15	10
Disciplinary Points	0	0

0-2

Plymouth Argyle ○
Reading ○

▶ Kevin Doyle secures the points for Reading

Event Line

20 ○	⊕	Little / RF / OP / IA
22 ○	■	Sidwell
24 ○	■	Buzsaky
Half time 0-1		
46 ○	⇄	Djordjic > Buzsaky
57 ○	⊕	Doyle / RF / OP / 6Y
		Assist: Convey
58 ○	■	Doyle
73 ○	■	Aljofree
81 ○	⇄	Derbyshire > Evans
82 ○	⇄	Oster > Little
84 ○	⇄	Hunt > Convey
90 ○	⇄	Cox > Doyle
Full time 0-2		

Argyle failed to repeat the shock result of the Coca-Cola Championship season as the gap between the top of the table and the nail-biting zone was amply demonstrated at Home Park.

The Pilgrims were by no means outclassed, and certainly not outfought, in the return but suffered in the ultimate comparison – outscored.

The first goal was a special one. Glen Little danced through the Argyle defence before beating Larrieu with an exquisite chip from the right edge of the penalty area.

The Pilgrims almost grabbed an equalizer from a sizzling drive by Norris that flew inches wide, but their fate was sealed minutes later when Leroy Lita broke down the left and his square pass found Kevin Doyle at the back post for the simplest of tap-ins.

Player of the Match	Quote	Championship Milestone
7 David Norris	🗨 **Tony Pulis**	▶ **25**
He again excelled in what was, for the most part, a lost cause.	They are the best counter-attacking side in the league. They have got good pace in the team that can cause you problems.	Jason Jarrett made his 25th appearance in the Championship and first in the competition for Plymouth.

Venue:	Home Park	Referee:	K.Wright - 05/06		Plymouth Argyle
Attendance:	14,020	Matches:	13		Reading
Capacity:	20,922	Yellow Cards:	49		
Occupancy:	67%	Red Cards:	4		

Form Coming into Fixture

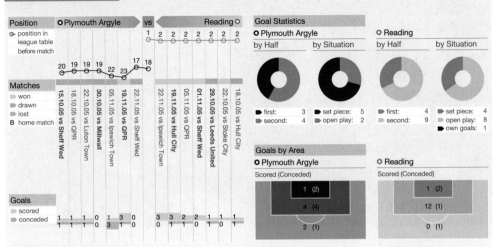

Position
- ⊙ position in league table before match

○ Plymouth Argyle   vs   Reading ○

Matches
- won
- drawn
- lost
- B home match

Plymouth Argyle positions: 20 19 19 19 22 23 17 18
- 15.10.05 vs Sheff Wed
- 18.10.05 vs QPR
- 22.10.05 vs Luton Town
- 30.10.05 vs Millwall
- 05.11.05 vs Ipswich Town
- 19.11.05 vs QPR
- 22.11.05 vs Sheff Wed

Reading:
- 22.11.05 vs Ipswich Town
- 19.11.05 vs Hull City
- 05.11.05 vs QPR
- 01.11.05 vs Sheff Wed
- 29.10.05 vs Leeds United
- 22.10.05 vs Stoke City
- 18.10.05 vs Hull City

Goals
- scored
- conceded

scored	1	1	1	0	1	3	0		3	3	2	2	1	1	1
conceded	1	1	1	0	3	1	0		0	1	1	0	1	0	1

Goal Statistics

○ Plymouth Argyle
- by Half — first: 3, second: 4
- by Situation — set piece: 5, open play: 2

○ Reading
- by Half — first: 4, second: 9
- by Situation — set piece: 4, open play: 8, own goals: 1

Goals by Area

○ Plymouth Argyle — Scored (Conceded): 1 (2), 4 (4), 2 (1)

○ Reading — Scored (Conceded): 1 (2), 12 (1), 0 (1)

Team Statistics

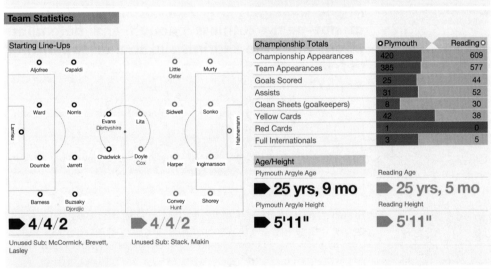

Starting Line-Ups

Plymouth Argyle — 4/4/2
Larrieu; Barness, Doumbe, Jarrett, Buzsaky/Djordjic; Ward, Norris, Chadwick, Aljofree, Capaldi; Evans/Derbyshire, Lita

Reading — 4/4/2
Hahnemann; Shorey, Ingimarsson, Sonko, Murty; Convey/Hunt, Harper, Sidwell, Little/Oster; Doyle/Cox, ...

Unused Sub: McCormick, Brevett, Lasley
Unused Sub: Stack, Makin

Championship Totals

	○ Plymouth	Reading ○
Championship Appearances	420	609
Team Appearances	385	577
Goals Scored	25	44
Assists	31	52
Clean Sheets (goalkeepers)	8	30
Yellow Cards	42	38
Red Cards	1	0
Full Internationals	3	5

Age/Height

	Plymouth Argyle	Reading
Age	25 yrs, 9 mo	25 yrs, 5 mo
Height	5'11"	5'11"

Match Statistics

League Table after Fixture

	Played	Won	Drawn	Lost	For	Against	Pts
● 1 Reading	21	15	5	1	38	11	50
...	...	...	...	...	...	...	...
↑ 18 Hull	21	4	8	9	18	25	20
↓ 19 Plymouth	20	4	8	8	16	25	20
↓ 20 Sheff Wed	21	4	8	9	17	27	20
↑ 21 Coventry	21	3	10	8	24	33	19
↓ 22 Crewe	21	4	7	10	23	41	19
● 23 Brighton	21	2	12	7	20	29	18
● 24 Millwall	21	3	7	11	16	33	16

Statistics

	○ Plymouth	Reading ○
Goals	0	2
Shots on Target	4	6
Shots off Target	7	7
Hit Woodwork	1	0
Possession %	52	48
Corners	9	7
Offsides	2	4
Fouls	14	23
Disciplinary Points	8	8

3-1

Coventry City ○
Plymouth Argyle ○

► Nick Chadwick battles for possession with Andy Morrell

Event Line

25 ○ ⊕	Norris / LF / OP / IA	
	Assist: Barness	
27 ○ ⇄	Shaw > Heath	
28 ○ ⇄	Impey > Hall	
28 ○ ⇄	Hutchison > Scowcroft	
36 ○ ⊕	Morrell / RF / OP / IA	
	Assist: Jorgensen	
41 ○ ■	Hutchison	
45 ○ ⊕	Hutchison / LF / OP / IA	
	Assist: Impey	

Half time 2-1

49 ○ ⊕	McSheffrey / LF / OP / OA	
54 ○ ■	Doyle	
63 ○ ⇄	Derbyshire > Aljofree	
73 ○ ⇄	Connolly > Barness	
78 ○ ■	Norris	
84 ○ ⇄	Taylor > Chadwick	
85 ○ ■	McSheffrey	

Full time 3-1

Argyle manager Tony Pulis accused his players of not being ruthless enough and defending poorly after the Pilgrims slid to a disappointing defeat.

The Pilgrims actually took a thoroughly deserved lead at the Ricoh Arena when David Norris neatly converted an Anthony Barness cross with a side-footed half-volley from 15 yards.

Unfortunately for the Greens, the lead lasted a mere 11 minutes before Andy Morrell smashed a close-range half-volley through the legs of Romain Larrieu.

The Sky Blues took the lead in first-half injury time after some quality work by Don Hutchison. The former Scotland international expertly controlled a cross by Andy Impey before slamming the ball past the advancing Larrieu.

Four minutes into the second half it was game over. A poor clearance from Hasney Aljofree fell straight at the feet of Gary McSheffrey, who let fly with an unstoppable low drive from 20 yards which cannoned in off the far post.

Player of the Match

7 David Norris

Again. And he will be again, you know.

Quote

❝ **Tony Pulis**

We had the game and we threw it away. I don't think there's any doubt about that. The goals were very, very poor goals.

Venue:	Ricoh Arena	Referee:	N.Miller - 05/06		Coventry City
Attendance:	18,796	Matches:	17		Plymouth Argyle
Capacity:	32,000	Yellow Cards:	42		
Occupancy:	59%	Red Cards:	8		

Form Coming into Fixture

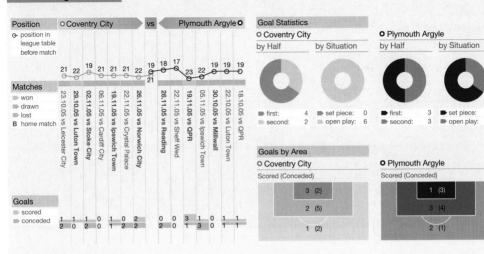

Position

○ Coventry City vs Plymouth Argyle ○

○- position in league table before match

Matches
- won
- drawn
- lost
- B home match

21 22 19 21 21 21 22 19 18 17 23 22 19 19 19
21

23.10.05 vs Leicester City
29.10.05 vs Luton Town
02.11.05 vs Stoke City
06.11.05 vs Cardiff City
19.11.05 vs Ipswich Town
22.11.05 vs Crystal Palace
26.11.05 vs Norwich City
26.11.05 vs Reading
22.11.05 vs Sheff Wed
19.11.05 vs QPR
05.11.05 vs Ipswich Town
30.10.05 vs Millwall
22.10.05 vs Luton Town
18.10.05 vs QPR

Goals
- scored
- conceded

1	1	1	0	1	0	2		0	0	3	1	0	1	1
2	0	2	0	1	2	2		2	0	1	3	0	1	1

Goal Statistics

○ Coventry City

by Half	by Situation
first: 4	set piece: 0
second: 2	open play: 6

● Plymouth Argyle

by Half	by Situation
first: 3	set piece: 4
second: 3	open play: 2

Goals by Area

○ Coventry City — Scored (Conceded)

3 (2)
2 (5)
1 (2)

● Plymouth Argyle — Scored (Conceded)

1 (3)
3 (4)
2 (1)

Team Statistics

Starting Line-Ups

Hall, Scowcroft, Impey, Hutchison
Heath, Shaw, Doyle, McSheffrey, Chadwick, Taylor
Fulop
Page, Jorgensen, Adebola, Evans
Whing, Morrell

Norris, Doumbe
Jarrett, Ward
Lamieu
Wotton, Aljofree, Derbyshire
Capaldi, Barness, Connolly

▷ 4/4/2   ▶ 4/4/2

Unused Sub: Ince, Thornton   Unused Sub: McCormick, Lasley

Championship Totals	○ Coventry	Plymouth ●
Championship Appearances	551	500
Team Appearances	419	465
Goals Scored	59	39
Assists	46	36
Clean Sheets (goalkeepers)	2	8
Yellow Cards	74	58
Red Cards	3	2
Full Internationals	5	2

Age/Height

Coventry City Age	Plymouth Argyle Age
▷ **28 yrs, 11 mo**	▶ **26 yrs, 3 mo**
Coventry City Height	Plymouth Argyle Height
▷ **6'**	▶ **5'11"**

Match Statistics

League Table after Fixture

		Played	Won	Drawn	Lost	For	Against	Pts
↓	16 Leicester	21	5	9	7	23	25	24
↑	17 Hull	22	5	8	9	20	25	23
↓	18 Norwich	22	6	5	11	21	29	23
↑	19 Coventry	22	4	10	8	27	34	22
↓	20 Plymouth	21	4	8	9	17	28	20
↓	21 Sheff Wed	22	4	8	10	17	28	20
↑	22 Brighton	22	2	13	7	21	30	19
↓	23 Crewe	22	4	7	11	23	43	19
●	24 Millwall	22	3	8	11	17	34	17

Statistics	○ Coventry	Plymouth ●
Goals	3	1
Shots on Target	4	4
Shots off Target	5	6
Hit Woodwork	1	0
Possession %	52	48
Corners	3	3
Offsides	2	1
Fouls	11	11
Disciplinary Points	12	4

1-1

Watford ○
Plymouth Argyle ○

► Nick Chadwick wheels away after opening the scoring

Event Line
Half time 0-0
48 ○ ⊕ Chadwick / RF / C / 6Y
Assist: Wotton
64 ○ ▇ Wotton
76 ○ ⇄ Chambers > Stewart
80 ○ ⇄ Bangura > Spring
82 ○ ⇄ Derbyshire > Evans
90 ○ ⊕ King / RF / OP / OA
Assist: Mackay
90 ○ ⇄ Aljofree > Chadwick
Full time 1-1

Nick Chadwick showed further signs that he was benefiting from a regular run in the Argyle side since Tony Pulis was appointed manager by setting up the Pilgrims' point at Vicarage Road.

A stunning save by Romain Larrieu from Gavin Mahon's point-blank drive enabled the Pilgrims to hold fourth-placed Watford to a goalless first period.

Chadwick broke the deadlock three minutes into the second half with a true poacher's goal. A Paul Connolly corner was headed goalwards by Wotton, and Chadwick spun round and forced the ball home from two yards.

The Pilgrims were seconds away from victory when Marlon King broke their hearts with an excellent finish from the edge of the box after some tricky wing play by the impressive Anthony McNamee.

Player of the Match

27 Jason Jarrett

In the third of his seven-match loan spell from Norwich, he was the stand-out performer in a disciplined midfield display.

Quote

❝ Tony Pulis

The way we played for 90 minutes was first class; in injury-time, we got a little bit panicky, and that's when I want the men to stand up and be counted.

Venue:	Vicarage Road	Referee:	S.W.Mathieson - 05/06		**Watford**
Attendance:	12,884	Matches:	13		**Plymouth Argyle**
Capacity:	22,100	Yellow Cards:	26		
Occupancy:	58%	Red Cards:	2		

Form Coming into Fixture

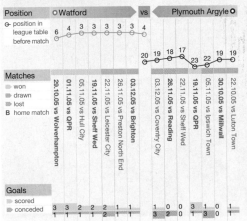

Goal Statistics

○ Watford

by Half	by Situation

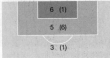

- ▶ first: 8 ▶ set piece: 6
- ▶ second: 6 ▶ open play: 8

● Plymouth Argyle

by Half	by Situation

- ▶ first: 3 ▶ set piece: 4
- ▶ second: 3 ▶ open play: 2

Goals by Area

○ Watford
Scored (Conceded)

	6 (1)	
	5 (6)	
	3 (1)	

● Plymouth Argyle
Scored (Conceded)

	1 (3)	
	4 (5)	
	1 (2)	

Team Statistics

Starting Line-Ups

▶ 4 / 4 / 2   ▶ 4 / 4 / 2

Unused Sub: Chamberlain, Mariappa, Grant

Unused Sub: McCormick, Djordjic, Lasley

Championship Totals	○ Watford	Plymouth ●
Championship Appearances	535	482
Team Appearances	399	447
Goals Scored	41	36
Assists	38	37
Clean Sheets (goalkeepers)	5	8
Yellow Cards	59	57
Red Cards	5	2
Full Internationals	3	2

Age/Height

Watford Age	Plymouth Argyle Age
▶ **25 yrs, 9 mo**	▶ **26 yrs**
Watford Height	Plymouth Argyle Height
▶ **5'11"**	▶ **5'11"**

Match Statistics

League Table after Fixture

		Played	Won	Drawn	Lost	For	Against	Pts
↑ 3	Watford	23	10	9	4	38	27	39
...		...	...	...	...	...	...	...
↑ 18	Coventry	23	5	10	8	28	34	25
↓ 19	Leicester	22	5	9	8	25	28	24
● 20	Plymouth	22	4	9	9	18	29	21
● 21	Sheff Wed	23	4	8	11	17	29	20
● 22	Brighton	23	2	13	8	22	35	19
● 23	Crewe	23	4	7	12	24	45	19
● 24	Millwall	23	3	8	12	17	35	17

Statistics	○ Watford	Plymouth ●
Goals	1	1
Shots on Target	5	3
Shots off Target	5	4
Hit Woodwork	0	0
Possession %	61	39
Corners	6	2
Offsides	7	4
Fouls	13	13
Disciplinary Points	0	4

2-0

Plymouth Argyle ○
Crystal Palace ○

► Nick Chadwick celebrates making history at Home Park

Event Line

1 ○ ⊕	Chadwick / RF / OP / IA	
	Assist: Evans	
Half time 1-0		
54 ○ ▢	Doumbe	
57 ○ ▢	Morrison	
67 ○ ⇄	McAnuff > Morrison	
67 ○ ⇄	Reich > Soares	
73 ○ ⇄	Buzsaky > Evans	
78 ○ ⇄	Macken > Popovic	
80 ○ ▢	Hughes	
82 ○ ▢	Hall F	
85 ○ ▢	Connolly	
88 ○ ▢	Chadwick	
89 ○ ▢	Boyce	
90 ○ ▢	McAnuff	
90 ○ ○ ⊕	Capaldi / LF / OP / IA	
	Assist: Norris	
Full time 2-0		

The fastest ever goal at Home Park and one 94 minutes later – has there ever been such a time between consecutive goals in any football match? – sent the Green Army into Christmas with a spring in their step.

Nick Chadwick made sure of his place in the Argyle record books with a goal in the 12th second of the match that turned out to be a blow from which Palace never recovered.

Mathias Doumbe launched a hopeful ball forward and Michael Evans climbed highest to glance a header into the path of Chadwick, who raced clear of a static Palace defence and lobbed over the helpless Julian Speroni.

Palace were never really at the races all afternoon, although England international Andrew Johnson did hit the post late in the first half, and Michael Hughes wasted a glorious opportunity to equalise before Capaldi sealed matters in injury-time with a neat finish over the spread-eagled Speroni, following an incisive run and pass from Norris.

Player of the Match

21 Elliott Ward

Another loan star, got one over his big brother Darren, who watched from the Home Park grandstand.

Quote

❝ **Tony Pulis**

They've probably got the best choice of front players in the league. For us to keep a clean sheet was a massive, massive bonus.

Venue:	Home Park	Referee:	R.J.Beeby - 05/06		Plymouth Argyle
Attendance:	14,582	Matches:	20		Crystal Palace
Capacity:	20,922	Yellow Cards:	49		
Occupancy:	70%	Red Cards:	6		

Form Coming into Fixture

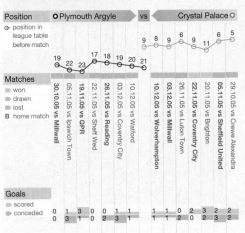

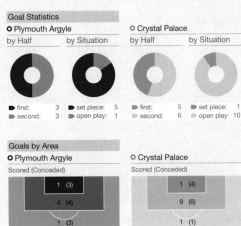

Goal Statistics

Plymouth Argyle

by Half — first: 3, second: 3
by Situation — set piece: 5, open play: 1

Crystal Palace

by Half — first: 5, second: 6
by Situation — set piece: 1, open play: 10

Goals by Area

Plymouth Argyle — Scored (Conceded)
1 (3)
4 (4)
1 (3)

Crystal Palace — Scored (Conceded)
1 (4)
9 (6)
1 (1)

Team Statistics

Starting Line-Ups

Plymouth Argyle: 4/4/2
Unused Sub: McCormick, Aljofree, Djordjic, Derbyshire

Crystal Palace: 4/3/3
Unused Sub: Kiraly, Hudson

Championship Totals	Plymouth	C. Palace
Championship Appearances	487	273
Team Appearances	452	192
Goals Scored	40	38
Assists	36	31
Clean Sheets (goalkeepers)	8	0
Yellow Cards	60	41
Red Cards	2	0
Full Internationals	3	8

Age/Height

Plymouth Argyle Age: 26 yrs, 3 mo
Crystal Palace Age: 26 yrs, 6 mo
Plymouth Argyle Height: 6'
Crystal Palace Height: 5'11"

Match Statistics

League Table after Fixture

	Played	Won	Drawn	Lost	For	Against	Pts
↓ 11 Crystal Palace	22	9	5	8	33	26	32
...	...	...	...	...	...	...	...
↑ 18 Leicester	23	5	10	8	26	29	25
↓ 19 Coventry	23	5	10	8	28	34	25
↑ 20 Plymouth	23	5	9	9	20	29	24
↓ 21 Brighton	24	3	13	8	24	36	22
● 22 Sheff Wed	24	4	8	12	17	30	20
● 23 Crewe	24	4	8	12	25	46	20
● 24 Millwall	24	3	8	13	17	37	17

Statistics	Plymouth	C. Palace
Goals	2	0
Shots on Target	5	4
Shots off Target	6	4
Hit Woodwork	0	1
Possession %	48	52
Corners	6	3
Offsides	7	2
Fouls	9	21
Disciplinary Points	12	20

0-2

Cardiff City ○
Plymouth Argyle ○

▶ David Norris is on target at Ninian Park

Event Line

32 ○ ▉	Jerome
44 ○ ▉	Capaldi
Half time 0-0	
65 ○ ⇄	Parry > Cooper
71 ○ ▉	Purse
	Foul
72 ○ ⊕	Wotton / RF / P / IA
	Assist: Chadwick
73 ○ ▉	Norris
75 ○ ⇄	Cox > Barker
77 ○ ⇄	Lee > Jerome
80 ○ ⊕	Norris / RF / OP / IA
	Assist: Evans
84 ○ ⇄	Lasley > Evans
90 ○	Whitley
Full time 0-2	

The boy from Newport returned home for Christmas and put one over the rivals from down the road, leaving Tony Pulis as perhaps the only happy Welshman inside Ninian Park.

It was the first time in the season that Argyle won two league games in succession and was thoroughly deserved. After dominating the first half, the only question was whether they would regret not taking the many chances they had created.

The answer came on 72 minutes when Bluebirds' skipper Darren Purse hauled down Nick Chadwick in the box, and Cardiff suffered a double blow. Purse was, perhaps harshly, dismissed and Mr Reliable, Paul Wotton, smashed the ball into the bottom right corner.

David Norris completed the victory eight minutes later. Mickey Evans' defence splitting pass found the run of Norris on the right-hand side, and he fired the penalty beyond Neil Alexander in the Cardiff goal and into the far corner.

Player of the Match

15 Paul Wotton

The skipper led by example and set the Pilgrims on their way to victory with a trademark unstoppable spot-kick.

Quote

🔊 **Tony Pulis**

I thought we started well in the first half, created some good opportunities. Cardiff had a good start to the second half, but once we scored the first goal that was the game.

Championship Milestone

▶ **50**

Mathias Doumbe made his 50th appearance in the Championship.

Venue:	Ninian Park	Referee:	L.Probert - 05/06		Cardiff City
Attendance:	16,403	Matches:	19		Plymouth Argyle
Capacity:	20,000	Yellow Cards:	81		
Occupancy:	82%	Red Cards:	2		

Form Coming into Fixture

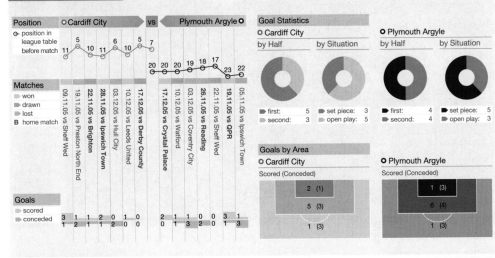

Goal Statistics

Cardiff City — by Half: first: 5, second: 3 — by Situation: set piece: 3, open play: 5

Plymouth Argyle — by Half: first: 4, second: 4 — by Situation: set piece: 5, open play: 3

Goals by Area

Cardiff City — Scored (Conceded): 2 (1), 5 (3), 1 (3)

Plymouth Argyle — Scored (Conceded): 1 (3), 6 (4), 1 (3)

Team Statistics

Starting Line-Ups

Cardiff City 4/4/2 — Unused Sub: Margetson, Ardley

Plymouth Argyle 4/4/2 — Unused Sub: McCormick, Buzsaky, Derbyshire, Taylor

Championship Totals	Cardiff	Plymouth
Championship Appearances	627	491
Team Appearances	483	456
Goals Scored	57	39
Assists	50	36
Clean Sheets (goalkeepers)	13	9
Yellow Cards	76	54
Red Cards	3	1
Full Internationals	7	2

Age/Height

	Cardiff City	Plymouth Argyle
Age	26 yrs, 2 mo	26 yrs, 11 mo
Height	6'	5'11"

Match Statistics

League Table after Fixture

		Played	Won	Drawn	Lost	For	Against	Pts
↓	10 Cardiff	25	9	8	8	33	28	35
...	...	...	...	...	...	...	...	...
•	18 Hull	25	6	9	10	24	29	27
↑	19 Plymouth	24	6	9	9	22	29	27
↓	20 Leicester	24	5	11	8	27	30	26
•	21 Brighton	25	4	13	8	25	36	25
•	22 Sheff Wed	25	4	9	12	17	30	21
•	23 Crewe	25	4	9	12	27	48	21
•	24 Millwall	25	3	9	13	18	38	18

Statistics	Cardiff	Plymouth
Goals	0	2
Shots on Target	2	7
Shots off Target	3	2
Hit Woodwork	0	0
Possession %	49	51
Corners	7	7
Offsides	2	4
Fouls	18	20
Disciplinary Points	20	8

1-1

Wolves ○
Plymouth Argyle ○

▶ Elliott Ward finds the net with a header

Event Line

22 ○ ⊕	Ward / H / C / 6Y
31 ○ ⊕	Cameron / RF / OP / IA
	Assist: Miller
Half time 1-1	
62 ○ ⇄	Ganea > Clarke
68 ○ ▢	Capaldi
69 ○ ⇄	Ince > Anderton
69 ○ ⇄	Seol > Ross
77 ○ ⇄	Lasley > Connolly
82 ○ ▢	Miller
90 ○ ⇄	Derbyshire > Chadwick
Full time 1-1	

Argyle survived a first-half pummelling to come away from Molineux with a point that owed as much to Argyle manager Tony Pulis's tactical prowess as it did to a resolute, disciplined, Pilgrims' performance.

On-loan centre-back Elliott Ward's first goal for the Pilgrims gave Argyle the lead midway through the first half, the goal coming against a tidal wave of Wolves' pressure. Colin Cameron equalised Ward's contribution as Wolves resumed their dominance before the interval.

Ward's goal was not the prettiest, as the West Ham defender converted with the side of his head/shoulder from close range after Stefan Postma had only managed to punch a Tony Capaldi corner straight up into the air.

Wolves got their deserved equaliser nine minutes later after another slick passing move found Scotland international Colin Cameron on the edge of the box, and he fired a precision shot past Larrieu's right hand and into the bottom corner.

Player of the Match	Quote	Championship Milestone
1 Romain Larrieu	🗨 **Tony Pulis**	▶ **75**
That Wolves' only goal came from a deflected shot speaks volumes for the defence, and, especially, the man between the sticks.	We changed it for the second half, matched their system and got up against them a little bit more.	Elliott Ward's goal was the 75th scored in the Championship by Plymouth and his first in the competition.

Venue:	Molineux	Referee:	P.Armstrong - 05/06	Wolverhampton Wanderers
Attendance:	22,790	Matches:	15	Plymouth Argyle
Capacity:	29,400	Yellow Cards:	34	
Occupancy:	78%	Red Cards:	3	

Form Coming into Fixture

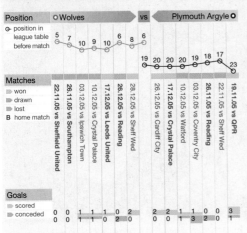

Position
○ Wolves vs Plymouth Argyle ○

⊙ position in league table before match

Wolves: 5, 7, 10, 9, 10, 8, 6
Plymouth Argyle: 19, 20, 20, 20, 19, 18, 17, 23

Matches
- ▶ won
- ▶ drawn
- ▶ lost
- B home match

Wolves matches:
22.11.05 vs Sheffield United
26.11.05 vs Southampton
03.12.05 vs Crystal Palace
10.12.05 vs Leeds United
17.12.05 vs Reading
26.12.05 vs Sheff Wed
28.12.05 vs Sheff Wed

Plymouth matches:
26.12.05 vs Cardiff City
17.12.05 vs Crystal Palace
10.12.05 vs Watford
03.12.05 vs Coventry City
26.11.05 vs Reading
22.11.05 vs Sheff Wed
19.11.05 vs QPR

Goals
	scored	conceded
Wolves	0 0 1 1 1 0 2	0 0 1 1 0 2 0
Plymouth	2 2 1 1 0 0 3	0 0 1 3 2 0 1

Goal Statistics

○ Wolverhampton Wanderers

by Half		by Situation	
▶ first:	3	▶ set piece:	0
▶ second:	2	▶ open play:	5

○ Plymouth Argyle

by Half		by Situation	
▶ first:	4	▶ set piece:	5
▶ second:	5	▶ open play:	4

Goals by Area

○ Wolverhampton Wanderers

Scored (Conceded)

1 (1)
2 (2)
2 (1)

○ Plymouth Argyle

Scored (Conceded)

1 (2)
8 (3)
0 (2)

Team Statistics

Starting Line-Ups

Wolves: Postma, Kennedy, Cameron, Lescott, Clarke Ganea, Craddock, Huddlestone, Chadwick Derbyshire, Miller, Evans, Gyepes, Anderton Ince, Ross Seol

Plymouth: Norris, Connolly Lasley, Wotton, Doumbe, Larrieu, Jarrett, Ward, Capaldi, Barness

▶ 5/3/2   ▶ 4/4/2

Unused Sub: Oakes, Ricketts

Unused Sub: McCormick, Aljofree, Buzsaky

Championship Totals

Championship Totals	○ Wolves	Plymouth ○
Championship Appearances	542	511
Team Appearances	496	476
Goals Scored	60	40
Assists	47	41
Clean Sheets (goalkeepers)	6	10
Yellow Cards	61	62
Red Cards	2	2
Full Internationals	9	2

Age/Height

Wolverhampton Wanderers Age	Plymouth Argyle Age
▶ 28 yrs, 1 mo	▶ 26 yrs
Wolverhampton Wanderers Height	Plymouth Argyle Height
▶ 6'	▶ 5'11"

Match Statistics

League Table after Fixture

		Played	Won	Drawn	Lost	For	Against	Pts
●	6 Wolverhampton	27	9	12	6	32	23	39
...		...	...	...	...	...	...	...
↓	18 Coventry	27	6	11	10	32	41	29
●	19 Plymouth	25	6	10	9	23	30	28
●	20 Leicester	26	5	11	10	27	33	26
●	21 Brighton	27	4	13	10	26	41	25
↑	22 Sheff Wed	27	5	9	13	19	33	24
↑	23 Millwall	27	4	10	13	20	39	22
↓	24 Crewe	27	4	10	13	31	53	22

Statistics

Statistics	○ Wolves	Plymouth ○
Goals	1	1
Shots on Target	8	2
Shots off Target	13	5
Hit Woodwork	1	1
Possession %	60	40
Corners	8	5
Offsides	4	1
Fouls	10	6
Disciplinary Points	4	4

0-3

Plymouth Argyle ○
Leeds United ○

▶ Micky Evans challenges Jonathan Douglas

Event Line

Half time 0-0

53 ○ ⊕	Cresswell / H / C / 6Y
	Assist: Lewis
60 ○ ⊕	Blake / RF / OP / 6Y
	Assist: Lewis
66 ○ ⇄	Djordjic > Connolly
71 ○ ⇄	Lasley > Buzsaky
79 ○ ⇄	Derbyshire > Taylor
82 ○ ⇄	Hulse > Blake
86 ○ ⊕	Hulse / RF / P / IA
	Assist: Miller

Full time 0-3

Sky proved the limit for Argyle as they crashed to their first defeat of the festive period to old boy Kevin Blackwell's rampant Leeds in front of the TV cameras.

American international Eddie Lewis was the star performer, giving the Argyle defence a torrid evening.

After an even first half, the Yorkshire side took control. Lewis fired in a powerful shot following a deep corner by Gary Kelly, and Richard Cresswell managed to get his head on the ball and divert it past the already committed dive of Larrieu.

The match was effectively over on the hour mark; Robbie Blake firing home from close range after another weaving left-wing run, and a deep cross by Lewis.

Substitute Rob Hulse rubbed salt in the wounds five minutes from the end. He cracked an unstoppable penalty into the roof of the net, after Matty Doumbe's clumsy challenge on Liam Miller.

Player of the Match

8 Akos Buzsaky

He was entertaining in another match when 'no-one' would be the right answer.

Quote

🎙 **Tony Pulis**

There's no way I'm going to criticise the players. We haven't got the quality at the moment to chase the better clubs.

76

Venue:	Home Park	Referee:	P.Taylor - 05/06	Plymouth Argyle
Attendance:	17,726	Matches:	18	Leeds United
Capacity:	20,922	Yellow Cards:	49	
Occupancy:	85%	Red Cards:	4	

Form Coming into Fixture

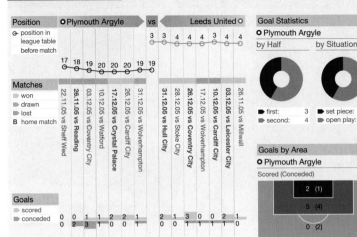

Goal Statistics

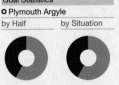

O Plymouth Argyle

by Half	by Situation
first: 3	set piece: 3
second: 4	open play: 4

O Leeds United

by Half	by Situation
first: 3	set piece: 3
second: 6	open play: 5
	own goals: 1

Goals by Area

O Plymouth Argyle — Scored (Conceded)

2 (1)
5 (4)
0 (2)

O Leeds United — Scored (Conceded)

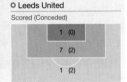

1 (0)
7 (2)
1 (2)

Team Statistics

Starting Line-Ups

Barness, Capaldi, Miller, Kelly
Ward, Jarrett, Evans, Blake Hulse, Derry, Butler
Larrieu, Taylor Derbyshire, Cresswell, Sullivan
Doumbe, Wotton, Douglas, Kilgallon
Connolly Djordjic, Buzsaky Lasley, Lewis, Crainey

4/4/2   **4/4/2**

Unused Sub: McCormick, Aljofree

Unused Sub: Bennett, Pugh, Richardson, Healy

Championship Totals

	O Plymouth	Leeds O
Championship Appearances	512	543
Team Appearances	477	413
Goals Scored	40	62
Assists	33	54
Clean Sheets (goalkeepers)	10	18
Yellow Cards	60	79
Red Cards	2	5
Full Internationals	3	7

Age/Height

Plymouth Argyle Age	Leeds United Age
26 yrs, 2 mo	**28 yrs, 4 mo**
Plymouth Argyle Height	Leeds United Height
5'11"	**5'11"**

Match Statistics

League Table after Fixture

		Played	Won	Drawn	Lost	For	Against	Pts
● 3	Leeds	27	15	6	6	37	22	51
...		...	...	...	...	...	...	...
↓ 18	Derby	28	5	14	9	34	40	29
● 19	Plymouth	26	6	10	10	23	33	28
↑ 20	Sheff Wed	28	6	9	13	22	33	27
↓ 21	Leicester	27	5	11	11	27	35	26
↓ 22	Brighton	28	4	13	11	27	43	25
● 23	Millwall	28	5	10	13	22	40	25
● 24	Crewe	28	4	10	14	31	56	22

Statistics

	O Plymouth	Leeds O
Goals	0	3
Shots on Target	5	8
Shots off Target	2	1
Hit Woodwork	0	0
Possession %	47	53
Corners	5	10
Offsides	0	3
Fouls	15	13
Disciplinary Points	0	0

1-0

Wolves ○
Plymouth Argyle ○

FA Cup
07.01.06

▶ Micky Evans prepares to get a shot away

Event Line

26 ○ ⊕ Clarke / RF / OP / IA	
	Assist: Cameron
Half time 1-0	
69 ○ ⇄ Taylor > Buzsaky	
69 ○ ⇄ Djordjic > Hodges	
73 ○ ⇄ Cort > Seol	
80 ○ ⇄ Rosa > Cameron	
Full time 1-0	

If the FA Cup really is a romantic competition, Argyle received a not unexpected footballing elbow at Molineux.

Future Argyle player Leon Clarke's goal, from a suspiciously offside position, midway through the first half of a game which lacked the passion or imagination to distinguish it as a 'typical cup-tie', proved enough to dump Argyle out of the 2005-06 tournament.

After forcing Wolves on to the defence for a significant period, Argyle were then subjected to a sustained assault which led to Clarke's opener.

First, Paul Ince, possibly tired with seeing his forwards spurn the opportunities provided from midfield, fired off a shot from long range that Romain Larrieu tipped wide for a corner. Then, from Tony Capaldi's flag-kick, Akos Buzsaky stooped to keep a strong downward header from fellow countryman Gabor Gyepes from the goal-line.

Finally, the Pilgrims' resistance was broken when Ki-Hyeon Seol's long ball from the right flank found Clarke in plenty of space beyond the last line of the Argyle defence, and he finished with ease.

▶ Tony Capaldi battles with future loanee Leon Clarke

Match Statistics

Starting Line-Ups

▶ 4/3/3

▶ 4/4/1/1

Unused Sub: Edwards, Anderton, Ganea

Unused Sub: McCormick, Lasley, Zebroski

Statistics	○ Wolves	Plymouth ○
Goals	1	0
Shots on Target	7	4
Shots off Target	3	1
Hit Woodwork	0	0
Possession %	56	44
Corners	4	3
Offsides	2	5
Fouls	11	11
Disciplinary Points	0	0

Age/Height

Wolverhampton Wanderers Age

▶ 27 yrs, 1 mo

Plymouth Argyle Age

▶ 27 yrs, 7 mo

Wolverhampton Wanderers Height

▶ 6'

Plymouth Argyle Height

▶ 5'11"

Player of the Match

13 Mat Doumbe

He seems to enjoy Molineux and reserved another top-quality showing for this second successive visit to the Blackcountry.

Quote

🔘 Tony Pulis

I thought the best team won – I've no qualms about that, although we did better in the second half than the first.

1-1

Plymouth Argyle ○
Norwich City ○

▶ Nick Chadwick is denied by Robert Green

Event Line	
24 ○ ⊕	Chadwick / RF / C / 6Y
	Assist: Capaldi
30 ○ ▪	Wotton
Half time 1-0	
48 ○ ⊕	Huckerby / RF / OP / IA
55 ○ ⇄	Hughes > Jarrett
74 ○	Huckerby
75 ○	Colin
81 ○ ⇄	Thorne > Ashton
83 ○ ⇄	Taylor > Chadwick
Full time 1-1	

Jason Jarrett's quick return to Home Park proved to be an unhappy one as his then current side's away run was brought to an end by his previous side.

Midfielder Jarrett, who had lined up for Argyle in their previous league game, was back for Norwich following his successful seven-game loan spell for the Pilgrims.

Jarrett's replacement, Lilian Nalis, made his Argyle debut and saw his new team take the lead through Nick Chadwick, although it took two weeks for the former Everton striker to be credited with the goal.

The ball seemed to ricochet of a number of legs, but intense scrutiny and considerable lobbying from behind the scenes at Home Park saw the goal eventually awarded to its rightful owner. Chadwick's leg was, unquestionably, the last to touch the ball.

The equalizer definitely belonged to Darren Huckerby, as the Norwich dangerman cut in from the left, and scooped the ball over Larrieu from a seemingly impossible angle for an excellent goal.

Player of the Match	Quote	Championship Milestone
9 Michael Evans	**Tony Pulis**	▶ **50**
Chadwick's goal might have been shrouded in doubt, but there no doubt about Michael Evans' supremacy over his opponents.	We're disappointed not to win the game. It was a cracking game.	Lilian Nalis made his 50th appearance in the Championship and first in the competition for Plymouth.

Venue:	Home Park	Referee:	A.Penn - 05/06		Plymouth Argyle
Attendance:	13,906	Matches:	13		Norwich City
Capacity:	20,922	Yellow Cards:	28		
Occupancy:	66%	Red Cards:	1		

Form Coming into Fixture

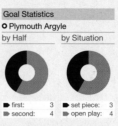

Goal Statistics

Plymouth Argyle

by Half
- first: 3
- second: 4

by Situation
- set piece: 3
- open play: 4

Norwich City

by Half
- first: 4
- second: 7

by Situation
- set piece: 5
- open play: 5
- own goals: 1

Goals by Area

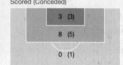

Plymouth Argyle — Scored (Conceded)

| 2 (3) |
| 5 (5) |
| 0 (2) |

Norwich City — Scored (Conceded)

| 3 (3) |
| 8 (5) |
| 0 (1) |

Team Statistics

Starting Line-Ups

Plymouth: **4/4/2**

Norwich: **4/3/3**

Unused Sub: McCormick, Aljofree, Djordjic, Hodges

Unused Sub: Gallacher, Brennan, Shackell

Championship Totals

	Plymouth	Norwich
Championship Appearances	545	413
Team Appearances	485	246
Goals Scored	52	54
Assists	37	35
Clean Sheets (goalkeepers)	10	5
Yellow Cards	66	32
Red Cards	2	2
Full Internationals	2	2

Age/Height

Plymouth Argyle Age	Norwich City Age
27 yrs, 6 mo	**27 yrs, 5 mo**

Plymouth Argyle Height	Norwich City Height
6'	**6'**

Match Statistics

League Table after Fixture

	Played	Won	Drawn	Lost	For	Against	Pts
↑ 10 Norwich	29	11	6	12	33	37	39
...	...	...	...	...	...	...	...
↓ 18 Hull	29	7	9	13	28	36	30
↑ 19 Sheff Wed	29	7	9	13	24	34	30
↓ 20 Plymouth	27	6	11	10	24	34	29
↑ 21 Brighton	29	5	13	11	29	44	28
↓ 22 Leicester	28	5	11	12	28	37	26
● 23 Millwall	29	5	10	14	22	42	25
● 24 Crewe	29	4	10	15	32	61	22

Statistics

	Plymouth	Norwich
Goals	1	1
Shots on Target	10	5
Shots off Target	7	10
Hit Woodwork	0	0
Possession %	56	44
Corners	5	7
Offsides	3	1
Fouls	7	21
Disciplinary Points	4	8

1-2

Crewe Alexandra ○
Plymouth Argyle ○

▶ Paul Wotton converts an early penalty

Event Line

3 ○ ⊕ Wotton / RF / P / IA	
	Assist: Norris
6 ○ ⇄ Foster > Moses	
32 ○ ▪ Otsemobor	
45 ○ ⊕ Wotton / RF / DFK / OA	
	Assist: Evans
Half time 0-2	
59 ○ ▪ Chadwick	
62 ○ ⇄ Rodgers > Vaughan	
68 ○ ⊕ Rodgers / RF / IFK / IA	
	Assist: Taylor
84 ○ ⇄ Hodges > Chadwick	
Full time 1-2	

Paul Wotton produced a captain's display at Gresty Road as Argyle secured a vital victory in their quest to break clear of the relegation pack.

Two goals from Wotton, one penalty and one free-kick, were enough to defeat Crewe Alexandra, despite a spirited late rally from the home side.

Captain Marvel blasted a third-minute penalty down the centre of the goal to give Argyle the lead, following a needless foul on Norris by the otherwise impressive Welsh international, David Vaughan.

Wotton doubled his, and Argyle's tally, in first-half injury-time, blasting a 25-yard free-kick through a flimsy defensive wall and under the body of keeper Ross Turnbull.

Crewe got their consolation when substitute Luke Rodgers smashed home from close range after Argyle had failed to deal with a seemingly harmless free-kick from the half-way line, but the Pilgrims held on for a deserved victory.

Player of the Match

15 Paul Wotton

Two goals, one choice.

Quote

❝ **Tony Pulis**

We're very pleased with the three points because it's a difficult place to come to. The crowd get behind them and they've got some good players.

Venue:	Gresty Road	Referee:	D.Drysdale - 05/06	Crewe Alexandra
Attendance:	5,984	Matches:	19	Plymouth Argyle
Capacity:	10,066	Yellow Cards:	64	
Occupancy:	59%	Red Cards:	4	

Form Coming into Fixture

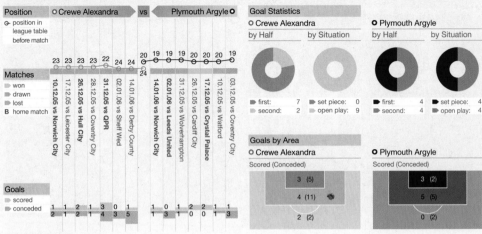

Position — Crewe Alexandra vs Plymouth Argyle

position in league table before match

Matches
- won
- drawn
- lost
- B home match

23 23 23 23 22 24 24 | 20 19 19 19 20 20 20 19
24

10.12.05 vs Norwich City
17.12.05 vs Leicester City
26.12.05 vs Hull City
28.12.05 vs Coventry City
31.12.05 vs QPR
02.01.06 vs Sheff Wed
14.01.06 vs Derby County
14.01.06 vs Norwich City
02.01.06 vs Leeds United
31.12.05 vs Wolverhampton
26.12.05 vs Cardiff City
17.12.05 vs Crystal Palace
10.12.05 vs Watford
03.12.05 vs Coventry City

Goals
- scored: 1 1 2 1 3 0 1 | 1 0 1 2 2 1 1
- conceded: 2 1 2 1 4 3 5 | 1 3 1 0 0 1 3

Goal Statistics

Crewe Alexandra

by Half | by Situation
- first: 7 | set piece: 0
- second: 2 | open play: 9

Plymouth Argyle

by Half | by Situation
- first: 4 | set piece: 4
- second: 4 | open play: 4

Goals by Area

Crewe Alexandra — Scored (Conceded)
- 3 (5)
- 4 (11)
- 2 (2)

Plymouth Argyle — Scored (Conceded)
- 3 (2)
- 5 (5)
- 0 (2)

Team Statistics

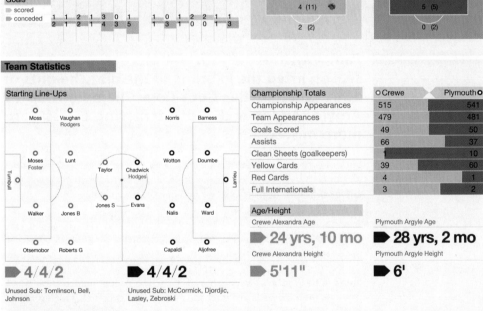

Starting Line-Ups

Crewe Alexandra (left)
- Turnbull
- Moss, Vaughan Rodgers
- Moses, Lunt
- Foster
- Taylor, Chadwick Hodges
- Walker, Jones B
- Jones S, Evans
- Otsemobor, Roberts G

4/4/2

Plymouth Argyle (right)
- Norris, Barness
- Wotton, Doumbe
- Nalis, Ward
- Capaldi, Aljofree
- Larrieu

4/4/2

Unused Sub: Tomlinson, Bell, Johnson

Unused Sub: McCormick, Djordjic, Lasley, Zebroski

Championship Totals

	Crewe	Plymouth
Championship Appearances	515	541
Team Appearances	479	481
Goals Scored	49	50
Assists	66	37
Clean Sheets (goalkeepers)	1	10
Yellow Cards	39	60
Red Cards	4	1
Full Internationals	3	2

Age/Height

Crewe Alexandra Age: **24 yrs, 10 mo**
Plymouth Argyle Age: **28 yrs, 2 mo**

Crewe Alexandra Height: **5'11"**
Plymouth Argyle Height: **6'**

Match Statistics

League Table after Fixture

	Played	Won	Drawn	Lost	For	Against	Pts
↓ 16 Southampton	29	7	13	9	29	32	34
↑ 17 Hull	30	8	9	13	31	36	33
↓ 18 Derby	30	6	14	10	40	47	32
↑ 19 Plymouth	28	7	11	10	26	35	32
↓ 20 Sheff Wed	30	7	9	14	24	37	30
● 21 Brighton	30	5	13	12	30	47	28
● 22 Leicester	29	5	11	13	29	39	26
● 23 Millwall	30	5	11	14	22	42	26
● 24 Crewe	30	4	10	16	33	63	22

Statistics

	Crewe	Plymouth
Goals	1	2
Shots on Target	4	8
Shots off Target	5	3
Hit Woodwork	0	1
Possession %	46	54
Corners	3	5
Offsides	2	2
Fouls	9	11
Disciplinary Points	4	4

1-0

Plymouth Argyle ○
Leicester City ○

▶ Paul Wotton is congratulated after scoring the only goal of the game

Event Line	
40 ○ ■	Gudjonsson
Half time 0-0	
47 ○ ⊕	Wotton / RF / DFK / OA
	Assist: Evans
57 ○ ⇄	Smith > Maybury
70 ○ ⇄	Hume > de Vries
70 ○ ⇄	Hammond > Fryatt
75 ○ ■	Capaldi
Full time 1-0	

Paul Wotton's eighth set-piece special of the season lifted the Pilgrims to the dizzy heights of 16th place in the Coca-Cola Championship as Argyle condemned under-achieving Leicester to more misery.

With the skipper firing on all cylinders, taking his goals total to five penalties and three direct free-kicks to head the scoring charts, Argyle had won four and drawn three of their most recent eight league matches.

Tony Capaldi almost stole the plaudits in the first half, but his curling free-kick sailed inches over the bar with Leicester's Scottish international goalkeeper Rab Douglas well beaten.

It was to be Wotton's evening, however, and the skipper fired in a trademark free-kick from 25 yards just after the interval. The excellent Douglas had no chance as the ball flew into top left-hand corner before anyone could even blink.

The defeat was to prove the final straw for the Leicester board, and manager Craig Levein was dismissed the next day.

Player of the Match

21 Elliott Ward

Wotton was again the match-winner, but Elliott Ward was head and shoulders above everyone in a blue shirt.

Quote

❝ **Tony Pulis**

It was a fantastic free-kick – Paul Wotton is a massive asset for the club. We've put a couple of our players in the wall and it makes it difficult for the keeper to get a clear view.

Venue:	Home Park	Referee:	A.Woolmer - 05/06	Plymouth Argyle
Attendance:	12,591	Matches:	23	Leicester City
Capacity:	20,922	Yellow Cards:	66	
Occupancy:	60%	Red Cards:	5	

Form Coming into Fixture

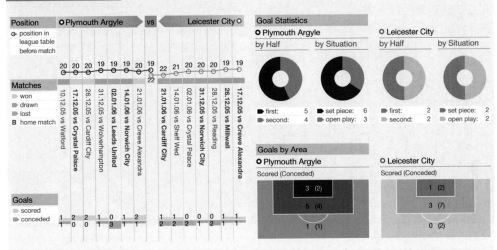

Position
- position in league table before match

Matches
- won
- drawn
- lost
- B home match

Plymouth Argyle vs Leicester City

20	20	20	19	19	19	20	19	22	21	20	20	20	19	19
							22						

10.12.05 vs Watford
17.12.05 vs Crystal Palace
26.12.05 vs Wolverhampton
31.12.05 vs Leeds United
02.01.06 vs Norwich City
14.01.06 vs Crewe Alexandra
21.01.06 vs Cardiff City

21.01.06 vs Cardiff City
14.01.06 vs Sheff Wed
02.01.06 vs Crystal Palace
31.12.05 vs Norwich City
28.12.05 vs Reading
26.12.05 vs Millwall
17.12.05 vs Crewe Alexandra

Goals
- scored
- conceded

| scored | 1 | 2 | 2 | 1 | 0 | 1 | 2 | | 1 | 1 | 0 | 0 | 0 | 1 | 1 |
| conceded | 1 | 0 | 0 | 1 | 3 | 1 | 1 | | 2 | 2 | 1 | 2 | 1 | 1 | 1 |

Goal Statistics

Plymouth Argyle

by Half
- first: 5
- second: 4

by Situation
- set piece: 6
- open play: 3

Leicester City

by Half
- first: 2
- second: 2

by Situation
- set piece: 2
- open play: 2

Goals by Area

Plymouth Argyle
Scored (Conceded)
3 (2)
5 (4)
1 (1)

Leicester City
Scored (Conceded)
1 (2)
3 (7)
0 (2)

Team Statistics

Starting Line-Ups

Aljofree, Capaldi
Stearman
Wesolowski
Ward, Nalis, McCarthy
Larrieu
Evans, Fryatt Hammond
Doumbe, Wotton, Chadwick, de Vries Hume, Gudjonsson, Kisnorbo, Douglas
Johansson
Hughes
Barness, Norris
Maybury Smith

4/4/2   **5/3/2**

Unused Sub: McCormick, Buzsaky, Djordjic, Hodges, Zebroski

Unused Sub: Hamill, O'Grady

Championship Totals	Plymouth	Leicester
Championship Appearances	533	380
Team Appearances	473	380
Goals Scored	52	31
Assists	39	23
Clean Sheets (goalkeepers)	10	5
Yellow Cards	60	74
Red Cards	1	3
Full Internationals	2	6

Age/Height

	Plymouth Argyle	Leicester City
Age	27 yrs, 9 mo	24 yrs, 1 mo
Height	6'	5'11"

Match Statistics

League Table after Fixture

		Played	Won	Drawn	Lost	For	Against	Pts
•	14 Ipswich	30	9	10	11	33	43	37
•	15 Coventry	30	8	11	11	40	44	35
↑	16 Plymouth	29	8	11	10	27	35	35
↓	17 Southampton	29	7	13	9	29	32	34
↓	18 Hull	30	8	9	13	31	36	33
↓	19 Derby	30	6	14	10	40	47	32
•	20 Sheff Wed	30	7	9	14	24	37	30
•	21 Brighton	30	5	13	12	30	47	28
•	22 Leicester	30	5	11	14	29	40	26

Statistics	Plymouth	Leicester
Goals	1	0
Shots on Target	5	5
Shots off Target	4	2
Hit Woodwork	0	0
Possession %	45	55
Corners	5	7
Offsides	2	7
Fouls	13	14
Disciplinary Points	4	4

2-1

Plymouth Argyle o
Southampton o

▶ Romain Larrieu is beaten from close range

Event Line

45 o	▦	Pahars
45 o	⊕	Chadwick / LF / OP / IA
Half time 1-0		
46 o	⇄	Jones > Pahars
46 o		Aljofree
47 o	⇄	Kenton > Brennan
57 o	⇄	Connolly > Aljofree
70 o	⊕	Surman / H / OP / 6Y
		Assist: Oakley
78 o		Kenton
79 o	⇄	Djordjic > Buzsaky
84 o	⊕	Wotton / RF / P / IA
Full time 2-1		

A controversial late penalty, coolly converted by – who else? – Paul Wotton gave Argyle a third consecutive victory for the first time since August 2004.

The Pilgrims' had taken the lead in first-half injury-time thanks to an excellent finish from Nick Chadwick. Southampton failed to deal with a long throw from Capaldi, and Chadwick controlled the ball on his thigh and, in one swift movement, fired a left-foot volley into the bottom right corner.

Another long throw, this time from Southampton, brought the equalizer. The Pilgrims' defence allowed the ball to bounce in the box and substitute Andrew Surman was the first to react, powering a close range header past Romain Larrieu.

The winner came after referee Andy Hall awarded Argyle a soft penalty for an apparent push on Michael Evans. Wotton stepped up to the plate, and fired an unstoppable penalty into the top corner.

The victory was secured by a truly fantastic save from Larrieu in the dying seconds.

Player of the Match	Quote
11 Nick Chadwick	🗨 **Tony Pulis**
In a sometimes difficult season for the former Everton man, he showed his character, and talent.	I thought it was a scrappy game, but the effort, commitment and togetherness of the lads was first class.

Venue:	Home Park	Referee:	A.R.Hall - 05/06	**Plymouth Argyle**
Attendance:	15,936	Matches:	24	**Southampton**
Capacity:	20,922	Yellow Cards:	78	
Occupancy:	76%	Red Cards:	9	

Form Coming into Fixture

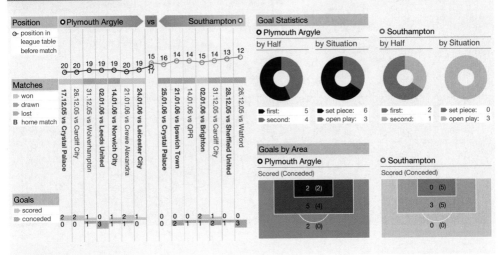

Position
- position in league table before match

Matches
- won
- drawn
- lost
- B home match

Plymouth Argyle — positions: 20, 20, 19, 19, 19, 20, 19, 15, 17
Southampton — positions: 16, 14, 14, 15, 14, 13, 12

Plymouth Argyle matches:
- 17.12.05 vs Crystal Palace
- 26.12.05 vs Cardiff City
- 31.12.05 vs Wolverhampton
- 02.01.06 vs Leeds United
- 14.01.06 vs Norwich City
- 21.01.06 vs Crewe Alexandra
- 24.01.06 vs Leicester City

Southampton matches:
- 25.01.06 vs Crystal Palace
- 21.01.06 vs Ipswich Town
- 14.01.06 vs QPR
- 02.01.06 vs Brighton
- 31.12.05 vs Cardiff City
- 28.12.05 vs Sheffield United
- 26.12.05 vs Watford

Goals
- scored
- conceded

Plymouth Argyle Goals scored: 2, 2, 1, 0, 1, 2, 1
Plymouth Argyle Goals conceded: 0, 0, 1, 3, 1, 1, 0
Southampton Goals scored: 0, 0, 0, 2, 1, 0, 0
Southampton Goals conceded: 0, 2, 1, 1, 2, 1, 3

Goal Statistics

O Plymouth Argyle

by Half — first: 5, second: 4
by Situation — set piece: 6, open play: 3

O Southampton

by Half — first: 2, second: 1
by Situation — set piece: 0, open play: 3

Goals by Area

O Plymouth Argyle — Scored (Conceded)

2 (2)
5 (4)
2 (0)

O Southampton — Scored (Conceded)

0 (5)
3 (5)
0 (0)

Team Statistics

Starting Line-Ups

Plymouth Argyle (left): Larrieu; Aljofree / Connolly, Buzsaky / Djordjic, Ward, Nalis, Evans, Pahars / Jones, Chadwick, Blackstock, Doumbe, Wotton, Barness, Norris

Southampton (right): Blalkowski; Dyer, Baird, Oakley, Lundekvam, Potter, Higginbotham, Surman, Brennan / Kenton

▶ 4/4/2 **▶ 4/4/2**

Unused Sub: McCormick, Hodges, Zebroski

Unused Sub: Smith, Cranie, Fuller

Championship Totals	O Plymouth	Southampton O
Championship Appearances	572	202
Team Appearances	512	133
Goals Scored	54	22
Assists	40	15
Clean Sheets (goalkeepers)	11	
Yellow Cards	67	18
Red Cards	2	1
Full Internationals	2	5

Age/Height

Plymouth Argyle Age	Southampton Age
▶ **27 yrs**	▶ **24 yrs, 4 mo**
Plymouth Argyle Height	Southampton Height
▶ **5'11"**	▶ **6'**

Match Statistics

League Table after Fixture

		Played	Won	Drawn	Lost	For	Against	Pts
↓	9 Wolverhampton	30	10	13	7	34	26	43
●	10 Burnley	31	11	7	13	39	40	40
↑	11 QPR	31	10	9	12	36	44	39
↓	12 Norwich	31	11	6	14	35	44	39
↑	13 Coventry	31	9	11	11	42	45	38
↑	14 Plymouth	30	9	11	10	29	36	38
↓	15 Stoke	30	12	2	16	35	44	38
↓	16 Ipswich	31	9	11	11	34	44	38
↓	17 Southampton	31	7	14	10	30	34	35

Statistics	O Plymouth	Southampton O
Goals	2	1
Shots on Target	4	5
Shots off Target	3	2
Hit Woodwork	0	0
Possession %	52	48
Corners	2	2
Offsides	3	2
Fouls	15	14
Disciplinary Points	4	8

1-0

Burnley ○
Plymouth Argyle ○

▶ Akos Buzsaky takes a tumble

Event Line

24 ○ ⊕ Ricketts / RF / OP / IA	
Assist: Hyde	
Half time 1-0	
72 ○ ⇄ Elliott > O'Connor G	
75 ○ ⇄ Buzsaky > Barness	
76 ○ ⇄ Zebroski > Evans	
87 ○ Harley	
Full time 1-0	

Punk poet John Cooper Clarke once wrote a poem which began by telling the reader firmly that he never wanted to go to Burnley; he must have been an Argyle fan.

The Pilgrims' three-match unbeaten run made this encounter a Coca-Cola Championship mid-table clash and it went the way of the home side through a goal midway through the first half from Michael Ricketts.

The only goal started with an incisive break from midfield by Micah Hyde, and he found Ricketts in space just inside the Argyle box.

The big striker still had plenty to do, however, and he was helped by the normally composed Elliott Ward diving in for a desperate challenge. Ricketts side-stepped him with ease and planted a low right-footed shot into the corner, leaving Romain Larrieu with no chance.

Argyle poured forward in the second half, but their relentless bombardment of the Burnley penalty box brought no reward, and the Green Army faced a long journey home without the point they deserved.

Player of the Match

7 David Norris

It might have been Nalis, apart from an error which led to the goal, so Norris gets the vote.

Quote

Tony Pulis

We let ourselves down today in the final third. We had enough possession, enough opportunities, and we've got to start taking out chances.

Venue:	Turf Moor	Referee:	T.Kettle - 05/06		Burnley
Attendance:	11,292	Matches:	24		Plymouth Argyle
Capacity:	22,546	Yellow Cards:	104		
Occupancy:	50%	Red Cards:	7		

Form Coming into Fixture

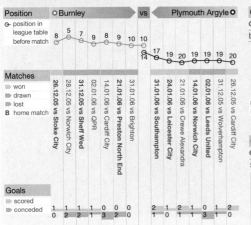

Position — Burnley vs Plymouth Argyle
- position in league table before match

Burnley: 8, 5, 7, 9, 8, 9, 10, 10
Plymouth Argyle: 14, 17, 19, 20, 19, 19, 19, 20

Matches
- won
- drawn
- lost
- B home match

Burnley matches: 26.12.05 vs Stoke City, 28.12.05 vs Norwich City, 31.12.05 vs Sheff Wed, 02.01.06 vs QPR, 14.01.06 vs Cardiff City, 21.01.06 vs Preston North End, 31.01.06 vs Brighton

Plymouth matches: 31.01.06 vs Southampton, 24.01.06 vs Leicester City, 21.01.06 vs Crewe Alexandra, 14.01.06 vs Norwich City, 02.01.06 vs Leeds United, 31.12.05 vs Wolverhampton, 26.12.05 vs Cardiff City

Goals
- scored
- conceded

Burnley scored: 1 1 1 0 0 0
Burnley conceded: 0 2 2 1 3 2 0
Plymouth scored: 2 1 2 1 0 1 2
Plymouth conceded: 1 0 1 1 3 1 0

Goal Statistics

Burnley

by Half / by Situation
- first: 1
- second: 3
- set piece: 1
- open play: 2
- own goals: 1

Plymouth Argyle

by Half / by Situation
- first: 5
- second: 4
- set piece: 7
- open play: 2

Goals by Area

Burnley

Scored (Conceded)
- 1 (2)
- 1 (8)
- 2 (0)

Plymouth Argyle

Scored (Conceded)
- 2 (3)
- 5 (4)
- 2 (0)

Team Statistics

Starting Line-Ups

Harley, Branch, Norris, Connolly
McGreal, Hyde, Ricketts, Chadwick, Wotton, Doumbe
Jensen, Larrieu
Sinclair, O'Connor J, Noel-Williams, Evans Zebroski, Nalis, Ward
Duff, O'Connor G Elliott, Capaldi, Barness Buzsaky

4/4/2 — 4/4/2

Unused Sub: Courtney, Karbassiyoon, McCann, Spicer
Unused Sub: McCormick, Aljofree, Hodges

Championship Totals	Burnley	Plymouth
Championship Appearances	680	592
Team Appearances	533	532
Goals Scored	46	58
Assists	42	43
Clean Sheets (goalkeepers)	19	11
Yellow Cards	103	71
Red Cards	8	2
Full Internationals	4	3

Age/Height

Burnley Age: **29 yrs, 3 mo**
Plymouth Argyle Age: **26 yrs, 5 mo**

Burnley Height: **5'11"**
Plymouth Argyle Height: **6'**

Match Statistics

League Table after Fixture

		Played	Won	Drawn	Lost	For	Against	Pts
●	10 Burnley	32	12	7	13	40	40	43
↑	11 Coventry	32	10	11	11	44	45	41
●	12 Norwich	31	11	6	14	35	44	39
↑	13 Stoke	31	12	3	16	35	44	39
↓	14 QPR	32	10	9	13	36	46	39
↓	15 Plymouth	31	9	11	11	29	37	38
●	16 Ipswich	31	9	11	11	34	44	38
●	17 Southampton	32	7	15	10	30	34	36
●	18 Hull	32	9	9	14	35	40	36

Statistics	Burnley	Plymouth
Goals	1	0
Shots on Target	3	8
Shots off Target	2	3
Hit Woodwork	0	0
Possession %	50	50
Corners	3	6
Offsides	6	1
Fouls	16	15
Disciplinary Points	4	0

0-0

Plymouth Argyle ○
Sheffield United ○

▶ David Norris spins away from Chris Armstrong

Event Line	
43 ○ ▢ Nalis	
Half time 0-0	
58 ○ ⇄ Pericard > Evans	
67 ○ ▢ Doumbe	
71 ○ ⇄ Gillespie > Quinn A	
76 ○ ⇄ Shipperley > Kabba	
77 ○ ⇄ Montgomery > Flitcroft	
Full time 0-0	

For the second season running, there was no happy homecoming for Stoke Climsland's most famous resident as Sheffield United manager Neil Warnock was forced to concede further ground to runaway Championship leaders Reading.

The point from a hard-fought draw against resurgent Argyle at least allowed the man who guided them to promotion from the old Third Division a decade ago to leave his old stamping ground with his head held higher than it had been a year previously, when the Pilgrims won 3-0.

In a game of precious few chances, it wasn't until the last minute when Argyle midfielder David Norris's powerful shot was saved by Blades' keeper Paddy Kenny that either side truly looked capable of breaking the deadlock.

The game was overshadowed by a controversy surrounding former Blades midfielder Lilian Nalis. Warnock had apparently sold the Frenchman to Argyle on the understanding that he would not play in this fixture. Pulis was oblivious to the agreement and didn't hesitate to play the influential Nalis.

Player of the Match

4 Lilian Nalis

And not just for the controversy value when he lined up against his former side.

Quote

❝ Tony Pulis

We took the game to them in the second half, and we're disappointed not to have won.

Championship Milestone

▶ Debut

Vincent Pericard made his first appearance in the Championship for Plymouth.

Form Coming into Fixture

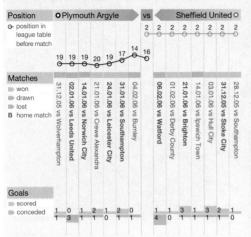

Goal Statistics

O Plymouth Argyle

by Half | by Situation

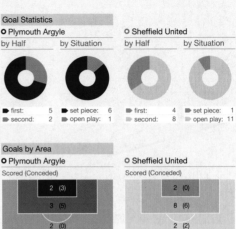

- first: 5
- second: 2
- set piece: 6
- open play: 1

O Sheffield United

by Half | by Situation

- first: 4
- second: 8
- set piece: 1
- open play: 11

Goals by Area

O Plymouth Argyle — Scored (Conceded)

- 2 (3)
- 3 (5)
- 2 (0)

O Sheffield United — Scored (Conceded)

- 2 (0)
- 8 (6)
- 2 (2)

Team Statistics

Starting Line-Ups

Plymouth Argyle: Larrieu; Barness, Capaldi, Ward, Nalis, Evans Pericard, Doumbe, Wotton, Chadwick, Kabba Shipperley, Connolly, Norris

Sheffield United: Kenny; Ifill, Bromby, Jagielka, Short, Akinbiyi, Flitcroft Montgomery, Morgan, Quinn A Gillespie, Armstrong

▶ 4/4/2   ▶ 4/4/2

Unused Sub: McCormick, Aljofree, Buzsaky, Hodges

Unused Sub: Barnes, Kozluk

Championship Totals

	O Plymouth	Sheff Utd O
Championship Appearances	575	678
Team Appearances	504	562
Goals Scored	56	90
Assists	42	74
Clean Sheets (goalkeepers)	11	25
Yellow Cards	67	70
Red Cards	2	7
Full Internationals	2	5

Age/Height

Plymouth Argyle Age	Sheffield United Age
▶ **27 yrs**	▶ **28 yrs, 3 mo**
Plymouth Argyle Height	Sheffield United Height
▶ **6'**	▶ **5'11"**

Match Statistics

League Table after Fixture

		Played	Won	Drawn	Lost	For	Against	Pts
● 2	Sheff Utd	33	21	7	5	59	32	70
...		...	...	...	...	...	...	...
↑ 15	Plymouth	32	9	12	11	29	37	39
↓ 16	Stoke	32	12	3	17	35	47	39
● 17	Hull	33	9	10	14	36	41	37
● 18	Southampton	33	7	15	11	30	36	36
↑ 19	Leicester	33	8	11	14	35	43	35
↓ 20	Derby	33	6	16	11	40	48	34
↓ 21	Sheff Wed	33	8	10	15	25	39	34

Statistics

	O Plymouth	Sheff Utd O
Goals	0	0
Shots on Target	5	7
Shots off Target	4	4
Hit Woodwork	0	0
Possession %	53	47
Corners	5	3
Offsides	2	0
Fouls	9	15
Disciplinary Points	8	0

0-0

Stoke City ○
Plymouth Argyle ○

► Anthony Barness clears the danger

Event Line

15 ○ ▢	Doumbe	
18 ○ ⇄	Sigurdsson > Sidibe	
Half time 0-0		
60 ○ ⇄	Evans > Chadwick	
67 ○ ⇄	Sweeney > Kopteff	
81 ○ ▢	Barness	
83 ○ ▢	Chadwick	
Full time 0-0		

Appropriately enough for Valentine's Day, a love match.

There was plenty of passion at the Britannia on Tony Pulis's return to the club that elbowed him in the summer, but not even an Argyle side containing four men from that most traditional of romantic countries, France, could kiss and run from the Potteries with all three points.

The Pilgrims' fans' real heart-breaker was striker Nick Chadwick, who missed two simple chances to score in the opening stages of the second half.

The first Chadwick chance came after Norris angled a shot across goal; Chadwick saw it and ran in unopposed, but failed to connect with the dolly.

The second opportunity, within seconds, was, if anything, even easier. This time Vincent Péricard embarrassed left-back Marlon Broomes and sent in a low cross across the face of the goal that Chadwick again homed in on at the far post. Again, no connection.

Pulis could only take heart in the warm reception he received from the Stoke faithful, and a fantastic late save by Larrieu.

Player of the Match	Quote	Championship Milestone
1 Romain Larrieu	🗨 **Tony Pulis**	► **75**
Another point-preserving save for the 'keeper, late in the game, was the cherry on a fine rearguard operation.	It was a fantastic reception. I'm very, very pleased. You sometimes worry about what people might think of your time here.	Micky Evans made his 75th appearance in the Championship.

Venue:	Britannia Stadium	Referee:	M.A.Riley - 05/06		Stoke City
Attendance:	10,242	Matches:	28		Plymouth Argyle
Capacity:	28,218	Yellow Cards:	94		
Occupancy:	36%	Red Cards:	7		

Form Coming into Fixture

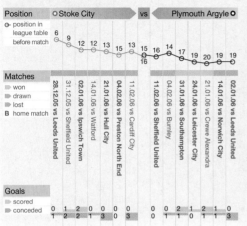

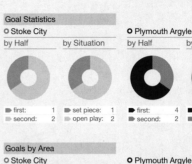

Goal Statistics

Stoke City

by Half | by Situation

first: 1 | set piece: 1
second: 2 | open play: 2

Plymouth Argyle

by Half | by Situation

first: 4 | set piece: 5
second: 2 | open play: 1

Goals by Area

Stoke City

Scored (Conceded)

1 (2)
2 (7)
0 (3)

Plymouth Argyle

Scored (Conceded)

1 (3)
3 (4)
2 (0)

Team Statistics

Starting Line-Ups

Stoke City: Simonsen; Broomes, Kopteff, Sweeney, Hill, Skoko, Sidibe, Sigurdsson, Pericard, Duberry, Brammer, Bangoura, Chadwick Evans, Hoefkens, Chadwick

Plymouth Argyle: Larrieu; Norris, Connolly, Wotton, Doumbe, Nalis, Ward, Capaldi, Barness

Stoke ▶ 4/4/2   Plymouth ▶ 4/4/2

Unused Sub: de Goey, Dickinson, Junior

Unused Sub: McCormick, Aljofree, Buzsaky, Hodges

Championship Totals

	Stoke	Plymouth
Championship Appearances	484	587
Team Appearances	378	516
Goals Scored	26	56
Assists	42	42
Clean Sheets (goalkeepers)	21	12
Yellow Cards	58	69
Red Cards	6	2
Full Internationals	6	2

Age/Height

Stoke City Age	Plymouth Argyle Age
▶ 26 yrs, 9 mo	▶ 27 yrs
Stoke City Height	Plymouth Argyle Height
▶ 6'	▶ 6'

Match Statistics

League Table after Fixture

		Played	Won	Drawn	Lost	For	Against	Pts
●	8 Wolverhampton	33	11	14	8	36	28	47
↑	9 Ipswich	34	12	11	11	40	47	47
↓	10 Luton	34	13	6	15	51	52	45
●	11 Burnley	34	12	7	15	41	43	43
↑	12 Norwich	34	12	7	15	40	47	43
↓	13 QPR	34	11	9	14	38	48	42
↓	14 Coventry	33	10	11	12	44	49	41
●	15 Plymouth	33	9	13	11	29	37	40
●	16 Stoke	33	12	4	17	35	47	40

Statistics

	Stoke	Plymouth
Goals	0	0
Shots on Target	2	1
Shots off Target	1	3
Hit Woodwork	0	0
Possession %	56	44
Corners	4	3
Offsides	3	0
Fouls	10	11
Disciplinary Points	4	8

3-1

Plymouth Argyle ○
Coventry City ○

▶ Vincent Pericard is the hat-trick hero at Home Park

Event Line

13 ○ ⊕	Pericard / LF / OP / IA	
41 ○ ■	Williams	
41 ○ ⊕	Pericard / RF / OP / OA	
	Assist: Evans	
Half time 2-0		
60 ○ ⇄	Chadwick > Evans	
74 ○ ⊕	Pericard / RF / OP / 6Y	
	Assist: Capaldi	
78 ○ ⇄	Morrell > Adebola	
78 ○ ⇄	Wise > Doyle	
78 ○ ⇄	Jorgensen > Scowcroft	
79 ○ ■	Wise	
81 ○ ⇄	Djordjic > Aljofree	
81 ○ ⇄	Buzsaky > Norris	
84 ○ ⊕	Wise / LF / OP / IA	
	Assist: Jorgensen	
90 ○ ■	McSheffrey	
Full time 3-1		

On the afternoon that defender Elliott Ward made an emotional final appearance of his three-month loan spell from West Ham, a new Green hero emerged.

Vincent Péricard became the first Argyle player to net a hat-trick since his compatriot David Friio delivered a similar triple whammy in the 7-0 January 2004 thrashing of Chesterfield.

The first was a left-foot snap-shot from 12 yards that nestled into the bottom corner after Coventry had failed to deal with a long throw by Paul Connolly.

The next arrived courtesy of a headed pass by Evans. Péricard broke into the gap and placed a neat right-foot shot beyond the diving Marton Fulop.

The hat-trick goal was a calamity for the Sky Blues' defence. Fulop collided with defender Ady Williams, and Péricard picked up the pieces for the simplest of tap-ins.

Denis Wise made a cameo appearance for Coventry, earning a customary booking before netting a consolation from the edge of the box.

Player of the Match	Quote	Championship Milestone
10 Vincent Péricard	🔵 **Tony Pulis**	▶ **First Goal**
The first man to score a hat-trick on his full Home park debut since Steve Guinan.	Vincent took his goals well and everything fell for him today but, to be fair, there were good performances all over the park.	Vincent Pericard netted his first goals in the Championship for Plymouth.

Venue:	Home Park	Referee:	P.Armstrong - 05/06		Plymouth Argyle
Attendance:	12,958	Matches:	23		Coventry City
Capacity:	20,922	Yellow Cards:	49		
Occupancy:	62%	Red Cards:	3		

Form Coming into Fixture

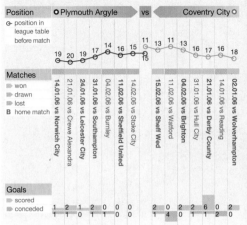

Position
- position in league table before match

Matches
- won
- drawn
- lost
- B home match

Plymouth Argyle: 19, 20, 19, 17, 14, 16, 15, 11, 15

14.01.06 vs Norwich City · 21.01.06 vs Crewe Alexandra · 24.01.06 vs Leicester City · 31.01.06 vs Southampton · 04.02.06 vs Burnley · 11.02.06 vs Sheffield United · 14.02.06 vs Stoke City

Coventry City: 13, 11, 13, 16, 17, 16, 18

15.02.06 vs Sheff Wed · 11.02.06 vs Watford · 04.02.06 vs Brighton · 31.01.06 vs Hull City · 21.01.06 vs Derby County · 14.01.06 vs Reading · 02.01.06 vs Wolverhampton

Goals
- scored
- conceded

Plymouth scored: 1 2 1 2 0 0 0 / conceded: 1 1 0 1 1 0 0

Coventry scored: 2 0 2 2 6 0 2 / conceded: 1 4 0 1 1 2 0

Goal Statistics

Plymouth Argyle

by Half | by Situation
- first: 4
- second: 2
- set piece: 5
- open play: 1

Coventry City

by Half | by Situation
- first: 5
- second: 9
- set piece: 4
- open play: 9
- own goals: 1

Goals by Area

Plymouth Argyle — Scored (Conceded)

1 (1)
3 (3)
2 (0)

Coventry City — Scored (Conceded)

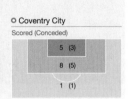

5 (3)
8 (5)
1 (1)

Team Statistics

Starting Line-Ups

Plymouth (4/4/2): Larrieu; Aljofree, Djordjic, Capaldi, Ward, Nalis, Pericard, Doumbe, Wotton, Evans/Chadwick, Connolly, Norris/Buzsaky

Coventry (4/4/2): Fulop; McSheffrey, Impey, Adebola/Morrell, Hutchison, Williams, John, Doyle/Wise, Heath, Scowcroft/Jorgensen, Whing

Unused Sub: McCormick, Hodges

Unused Sub: Ince, Thornton

Championship Totals	Plymouth	Coventry
Championship Appearances	661	684
Team Appearances	590	515
Goals Scored	62	96
Assists	45	66
Clean Sheets (goalkeepers)	13	6
Yellow Cards	78	98
Red Cards	2	4
Full Internationals	3	7

Age/Height

	Plymouth Argyle	Coventry City
Age	26 yrs, 2 mo	29 yrs, 5 mo
Height	6'	6'

Match Statistics

League Table after Fixture

	Played	Won	Drawn	Lost	For	Against	Pts
↓ 12 Coventry	35	11	11	13	47	53	44
↓ 13 Burnley	34	12	7	15	41	43	43
↑ 14 Plymouth	34	10	13	11	32	38	43
↓ 15 QPR	34	11	9	14	38	48	42
• 16 Stoke	33	12	4	17	35	47	40
• 17 Hull	35	9	11	15	37	43	38
• 18 Southampton	34	7	16	11	30	36	37
• 19 Leicester	35	8	13	14	38	46	37
• 20 Derby	35	6	17	12	42	52	35

Statistics	Plymouth	Coventry
Goals	3	1
Shots on Target	11	11
Shots off Target	5	2
Hit Woodwork	0	0
Possession %	68	32
Corners	5	3
Offsides	4	2
Fouls	13	10
Disciplinary Points	0	12

1-0

Derby County o
Plymouth Argyle o

► Derby's Inigo Idiakez is beaten for pace

Event Line

2 o ⊕ Bolder / H / OP / IA	
Assist: Smith	
Half time 1-0	
65 o ⇄ Buzsaky > Hodges	
70 o ⇄ Evans > Chadwick	
73 o ◢ Connolly	
2nd Bookable Offence	
76 o ⇄ Holmes > Peschisolido	
84 o Moore	
90 o ⇄ Ainsworth > Lisbie	
Full time 1-0	

Argyle paid the ultimate price for a dozy start at Derby, losing all three points inside the opening two minutes at Pride Park.

Despite dominating the game for the bulk of the remaining 88 minutes, they were unable to peg back Adam Bolder's early headed conversion of Tommy Smith's left-wing cross.

The goal was agonising to watch as Bolder popped up at the far post to loop a header back across goal and beyond the reach of Romain Larrieu, and his frantically retreating defence.

The outstanding David Norris had enough chances of his own to take home a couple of match-balls, but for a series of saves from Derby goalkeeper Lee Camp, while Camp's Argyle counterpart Larrieu's greatest danger was from the biting north-easterly whipping off the Trent.

The Pilgrims even held sway without defender Paul Connolly for the final 20 minutes, the young Scouser sitting in the dressing-room after becoming the only Pilgrim in the season to be red carded following a couple of injudicious tackles.

Player of the Match

4 Lilian Nalis

He showed his versatility by ending up playing centre-back following Paul Connolly's dismissal.

Quote

🔘 **Tony Pulis**

It was a good header on the back post. Give credit to the kid – it was a good header.

Venue:	Pride Park	Referee:	K.Wright - 05/06		Derby County
Attendance:	25,170	Matches:	23		Plymouth Argyle
Capacity:	33,597	Yellow Cards:	79		
Occupancy:	75%	Red Cards:	5		

Form Coming into Fixture

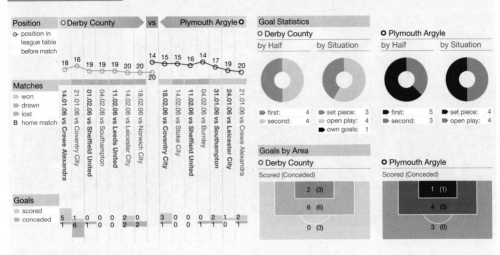

Position — position in league table before match

Derby County vs Plymouth Argyle

Matches: won / drawn / lost / B home match

Goals: scored / conceded

Goal Statistics

Derby County — by Half: first 4, second 4 — by Situation: set piece 3, open play 4, own goals 1

Plymouth Argyle — by Half: first 5, second 3 — by Situation: set piece 4, open play 4

Goals by Area

Derby County — Scored (Conceded): 2 (3), 6 (6), 0 (3)

Plymouth Argyle — Scored (Conceded): 1 (1), 4 (3), 3 (0)

Team Statistics

Starting Line-Ups

Derby County: Camp; Wright, Smith, Nyatanga, Barnes, Peschisolido, Holmes, Pericard, Moore, Idiakez, Lisbie Ainsworth, Edworthy, Bolder

Plymouth Argyle: Larrieu; Norris, Connolly, Nalis, Wotton, Chadwick Evans, Hodges Buzsaky, Aljofree, Capaldi, Barness

Derby 4/4/2   Plymouth 4/4/2

Unused Sub: Poole, Hajto, Thirlwell
Unused Sub: McCormick, Djordjic, Summerfield

Championship Totals	Derby	Plymouth
Championship Appearances	426	619
Team Appearances	400	559
Goals Scored	50	60
Assists	50	44
Clean Sheets (goalkeepers)	19	13
Yellow Cards	42	68
Red Cards	1	1
Full Internationals	3	3

Age/Height

Derby County Age: 26 yrs, 1 mo
Plymouth Argyle Age: 27 yrs, 9 mo
Derby County Height: 5'10"
Plymouth Argyle Height: 6'

Match Statistics

League Table after Fixture

		Played	Won	Drawn	Lost	For	Against	Pts
↑	11 Coventry	36	12	11	13	48	53	47
↓	12 Norwich	36	13	7	16	43	51	46
↑	13 QPR	35	12	9	14	41	50	45
↓	14 Burnley	35	12	7	16	41	44	43
↓	15 Plymouth	35	10	13	12	32	39	43
●	16 Stoke	34	13	4	17	37	48	43
↑	17 Southampton	35	8	16	11	33	36	40
↓	18 Hull	36	9	11	16	39	46	38
↑	19 Derby	36	9	17	12	43	52	38

Statistics	Derby	Plymouth
Goals	1	0
Shots on Target	6	8
Shots off Target	4	3
Hit Woodwork	1	0
Possession %	49	51
Corners	5	1
Offsides	5	9
Fouls	15	17
Disciplinary Points	4	10

1-0

Plymouth Argyle ○
Brighton & Hove Albion ○

▶ Lilian Nalis is mobbed after scoring the winner

Event Line

37 ○ ⊕	Nalis / RF / OP / IA
45 ○ ▪	Hammond
Half time 1-0	
63 ○ ⇄	Mayo > Frutos
66 ○ ⇄	Evans > Chadwick
75 ○ ▪	El-Abd
77 ○ ▪	Hinshelwood
80 ○ ⇄	McPhee > Gatting
86 ○ ▪	Butters
Full time 1-0	

For the second successive home Saturday, a French Green was the toast of Home Park.

After Vincent Péricard's hat-trick against Coventry a fortnight earlier, it was the turn of his compatriot Lilian Nalis to edge Argyle closer to Coca-Cola Championship safety with a first-half winner in a stodgy Home Park encounter.

The midfielder's cool finish after a defensive mix-up in the Brighton penalty area proved the ultimate difference between two sides whose anxious, unedifying, performances pointed to the obvious conclusion that winning points was everything at that stage of the season.

A Tony Capaldi throw was the catalyst; Brighton failed to deal properly with a ball that eventually broke for Nalis, who lob-volleyed it back over the heads of the Seagull's defenders, and goalkeeper Wayne Henderson, into an unguarded net.

Player of the Match

7 David Norris

Like the Duracell bunny, when others around him have stopped, David Norris keeps on going.

Quote

Tony Pulis

It's probably the first time we've come into a game as favourites, which means the pressure was on us, so I'm very pleased.

Championship Milestone

▶ First Goal

Lilian Nalis netted his first goal in the Championship for Plymouth.

Venue:	Home Park	Referee:	P.J.Joslin - 05/06		Plymouth Argyle
Attendance:	13,650	Matches:	29		Brighton & Hove Albion
Capacity:	20,922	Yellow Cards:	83		
Occupancy:	65%	Red Cards:	3		

Form Coming into Fixture

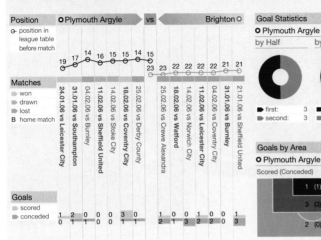

Position
O Plymouth Argyle   vs   Brighton O

- position in league table before match

19 17 14 16 15 15 14 15
23 23 22 22 22 22 21 21

Matches
- won
- drawn
- lost
- B home match

| 24.01.06 vs Leicester City | 31.01.06 vs Southampton | 04.02.06 vs Burnley | 11.02.06 vs Sheffield United | 14.02.06 vs Stoke City | 18.02.06 vs Coventry City | 25.02.06 vs Derby County | | 25.02.06 vs Crewe Alexandra | 18.02.06 vs Watford | 14.02.06 vs Norwich City | 11.02.06 vs Leicester City | 04.02.06 vs Coventry City | 31.01.06 vs Burnley | 21.01.06 vs Sheffield United |

Goals
- scored
- conceded

| 1 | 2 | 0 | 0 | 0 | 3 | 0 | | 1 | 0 | 0 | 1 | 0 | 0 | 1 |
| 0 | 1 | 1 | 0 | 0 | 1 | 1 | | 2 | 1 | 3 | 2 | 2 | 0 | 3 |

Goal Statistics

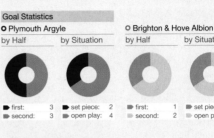

O Plymouth Argyle

by Half		by Situation	
first:	3	set piece:	2
second:	3	open play:	4

O Brighton & Hove Albion

by Half		by Situation	
first:	1	set piece:	1
second:	2	open play:	2

Goals by Area

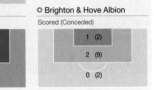

O Plymouth Argyle — Scored (Conceded)

1 (1)
3 (3)
2 (0)

O Brighton & Hove Albion — Scored (Conceded)

1 (2)
2 (9)
0 (2)

Team Statistics

Starting Line-Ups

Plymouth: Larrieu; Hodges, Capaldi, Aljofree, Nalis, Doumbe, Wotton, Barness, Norris, Pericard, Chadwick (Evans), Kazim-Richards

Brighton: Henderson; Carole, El-Abd, Carpenter, Hinshelwood, Hammond, Butters, Frutos (Mayo), Lynch, Gatting (McPhee)

4/4/2 **4/4/2**

Unused Sub: McCormick, Buzsaky, Djordjic, Zebroski

Unused Sub: Martin, Reid, Nicolas

Championship Totals

	O Plymouth	Brighton O
Championship Appearances	612	461
Team Appearances	552	461
Goals Scored	59	30
Assists	41	22
Clean Sheets (goalkeepers)	13	5
Yellow Cards	64	38
Red Cards	1	3
Full Internationals	2	1

Age/Height

Plymouth Argyle Age	Brighton & Hove Albion Age
28 yrs, 6 mo	**24 yrs, 2 mo**
Plymouth Argyle Height	Brighton & Hove Albion Height
6'	**5'11"**

Match Statistics

League Table after Fixture

		Played	Won	Drawn	Lost	For	Against	Pts
↑	7 Cardiff	37	15	10	12	51	43	55
↓	8 Wolverhampton	36	13	15	8	40	30	54
•	9 Ipswich	36	13	11	12	42	48	50
↑	10 Norwich	37	14	7	16	45	52	49
↓	11 Luton	37	14	6	17	56	58	48
↓	12 Coventry	37	12	12	13	49	54	48
↑	13 Plymouth	36	11	13	12	33	39	46
...	...	...	...	...	...	...	...	...
•	23 Brighton	37	5	14	18	32	58	29

Statistics

	O Plymouth	Brighton O
Goals	1	0
Shots on Target	7	1
Shots off Target	4	3
Hit Woodwork	0	0
Possession %	56	44
Corners	6	1
Offsides	2	1
Fouls	17	17
Disciplinary Points	0	16

0-0

Plymouth Argyle ○
Preston North End ○

▶ Micky Evans attempts an acrobatic effort

Event Line

44 ○ ⇄ Buzsaky > Doumbe	
Half time 0-0	
70 ○ ⬜ Pericard	
73 ○ ⇄ Agyemang > Dichio	
75 ○ ⇄ Barness > Hodges	
77 ○ ⇄ Ormerod > Nugent	
82 ○ ⇄ Chadwick > Evans	
83 ○ ⇄ Neal L > Whaley	
Full time 0-0	

As someone once said: "There are 0-0 draws and there are 0-0 draws." This one definitely fell in the latter category.

A highly entertaining game lacked only the essential element of football – goals – but did contain passion, commitment, aggression and finesse.

The irrepressible David Norris had the first opening of the game, surging through the middle of the North End defence but he eventually ran out of steam and Carlo Nash had little trouble blocking his weak shot.

Norris was a constant problem for the Lilywhites, and he could have atoned for his earlier miss after some muscular work by Vincent Péricard provided him with a great chance in the box. He snatched at the chance, unfortunately, and Preston escaped again.

Simon Whaley had Preston's best chance of the game but he blasted over from 12 yards with the goal gaping in front of him.

Player of the Match

7 David Norris

Still running, still chasing.

Quote

❝ **Tony Pulis**

The players have been fantastic and they showed that they'll always give it their best shot again today, against a very good Preston side.

100

Venue:	Home Park	Referee:	I.Williamson - 05/06	**Plymouth Argyle**
Attendance:	10,874	Matches:	25	**Preston North End**
Capacity:	20,922	Yellow Cards:	82	
Occupancy:	52%	Red Cards:	5	

Form Coming into Fixture

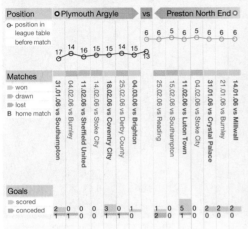

Position
- position in league table before match

Matches
- won
- drawn
- lost
- B home match

Goals
- scored
- conceded

Goal Statistics

Plymouth Argyle

by Half / by Situation

- first: 4
- second: 2
- set piece: 1
- open play: 5

Preston North End

by Half / by Situation

- first: 5
- second: 7
- set piece: 6
- open play: 6

Goals by Area

Plymouth Argyle — Scored (Conceded)

1 (1)
4 (3)
1 (0)

Preston North End — Scored (Conceded)

1 (2)
9 (1)
2 (0)

Team Statistics

Starting Line-Ups

4/4/2 — Unused Sub: McCormick, Djordjic

4/5/1 — Unused Sub: Ward, Stock

Championship Totals	Plymouth	Preston
Championship Appearances	704	697
Team Appearances	644	545
Goals Scored	64	76
Assists	46	68
Clean Sheets (goalkeepers)	14	18
Yellow Cards	76	79
Red Cards	3	5
Full Internationals	3	4

Age/Height

Plymouth Argyle Age	Preston North End Age
27 yrs, 8 mo	**27 yrs, 5 mo**
Plymouth Argyle Height	Preston North End Height
6'	**6'**

Match Statistics

League Table after Fixture

		Played	Won	Drawn	Lost	For	Against	Pts
● 6	Preston	35	13	17	5	45	25	56
↑ 7	Wolverhampton	37	13	16	8	40	30	55
↓ 8	Cardiff	37	15	10	12	51	43	55
● 9	Ipswich	36	13	11	12	42	48	50
● 10	Norwich	37	14	7	16	45	52	49
● 11	Luton	37	14	6	17	56	58	48
● 12	Coventry	37	12	12	13	49	54	48
● 13	Plymouth	37	11	14	12	33	39	47
● 14	QPR	36	12	10	14	41	50	46

Statistics	Plymouth	Preston
Goals	0	0
Shots on Target	4	0
Shots off Target	4	7
Hit Woodwork	0	0
Possession %	50	50
Corners	3	5
Offsides	1	5
Fouls	11	8
Disciplinary Points	4	0

1-0 Hull City ○ Plymouth Argyle ○

Championship

11.03.06

Vincent Pericard tussles with Damien Delaney

Event Line	
Half time 0-0	
46 ○	⇄ Fagan > Duffy
46 ○	⇄ Noble > Welsh
55 ○	⚽ Fagan / LF / OP / OA
	Assist: Parkin
67 ○	⇄ Djordjic > Barness
70 ○	⇄ Buzsaky > Hodges
84 ○	▯ Delaney
84 ○	⇄ Chadwick > Evans
88 ○	▯ Capaldi
89 ○	▯ Aljofree
Full time 1-0	

Argyle's narrow defeat on the Humber was, like baseball legend Yogi Berra once said, a case of déjà vu all over again.

Just as in their previous away outing, at Derby, the Pilgrims dominated enough of the game at the Kingston Communications Stadium to have a valid claim for at least a point

Lilian Nalis had Argyle's best opportunity of the first period after Hull goalkeeper Boaz Myhill found himself hopelessly out of position. Nalis rifled in a shot from the edge of the box that was amazingly cleared off the line by defender Leon Cort's knee.

The slightly undeserved winner arrived ten minutes into the second half. Lively substitute Craig Fagan was released by Keith Andrews following a rare mistake in midfield by Nalis. Fagan galloped clear and slotted the ball past the advancing Romain Larrieu.

The Pilgrims' frustration was compounded in the last minute when Hasney Aljofree tangled with Andrews in the box. The Tigers' skipper appeared to handle the ball, but referee Howard Webb waved away the protests.

Player of the Match

14 Tony Capaldi

In another fine all-round display he was again a consistent performer on the left-hand side of midfield.

Quote

Tony Pulis

It's a little bit déjà vu. We had enough chances and enough opportunities, but, when you are on top, you have got to score.

Venue:	Kingston	Referee:	H.M.Webb - 05/06		**Hull City**
Attendance:	20,137	Matches:	32		**Plymouth Argyle**
Capacity:	25,504	Yellow Cards:	84		
Occupancy:	79%	Red Cards:	3		

Form Coming into Fixture

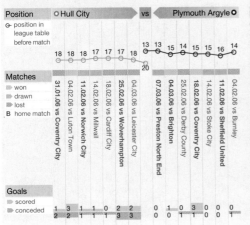

Position
○ Hull City vs Plymouth Argyle ○

○- position in league table before match

Matches
- won
- drawn
- lost
- B home match

Goals
- scored
- conceded

Goal Statistics

○ Hull City

by Half | by Situation

- first: 6
- second: 4
- set piece: 3
- open play: 6
- own goals: 1

○ Plymouth Argyle

by Half | by Situation

- first: 3
- second: 1
- set piece: 0
- open play: 4

Goals by Area

○ Hull City — Scored (Conceded)

2 (2)
5 (8)
3 (3)

○ Plymouth Argyle — Scored (Conceded)

1 (0)
2 (3)
1 (0)

Team Statistics

Starting Line-Ups

Rogers · Elliott · Norris · Connolly

Delaney · Andrews · Parkin · Evans (Chadwick) · Hodges Buzsaky · Wotton

Myhill · Larrieu

Cort · Welsh (Noble) · Duffy Fagan · Pericard · Nalis · Aljofree

Wiseman · Green · Capaldi · Barness Djordjic

▶ 4/4/2   ▶ 4/4/2

Unused Sub: Duke, Lynch, Paynter
Unused Sub: McCormick, Pulis

Championship Totals

	○ Hull	Plymouth ○
Championship Appearances	340	676
Team Appearances	274	616
Goals Scored	23	62
Assists	27	44
Clean Sheets (goalkeepers)	7	15
Yellow Cards	27	72
Red Cards	1	2
Full Internationals	1	3

Age/Height

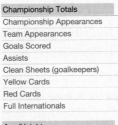

Hull City Age
▶ **24 yrs**

Plymouth Argyle Age
▶ **27 yrs, 7 mo**

Hull City Height
▶ **6'**

Plymouth Argyle Height
▶ **5'11"**

Match Statistics

League Table after Fixture

		Played	Won	Drawn	Lost	For	Against	Pts
↓	12 Luton	38	14	6	18	57	60	48
●	13 Plymouth	38	11	14	13	33	40	47
●	14 QPR	37	12	11	14	42	51	47
●	15 Stoke	36	13	5	18	38	50	44
↑	16 Leicester	38	10	13	15	43	51	43
↓	17 Burnley	37	12	7	18	41	50	43
↓	18 Southampton	37	8	18	11	35	38	42
●	19 Derby	38	8	18	12	48	54	42
●	20 Hull	38	10	11	17	42	49	41

Statistics

	○ Hull	Plymouth ○
Goals	1	0
Shots on Target	8	11
Shots off Target	11	3
Hit Woodwork	0	0
Possession %	49	51
Corners	6	5
Offsides	4	3
Fouls	18	13
Disciplinary Points	4	8

0-1

Plymouth Argyle ○
Cardiff City ○

▶ Hasney Aljofree challenges Cameron Jerome

Event Line

34 ○ ⊕	Thompson / H / OP / IA	
	Assist: Jerome	
35 ○ ▢	Purse	
40 ○ ▢	Ledley	
45 ○ ▢	Cooper	
Half time 0-1		
64 ○ ⇄	Djordjic > Hodges	
66 ○ ⇄	Zebroski > Evans	
71 ○ ▢	Doumbe	
80 ○ ⇄	Buzsaky > Connolly	
81 ○ ▢	Jerome	
89 ○ ▢	Loovens	
90 ○ ⇄	Ndumbu-Nsungu > Jerome	
Full time 0-1		

Better finishing against play-off chasing Cardiff may have seen a very different outcome, but just one goal from their five most recent games perfectly highlights the current problem with the Argyle team.

Michael Evans had a fantastic opportunity to dictate the shape of the game in the first two minutes, but the veteran evergreen diverted his close-range effort the wrong side of the post after good work from Vincent Péricard.

Not long after, Cardiff's Cameron Jerome was guilty of a far worse miss; probably the miss of the season in a game involving Argyle, or any other team for that matter. Jerome managed to not score, despite having an open goal from three yards out.

Jerome did redeem himself on 34 minutes with a pinpoint cross from the right for Scotland international Thompson, and the Scot wrong-footed Romain Larrieu with a powerful header back across goal and into the bottom corner.

The Pilgrims huffed and puffed, but it was not their day.

Player of the Match	Quote	Championship Milestone
1 Romain Larrieu	🔊 **Tony Pulis**	▶ **25**
When everything else is equal, vote for the goalkeeper. Another fine display from Larrieu, short-listed as March's Championship player of the month.	After they scored I thought we dominated the game but they were a threat on the break.	Lee Hodges made his 25th appearance in the Championship.

Venue:	Home Park	Referee:	R.J.Olivier - 05/06		Plymouth Argyle
Attendance:	13,494	Matches:	22		Cardiff City
Capacity:	20,922	Yellow Cards:	65		
Occupancy:	64%	Red Cards:	5		

Form Coming into Fixture

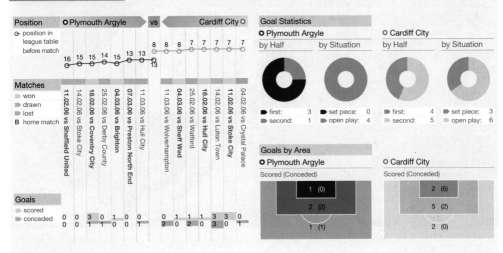

Goal Statistics

Plymouth Argyle

by Half — first: 3, second: 1
by Situation — set piece: 0, open play: 4

Cardiff City

by Half — first: 4, second: 5
by Situation — set piece: 3, open play: 6

Goals by Area

Plymouth Argyle — Scored (Conceded)

1 (0)
2 (2)
1 (1)

Cardiff City — Scored (Conceded)

2 (6)
5 (2)
2 (0)

Team Statistics

Starting Line-Ups

Plymouth Argyle: 4/4/2
Cardiff City: 4/4/2

Unused Sub: McCormick, Barness

Unused Sub: Worgan, Cox, Weston, Whitley

Championship Totals	Plymouth	Cardiff
Championship Appearances	672	512
Team Appearances	612	442
Goals Scored	58	61
Assists	42	56
Clean Sheets (goalkeepers)	15	17
Yellow Cards	75	39
Red Cards	3	3
Full Internationals	3	4

Age/Height

Plymouth Argyle Age	Cardiff City Age
26 yrs, 10 mo	26 yrs, 5 mo

Plymouth Argyle Height	Cardiff City Height
6'	6'

Match Statistics

League Table after Fixture

		Played	Won	Drawn	Lost	For	Against	Pts
● 8	Cardiff	39	16	10	13	52	45	58
↑ 9	Norwich	39	15	8	16	49	55	53
↓ 10	Coventry	39	13	13	13	52	55	52
↓ 11	Ipswich	39	13	13	13	46	54	52
● 12	Luton	39	15	6	18	58	60	51
↑ 13	QPR	38	12	12	14	43	52	48
↓ 14	Plymouth	39	11	14	14	33	41	47
● 15	Stoke	38	14	5	19	40	53	47
● 16	Leicester	39	11	13	15	44	51	46

Statistics	Plymouth	Cardiff
Goals	0	1
Shots on Target	3	6
Shots off Target	9	7
Hit Woodwork	0	0
Possession %	45	55
Corners	14	3
Offsides	3	4
Fouls	13	18
Disciplinary Points	4	20

0-0

Preston North End ○
Plymouth Argyle ○

▶ Mathias Doumbe slides in on Brett Ormerod

Event Line	
41 ○ ■ Hill	
42 ○ ■ Capaldi	
Half time 0-0	
60 ○ ■ Davis	
64 ○ ⇄ Agyemang > Stewart	
68 ○ ⇄ Whaley > Neal L	
78 ○ ⇄ Mears > Hill	
78 ○ ⇄ Barness > Connolly	
84 ○ ⇄ Chadwick > Clarke	
90 ○ ⇄ Evans > Pericard	
Full time 0-0	

Whatever familiarity might breed, it certainly is not a goalfest.

For the second time in less than three weeks, the only things separating Plymouth and Preston was about 300 miles of motorway and a handful of Coca-Cola Championship places.

The Pilgrims introduced Leon Clarke, the young striker on loan from Wolves, and Clarke had Argyle's best opportunity of the first period, but his heavy first touch enabled Youl Mawene to make a goal saving challenge.

Arguably the main talking point of the afternoon was a sickening clash of heads between Matt Hill and Paul Connolly. Hill raced in at full speed in an attempt to reach a hanging cross from the right; Connolly stood his ground and turned the header away but Hill was already committed to the challenge, and both men were forced to leave the field with blood all over the Deepdale pitch.

Both sides kept pressing until the final knockings, and, although there were hearts-in-mouth moments at both ends, the status quo was, inevitably, preserved.

Player of the Match

14 Tony Capaldi

He was busy and caused constant problems with his long throws into the Preston penalty area.

Quote

🔵 **Tony Pulis**

It's credit to the players, really. They give their maximum, win, lose or draw.

Championship Milestone

▶ **Debut**

Leon Clarke made his first appearance in the Championship for Plymouth.

Venue:	Deepdale	Referee:	N.Miller - 05/06
Attendance:	13,925	Matches:	30
Capacity:	22,225	Yellow Cards:	66
Occupancy:	63%	Red Cards:	9

Preston North End
Plymouth Argyle

Form Coming into Fixture

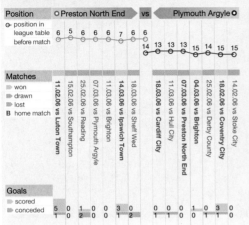

Position

position in league table before match

Preston North End: 6 5 6 6 6 7 6 6
Plymouth Argyle: 14 13 13 13 15 14 15 15

Matches
- won
- drawn
- lost
- B home match

Preston North End:
11.02.06 vs Luton Town
15.02.06 vs Southampton
25.02.06 vs Reading
07.03.06 vs Plymouth Argyle
11.03.06 vs Brighton
14.03.06 vs Ipswich Town
18.03.06 vs Sheff Wed

Plymouth Argyle:
18.03.06 vs Cardiff City
11.03.06 vs Hull City
07.03.06 vs Preston North End
04.03.06 vs Brighton
25.02.06 vs Derby County
18.02.06 vs Coventry City
14.02.06 vs Stoke City

Goals
- scored
- conceded

Preston: scored 5 0 1 0 0 3 0 | conceded 1 0 2 0 0 1 2
Plymouth: scored 0 0 0 1 0 3 0 | conceded 1 1 0 0 1 1 0

Goal Statistics

○ Preston North End

by Half | by Situation
- first: 2
- second: 7
- set piece: 2
- open play: 7

● Plymouth Argyle

by Half | by Situation
- first: 3
- second: 1
- set piece: 0
- open play: 4

Goals by Area

○ Preston North End
Scored (Conceded)

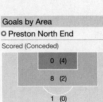

0 (4)
8 (2)
1 (0)

○ Plymouth Argyle
Scored (Conceded)

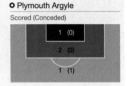

1 (0)
2 (3)
1 (1)

Team Statistics

Starting Line-Ups

Preston North End:
Nash
Hill / Mears, Neal L / Whaley
Davis, O'Neil
Stewart / Agyemang, Pericard / Evans
Mawene, McKenna, Ormerod, Clarke / Chadwick
Alexander, Sedgwick

Plymouth Argyle:
Larrieu
Norris, Connolly / Barness
Wotton, Doumbe
Nalis, Aljofree
Capaldi, Hodges

Preston: 4 / 4 / 2
Plymouth: 4 / 4 / 2

Unused Sub: Jarrett, Hibbert
Unused Sub: McCormick, Buzsaky

Championship Totals	○ Preston	Plymouth ○
Championship Appearances	748	753
Team Appearances	618	640
Goals Scored	70	68
Assists	65	50
Clean Sheets (goalkeepers)	20	15
Yellow Cards	90	82
Red Cards	2	3
Full Internationals	4	2

Age/Height

Preston North End Age
▶ **27 yrs, 11 mo**

Plymouth Argyle Age
▶ **27 yrs, 7 mo**

Preston North End Height
▶ **6'**

Plymouth Argyle Height
▶ **6'**

Match Statistics

League Table after Fixture

		Played	Won	Drawn	Lost	For	Against	Pts
● 6	Preston	39	14	19	6	48	28	61
● 7	Wolverhampton	40	14	17	9	44	34	59
● 8	Cardiff	40	16	11	13	52	45	59
● 9	Norwich	40	15	8	17	49	57	53
↑ 10	Ipswich	40	13	14	13	47	55	53
↑ 11	Luton	40	15	7	18	59	61	52
↓ 12	Coventry	40	13	13	14	53	59	52
● 13	QPR	39	12	13	14	43	52	49
● 14	Plymouth	40	11	15	14	33	41	48

Statistics	○ Preston	Plymouth ○
Goals	0	0
Shots on Target	3	5
Shots off Target	4	3
Hit Woodwork	0	0
Possession %	53	47
Corners	10	7
Offsides	5	1
Fouls	9	9
Disciplinary Points	8	4

2-0

Plymouth Argyle ○
Wolves ○

▶ Hasney Aljofree celebrates a rare goal

Event Line

9 ○ ⊕	Aljofree / LF / C / IA
	Assist: Capaldi
20 ○ ▪	Davies
20 ○ ▪	Wotton
34 ○ ▪	Miller
Half time 1-0	
62 ○ ⇄	Edwards > Jones
73 ○ ⇄	Frankowski > Miller
73 ○ ⇄	Ricketts > Ross
74 ○ ⇄	Evans > Chadwick
80 ○ ⊕	Ince / H / OG / 6Y
	Assist: Capaldi
84 ○ ▪	Aliadiere
90 ○ ⇄	Buzsaky > Capaldi
90 ○ ⇄	Pulis > Pericard
Full time 2-0	

A rare goal from Argyle centre-back Hasney Aljofree set Argyle on their way to a thoroughly deserved win against opposition who had arrived at Home Park with hearts, if not minds, set on earning a Coca-Cola Championship play-off place.

A pearl of a late own goal from veteran midfielder Paul Ince ensured that outcome had to be pursued more in hope than anticipation, as the Pilgrims came within two points of equalling last season's Championship total of 51 points.

The Pilgrims had already created decent chances for Vincent Péricard and Nick Chadwick, before Aljofree scored the opener, firing home from the edge of the box following a low corner by Tony Capaldi.

The Greens battered their illustrious opponents from start to finish and could have easily won the game by a margin of five or six. As it was, the only other goal came from the head of Ince. The former England international diverted a Capaldi free-kick into the top corner of his own net.

Player of the Match	Quote	Championship Milestone
10 Vincent Péricard	👍 **Tony Pulis**	▶ **75**
Can I have Paul Ince? No? Alright, then, Vincent Péricard.	We have out-played one of the best teams in the league.	David Norris made his 75th appearance in the Championship.

Venue:	Home Park	Referee:	P.Melin - 05/06		Plymouth Argyle
Attendance:	15,871	Matches:	28		Wolverhampton Wanderers
Capacity:	20,922	Yellow Cards:	85		
Occupancy:	76%	Red Cards:	8		

Form Coming into Fixture

Position

○ position in league table before match

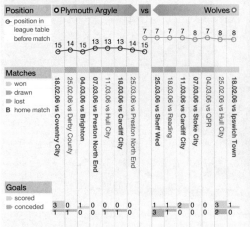

Matches

- won
- drawn
- lost
- **B** home match

Goals

- scored
- conceded

scored	3	0	1	0	0	0		1	1	2	0	3	1
conceded	1	1	0	0	1	1		3	1	0	0	2	0

Goal Statistics

○ Plymouth Argyle

by Half / by Situation

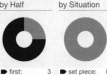

- first: 3
- second: 1
- set piece: 0
- open play: 4

○ Wolverhampton Wanderers

by Half / by Situation

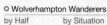

- first: 2
- second: 6
- set piece: 3
- open play: 5

Goals by Area

○ Plymouth Argyle

Scored (Conceded)

1 (0)
2 (3)
1 (1)

○ Wolverhampton Wanderers

Scored (Conceded)

2 (0)
6 (5)
0 (1)

Team Statistics

Starting Line-Ups

▶ **4/4/2**

Unused Sub: McCormick, Djordjic

▶ **4/3/3**

Unused Sub: Oakes, Little

Championship Totals	○ Plymouth	Wolves ○
Championship Appearances	720	542
Team Appearances	660	535
Goals Scored	64	69
Assists	45	43
Clean Sheets (goalkeepers)	16	12
Yellow Cards	78	57
Red Cards	3	1
Full Internationals	3	6

Age/Height

Plymouth Argyle Age

▶ **27 yrs**

Wolverhampton Wanderers Age

▶ **26 yrs, 6 mo**

Plymouth Argyle Height

▶ **6'**

Wolverhampton Wanderers Height

▶ **6'**

Match Statistics

League Table after Fixture

		Played	Won	Drawn	Lost	For	Against	Pts
● 7	Wolverhampton	41	14	17	10	44	36	59
● 8	Cardiff	41	16	11	14	54	48	59
● 9	Norwich	41	16	8	17	51	58	56
↑ 10	Luton	41	16	7	18	60	61	55
↓ 11	Ipswich	41	13	14	14	47	56	53
● 12	Coventry	41	13	13	15	53	60	52
● 13	Stoke	41	15	7	19	43	55	52
↑ 14	Plymouth	41	12	15	14	35	41	51
↓ 15	QPR	41	12	13	16	45	56	49

Statistics	○ Plymouth	Wolves ○
Goals	2	0
Shots on Target	5	2
Shots off Target	9	3
Hit Woodwork	0	0
Possession %	42	58
Corners	8	1
Offsides	3	6
Fouls	15	18
Disciplinary Points	4	12

0-0

Leeds United ○
Plymouth Argyle ○

▶ Vincent Pericard shows his commitment to the cause

Event Line	
6 ○ ▢	Healy
31 ○ ▢	Nalis
36 ○ ⇄	Beckford > Kelly
Half time 0-0	
51 ○ ▢	Connolly
68 ○ ⇄	Lewis > Healy
71 ○ ⇄	Evans > Clarke
74 ○ ⇄	Miller > Douglas
87 ○ ⇄	Buzsaky > Pericard
90 ○ ▢	Larrieu
90 ○ ⇄	Pulis > Hodges
Full time 0-0	

Unequiviocally, Argyle ensured their Coca-Cola Championship status. They did it with another performance in which they showed themselves to be the equal, or better, of a club that has pretensions to play at a higher level: not Reading, nor Sheffield United, nor Watford, nor Palace, nor Preston, nor Leeds took them for six points in the season.

They should have won at Elland Road, too.

With minutes to go, Argyle were denied a penalty when, for the second weekend in a row, the officials were unable to see a clear foul inside the 18-yard area.

Even the one-eyed homers around the Press box agreed that David Norris was hauled down two yards inside the box in front of the Leeds kop - referee Mike Thorpe and his unhelpful assistants bottled the decision and denied Argyle probable victory.

Player of the Match

7 David Norris

Winner of the match-turning penalty (well, that is what should have happened).

Quote

💬 **Tony Pulis**

I thought it was a definite penalty. It was two yards inside the box. I'm 120% biased, so I will see everything through green eyes, but I think it was a stone-banker penalty.

Venue:	Elland Road	Referee:	M.Thorpe - 05/06		Leeds United
Attendance:	20,650	Matches:	33		Plymouth Argyle
Capacity:	40,204	Yellow Cards:	83		
Occupancy:	51%	Red Cards:	3		

Form Coming into Fixture

Position — O Leeds United vs Plymouth Argyle O

G- position in league table before match

Leeds United: 4 4 3 3 3 4 4 4
Plymouth Argyle: 14 15 14 13 13 13 15 14

Matches
- won
- drawn
- lost
- B home match

Leeds matches: 25.02.06 vs Luton Town, 04.03.06 vs Crystal Palace, 11.03.06 vs Norwich City, 18.03.06 vs Coventry City, 21.03.06 vs Crystal Palace, 25.03.06 vs Stoke City, 01.04.06 vs Hull City

Plymouth matches: 01.04.06 vs Wolverhampton, 25.03.06 vs Preston North End, 18.03.06 vs Cardiff City, 11.03.06 vs Hull City, 07.03.06 vs Preston North End, 04.03.06 vs Brighton, 25.02.06 vs Derby County

Goals
- scored
- conceded

Leeds scored: 2 2 2 1 0 0 0
Leeds conceded: 1 1 2 1 1 0 1

Plymouth scored: 2 0 0 0 0 1 0
Plymouth conceded: 0 0 1 1 1 0 1

Goal Statistics

O Leeds United

by Half / by Situation

- first: 2
- second: 5
- set piece: 2
- open play: 5

O Plymouth Argyle

by Half / by Situation

- first: 2
- second: 1
- set piece: 1
- open play: 1
- own goals: 1

Goals by Area

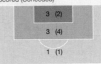

O Leeds United

Scored (Conceded)

3 (2)
3 (4)
1 (1)

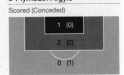

O Plymouth Argyle

Scored (Conceded)

1 (0)
2 (2)
0 (1)

Team Statistics

Starting Line-Ups

Leeds United:
Crainey, Healy, Lewis, Douglas, Miller, Gregan, Sullivan, Derry, Hulse, Butler, Richardson, Kelly, Beckford

4/3/3

Unused Sub: Bennett, Kilgallon

Plymouth Argyle:
Norris, Connolly, Wotton, Doumbe, Pericard, Buzsaky, Larrieu, Clarke, Evans, Nalis, Aljofree, Blake, Capaldi, Hodges, Pulis

4/4/2

Unused Sub: McCormick, Zebroski

Championship Totals

Championship Totals	O Leeds	Plymouth O
Championship Appearances	785	738
Team Appearances	693	625
Goals Scored	82	66
Assists	81	50
Clean Sheets (goalkeepers)	23	17
Yellow Cards	118	81
Red Cards	5	3
Full Internationals	8	3

Age/Height

	Leeds United Age	Plymouth Argyle Age
Age	28 yrs, 4 mo	26 yrs, 10 mo
	Leeds United Height	Plymouth Argyle Height
Height	5'10"	6'

Match Statistics

League Table after Fixture

		Played	Won	Drawn	Lost	For	Against	Pts
↑ 3	Leeds	42	20	13	9	54	34	73
...		...	...	...	...	...	...	...
● 14	Plymouth	42	12	16	14	35	41	52
↑ 15	Burnley	42	14	9	19	45	52	51
↓ 16	Leicester	42	12	14	16	48	54	50
↑ 17	Southampton	42	10	19	13	42	47	49
↓ 18	QPR	42	12	13	17	45	57	49
↓ 19	Hull	42	12	12	18	47	53	48
● 20	Derby	42	10	18	14	51	61	48

Statistics

Statistics	O Leeds	Plymouth O
Goals	0	0
Shots on Target	2	1
Shots off Target	6	7
Hit Woodwork	1	0
Possession %	45	55
Corners	4	3
Offsides	5	2
Fouls	10	16
Disciplinary Points	4	12

1-1

Millwall ○
Plymouth Argyle ○

► Vincent Pericard powers home an early header

Event Line

10 ○ ⊕	Pericard / H / C / 6Y
	Assist: Connolly
31 ○ ⊕	Williams / H / 1FK / IA
	Assist: Asaba
42 ○ ⇄	Powel > Asaba
44 ○ ▢	Wotton
Half time 1-1	
60 ○ ⇄	Buzsaky > Capaldi
62 ○ ▢	Williams
64 ○ ⇄	Evans > Clarke
76 ○ ⇄	Cogan > Dunne
79 ○ ⇄	Pulis > Pericard
87 ○ ▢	Pulis
Full time 1-1	

Argyle's first goal away from Home Park for more than two months secured the point that ensured that they still have three games to improve on last season's debut Championship total of 53 points. Given that only nine of those came in the first 11 matches, that is no mean boast.

The Pilgrims started at a gallop and could have scored within two minutes following a sweeping move involving Leon Clarke and David Norris, but ended with Vincent Péricard having a fresh-air swipe in front of goal.

Pericard atoned for the miss on ten minutes when he rose unopposed to head a Tony Capaldi corner into the corner of the Millwall net, prompting vociferous protests from the home crowd, with chairman Peter de Savary the target of their anger.

The Lions responded well to the set-back and Marvin Williams grabbed a brave equaliser, nodding past Larrieu after some fatal hesitation from the Argyle defence.

Player of the Match	Quote
22 Paul Connolly	🔵 **Tony Pulis**
He is adding some useful set-piece elements to his defensive abilities.	We just dropped off. For whatever reason, I don't know. We took a step back and invited pressure. That was disappointing for us.

Venue:	The New Den	Referee:	P.Walton - 05/06		Millwall
Attendance:	9,183	Matches:	38		Plymouth Argyle
Capacity:	20,146	Yellow Cards:	115		
Occupancy:	46%	Red Cards:	6		

Form Coming into Fixture

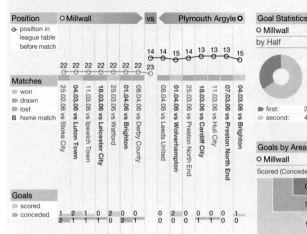

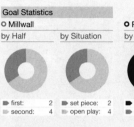

Goal Statistics

Millwall

by Half | by Situation

first: 2 | set piece: 2
second: 4 | open play: 4

Plymouth Argyle

by Half | by Situation

first: 2 | set piece: 1
second: 1 | open play: 1
| | own goals: 1

Goals by Area

Millwall

Scored (Conceded)

0 (1)

5 (5)

1 (2)

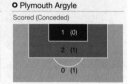

Plymouth Argyle

Scored (Conceded)

1 (0)

2 (1)

0 (1)

Team Statistics

Starting Line-Ups

Millwall:
Craig, Williams
Whitbread, Livermore
Doyle
May, Pericard Pulis
Asaba Powel, Clarke Evans
Phillips, Elliott
Lawrence, Dunne Cogan

Plymouth Argyle:
Norris, Connolly
Wotton, Doumbe
Larrieu
Nalis, Aljofree
Capaldi Buzsaky, Hodges

Millwall: 4/4/2
Plymouth Argyle: 4/4/2

Unused Sub: Marshall, Vincent, Braniff

Unused Sub: McCormick, Chadwick

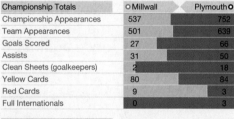

Championship Totals

Championship Totals	Millwall	Plymouth
Championship Appearances	537	752
Team Appearances	501	639
Goals Scored	27	66
Assists	31	50
Clean Sheets (goalkeepers)	2	18
Yellow Cards	80	84
Red Cards	9	3
Full Internationals	0	3

Age/Height

Millwall Age
24 yrs

Plymouth Argyle Age
26 yrs, 10 mo

Millwall Height
6'1"

Plymouth Argyle Height
6'

Match Statistics

League Table after Fixture

		Played	Won	Drawn	Lost	For	Against	Pts
● 7	Wolverhampton	43	14	19	10	47	39	61
● 8	Cardiff	43	16	11	16	56	54	59
● 9	Luton	43	16	8	19	62	64	56
↑ 10	Coventry	43	14	14	15	57	63	56
↓ 11	Norwich	43	16	8	19	51	61	56
↓ 12	Stoke	43	16	7	20	48	58	55
↑ 13	Plymouth	43	12	17	14	36	42	53
...		...	...	...	...	...	...	...
↓ 24	Millwall	43	7	16	20	32	56	37

Statistics

Statistics	Millwall	Plymouth
Goals	1	1
Shots on Target	6	2
Shots off Target	3	5
Hit Woodwork	0	0
Possession %	48	52
Corners	9	2
Offsides	5	3
Fouls	18	12
Disciplinary Points	4	8

1-2

Plymouth Argyle ○
Luton Town ○

▶ Akos Buzsaky fires Plymouth in front

Event Line		
40 ○ ▨	Showunmi	
Half time 0-0		
54 ○ ⇄	Evans > Clarke	
54 ○ ⇄	Buzsaky > Hodges	
68 ○ ⇄	Brkovic > Bell	
68 ○ ⇄	Vine > Feeney	
70 ○ ▨	Buzsaky	
70 ○ ⊕	Buzsaky / LF / OP / IA	
	Assist: Pericard	
72 ○ ▨	Heikkinen	
79 ○ ⊕	Vine / RF / OP / IA	
	Assist: Howard	
84 ○ ⇄	Andrew > Heikkinen	
88 ○ ⊕	Andrew / RF / OP / 6Y	
	Assist: Vine	
89 ○ ▨	Aljofree	
Full time 1-2		

Two goals in the last ten minutes from two Luton subs turned the game on its head to earn Mike Newell's side the distinction of becoming the first side since January 2 to score more than once against the Pilgrims.

It was a day for replacements. A super strike from supersub Akos Buzsaky had looked set to extend Argyle's unbeaten run to five matches.

Earlier, Vincent Péricard was denied a certain goal when his header was spilled over the line by Marlon Beresford, but Luton's luck soon ran out. Péricard released Akos Buzsaky on the left, and the Hungarian burst forward and smashed a left-foot shot past Marlon Beresford.

Impressive substitute Rowan Vine equalised with a cheeky overhead kick, and then, ten minutes later, the same player bamboozled the Argyle defence before sending the ball across the face of goal for the simplest of tap-ins for Calvin Andrew.

It was a particular disappointing end for keeper Luke McCormick, who turned in a competent performance in his first league start of the season.

Player of the Match

4 Lilian Nalis

Another game, another Frenchman.

Quote

❝ **Tony Pulis**

The equaliser knocked the stuffing out of us, and the second goal was a kick in the proverbials.

Venue:	Home Park	Referee:	A.R.Hall - 05/06		Plymouth Argyle
Attendance:	13,486	Matches:	32		Luton Town
Capacity:	20,922	Yellow Cards:	104		
Occupancy:	64%	Red Cards:	10		

Form Coming into Fixture

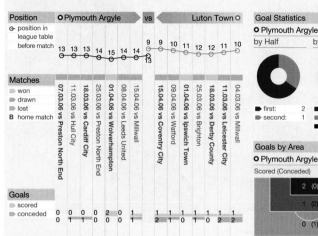

Position ○ Plymouth Argyle vs Luton Town ○

G- position in league table before match

Plymouth Argyle: 13 13 13 14 15 14 14 / 13
Luton Town: 9 9 10 11 12 12 11 10

Matches
- won
- drawn
- lost
- B home match

Plymouth matches: 07.03.06 vs Preston North End, 11.03.06 vs Hull City, 18.03.06 vs Cardiff City, 25.03.06 vs Preston North End, 01.04.06 vs Wolverhampton, 08.04.06 vs Leeds United, 15.04.06 vs Millwall

Luton matches: 15.04.06 vs Coventry City, 09.04.06 vs Watford, 01.04.06 vs Ipswich Town, 25.03.06 vs Brighton, 18.03.06 vs Derby County, 11.03.06 vs Leicester City, 04.03.06 vs Millwall

Goals
- scored: Plymouth 0 0 0 2 0 1 / Luton 1 1 1 1 1 1 1
- conceded: Plymouth 0 1 1 0 0 0 1 / Luton 2 1 0 1 0 2 2

Goal Statistics

○ Plymouth Argyle

by Half	by Situation
first: 2	set piece: 2
second: 1	open play: 0
	own goals: 1

○ Luton Town

by Half	by Situation
first: 0	set piece: 2
second: 7	open play: 3
	own goals: 2

Goals by Area

○ Plymouth Argyle — Scored (Conceded)

2 (0)
1 (2)
0 (1)

○ Luton Town — Scored (Conceded)

5 (1)
2 (7)
0 (0)

Team Statistics

Starting Line-Ups

Plymouth Argyle:
- McCormick
- Connolly, Doumbe, Aljofree, Hodges
- Norris, Wotton, Nalis, Capaldi
- Clarke Evans, Pericard, Buzsaky
- Feeney Vine

Luton Town:
- Beresford
- Keane, Heikkinen Andrew, Barnett, Edwards
- Morgan, Showunmi, Howard, Holmes, Brkovic
- Bell

Plymouth: ▶ 4 / 4 / 2
Luton: ▶ 4 / 4 / 2

Unused Sub: Pulis, Summerfield, Reid
Unused Sub: Brill, Stevens

Championship Totals

	○ Plymouth	Luton ○
Championship Appearances	720	401
Team Appearances	607	383
Goals Scored	67	51
Assists	51	45
Clean Sheets (goalkeepers)	9	9
Yellow Cards	85	33
Red Cards	3	2
Full Internationals	3	4

Age/Height

Plymouth Argyle Age	Luton Town Age
▶ **26 yrs, 8 mo**	▶ **25 yrs, 4 mo**

Plymouth Argyle Height	Luton Town Height
▶ **6'**	▶ **6'**

Match Statistics

League Table after Fixture

		Played	Won	Drawn	Lost	For	Against	Pts
●	9 Luton	44	17	8	19	64	65	59
↑	10 Norwich	44	17	8	19	54	63	59
↓	11 Coventry	44	14	15	15	58	64	57
↑	12 Southampton	44	12	19	13	46	48	55
↓	13 Stoke	44	16	7	21	49	61	55
↑	14 Burnley	44	14	11	19	45	52	53
↓	15 Plymouth	44	12	17	15	37	44	53
↓	16 Ipswich	44	13	14	17	50	64	53
●	17 Leicester	44	12	15	17	50	57	51

Statistics

	○ Plymouth	Luton ○
Goals	1	2
Shots on Target	3	10
Shots off Target	5	2
Hit Woodwork	0	0
Possession %	44	56
Corners	5	5
Offsides	5	4
Fouls	12	15
Disciplinary Points	8	8

1-0

Leicester City ○
Plymouth Argyle ○

▶ Vincent Pericard is denied by a sprawling save from Paul Henderson

Event Line

12 ○ ■ Stearman	
Half time 0-0	
54 ○ ⇄ Chadwick > Clarke	
55 ○ ⊕ Fryatt / H / OP / 6Y	
Assist: Welsh	
62 ○ ⇄ Buzsaky > Hodges	
63 ○ ⇄ Pulis > Connolly	
78 ○ ⇄ Tiatto > Welsh	
82 ○ ⇄ O'Grady > Fryatt	
Full time 1-0	

It was, all over, a black day for the Pilgrims.

Wearing their new away kit for the first time, they finished their away campaign having failed to win outside Devon for the 20th time this season. When you remember that one of their three wins came at runaway champions Reading on the opening day of the campaign, you can appreciate just how long and hard life on the road was since August.

In a real end-of-the-season encounter, all the action was compressed into the space of five second-half minutes.

Firstly, the Foxes took the lead after Matty Fryatt peeled off Lee Hodges at the far post to nod an Andy Welsh cross past the helpless Romain Larrieu.

Minutes later, and Richard Stearman's weak header back to his goalkeeper Paul Henderson was pounced on by Vincent Péricard, but Henderson spared his team-mates blushes with a brave block.

Player of the Match	Quote	Championship Milestone
7 David Norris	💬 **Tony Pulis**	▶ **75**
Man of the season.	I'm saying the same things every week – the team's got spirit, commitment, we just need that cutting edge.	Tony Capaldi made his 75th appearance in the Championship.

Venue:	Walkers Stadium	Referee:	P.J.Joslin - 05/06		Leicester City
Attendance:	22,796	Matches:	35		Plymouth Argyle
Capacity:	32,500	Yellow Cards:	103		
Occupancy:	70%	Red Cards:	3		

Form Coming into Fixture

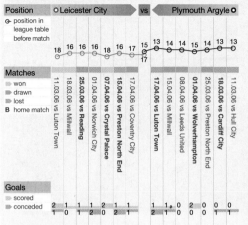

Goal Statistics

Leicester City

by Half | by Situation

first:	6	set piece:	0
second:	3	open play:	9

Plymouth Argyle

by Half | by Situation

first:	2	set piece:	2
second:	2	open play:	1
		own goals:	1

Goals by Area

Leicester City — Scored (Conceded)

| 1 (3) |
| 6 (2) |
| 2 (2) |

Plymouth Argyle — Scored (Conceded)

| 2 (1) |
| 2 (3) |
| 0 (1) |

Team Statistics

Starting Line-Ups

Leicester City: Maybury, Welsh, Tiatto, Johansson, Williams, Fryatt, O'Grady, Pericard, Hume, McCarthy, Gudjonsson, Stearman, Hughes, Henderson

4/4/2

Unused Sub: Douglas, Gerrbrand, Sylla

Plymouth Argyle: Norris, Connolly, Pulis, Wotton, Doumbe, Clarke, Chadwick, Nalis, Aljofree, Capaldi, Hodges, Buzsaky, Larrieu

4/4/2

Unused Sub: McCormick, Reid

Championship Totals

	Leicester	Plymouth
Championship Appearances	503	742
Team Appearances	496	629
Goals Scored	44	68
Assists	44	42
Clean Sheets (goalkeepers)	3	18
Yellow Cards	92	85
Red Cards	5	3
Full Internationals	6	2

Age/Height

Leicester City Age	Plymouth Argyle Age
24 yrs, 5 mo	26 yrs, 2 mo
Leicester City Height	Plymouth Argyle Height
5'11"	6'

Match Statistics

League Table after Fixture

		Played	Won	Drawn	Lost	For	Against	Pts
↑	15 Leicester	45	13	15	17	51	57	54
↓	16 Burnley	45	14	11	20	45	53	53
↓	17 Plymouth	45	12	17	16	37	45	53
•	18 Hull	45	12	15	18	49	55	51
•	19 Derby	45	10	20	15	53	65	50
•	20 QPR	45	12	14	19	49	63	50
•	21 Sheff Wed	45	12	13	20	37	52	49
↑	22 Millwall	45	8	16	21	33	58	40
↓	23 Crewe	45	8	15	22	53	84	39

Statistics

	Leicester	Plymouth
Goals	1	0
Shots on Target	2	3
Shots off Target	5	3
Hit Woodwork	0	0
Possession %	48	52
Corners	5	5
Offsides	3	4
Fouls	12	12
Disciplinary Points	4	0

2-1

Plymouth Argyle ○
Ipswich Town ○

▶ Micky Evans signs off with a trademark goal

Event Line

12 ○ ⊕ Forster / H / OP / 6Y	
	Assist: Casement
28 ○ ⊕ Capaldi / LF / OP / IA	
	Assist: Evans
40 ○ ▪ Nalis	
Half time 1-1	
50 ○ ▪ Naylor	
52 ○ ▪ De Vos	
53 ○ ⇄ Parkin > Brekke-Skard	
57 ○ ⊕ Evans / H / IFK / IA	
	Assist: Pericard
60 ○ ⇄ Magilton > Garvan	
78 ○ ⇄ Pulis > Buzsaky	
78 ○ ⇄ Chadwick > Evans	
78 ○ ⇄ Reid > Pericard	
80 ○ ⇄ Trotter > Westlake	
Full time 2-1	

Michael Evans scored the winning goal on an emotional day at Home Park.

Evans made the last of 432 appearances for the Pilgrims, but it was Nicky Forster who opened the scoring for Ipswich on 12 minutes with a well directed header after a fine run and deep cross from the right by young full-back Chris Casement.

Argyle responded positively, and gained a deserved equaliser on 28 minutes. Skipper Paul Wotton sent a long ball forward and Evans managed to flick the ball back into the danger area from the right side of the box, and into the path of Tony Capaldi.

The Northern Ireland international capped an excellent all-round performance with a neat finish that crept through the legs of Town's young keeper Shane Supple.

The winner arrived on 58 minutes, when Evans latched on to a Vincent Péricard flick-on to head past Supple, and send the Home Park crowd wild.

It would have been impossible to write a more perfect script for a true Argyle legend.

Player of the Match	Quote	Championship Milestone
9 Michael Evans	🎙 **Tony Pulis**	▶ **50**
Argyle legend.	The day has gone as planned; we've won the game and Micky's scored the winning goal. The reception afterwards shows the feelings people have for Micky.	Paul Connolly made his 50th appearance in the Championship.

Venue:	Home Park	Referee:	B.Curson - 05/06		Plymouth Argyle
Attendance:	15,921	Matches:	37		Ipswich Town
Capacity:	20,922	Yellow Cards:	87		
Occupancy:	76%	Red Cards:	7		

Form Coming into Fixture

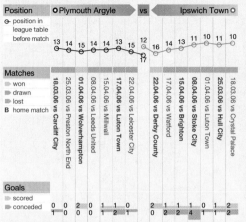

Goal Statistics

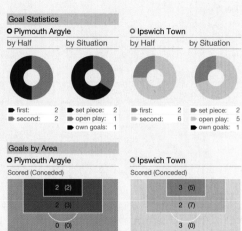

Plymouth Argyle

by Half: first: 2, second: 2
by Situation: set piece: 2, open play: 1, own goals: 1

Ipswich Town

by Half: first: 2, second: 6
by Situation: set piece: 2, open play: 5, own goals: 1

Goals by Area

Plymouth Argyle — Scored (Conceded): 2 (2), 2 (3), 0 (0)

Ipswich Town — Scored (Conceded): 3 (5), 2 (7), 3 (0)

Team Statistics

Starting Line-Ups

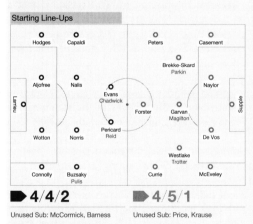

Plymouth Argyle: 4/4/2
Ipswich Town: 4/5/1

Unused Sub: McCormick, Barness

Unused Sub: Price, Krause

Championship Totals

	Plymouth	Ipswich
Championship Appearances	715	570
Team Appearances	655	508
Goals Scored	64	61
Assists	47	78
Clean Sheets (goalkeepers)	18	4
Yellow Cards	77	52
Red Cards	2	2
Full Internationals	3	3

Age/Height

Plymouth Argyle Age	Ipswich Town Age
27 yrs, 1 mo	24 yrs, 11 mo
Plymouth Argyle Height	Ipswich Town Height
6'	6'

Match Statistics

League Table after Fixture

		Played	Won	Drawn	Lost	For	Against	Pts
●	7 Wolverhampton	46	16	19	11	50	42	67
↑	8 Coventry	46	16	15	15	62	65	63
↓	9 Norwich	46	18	8	20	56	65	62
●	10 Luton	46	17	10	19	66	67	61
↓	11 Cardiff	46	16	12	18	58	59	60
↑	12 Southampton	46	13	19	14	49	50	58
↑	13 Stoke	46	17	7	22	54	63	58
↑	14 Plymouth	46	13	17	16	39	46	56
↓	15 Ipswich	46	14	14	18	53	66	56

Statistics

	Plymouth	Ipswich
Goals	2	1
Shots on Target	4	2
Shots off Target	8	1
Hit Woodwork	0	0
Possession %	52	48
Corners	3	4
Offsides	5	3
Fouls	14	13
Disciplinary Points	4	8

END OF SEASON REVIEW 2005/06

IT is tempting to suggest that the high point of Argyle's 2005-06 season came on its opening day.

Certainly, the 2-1 defeat of Reading, which turned out to be the only time the runaway Coca-Cola Championship champions were turned over at the Madejski, was one of the more satisfying victories of an eventful campaign.

Ironically, after the game, Reading manager Steve Coppell admitted to his Argyle counterpart Bobby Williamson that he was concerned for his future. Neither of the coaches could have envisioned then that, before September's first game, it would be Williamson who would be relieved of his duties.

The win in Berkshire was followed by a home 3-3 draw against another side which was promoted nine months later, Watford, but four successive league defeats – 1-0s at home to Derby and Hull, and at Crystal Palace (1-0) and Brighton (2-0) – persuaded the Pilgrims' board that a change was in the club's best interests.

Williamson's former lieutenant Jocky Scott was put in temporary charge while a permanent

replacement was sought. Scott tasted defeat a 2-0 defeat at Norwich before he broke the five-game losing streak with a 1-1 draw against rock-bottom Crewe and a 1-0 victory over Burnley, both at Home Park.

Scott's replacement was watching from the anonymity of the terraces as the Pilgrims were ignominiously dumped out of the Carling Cup 2-1 at League Two Barnet, having made rare progress to the second round by earlier beating Peterborough by the same score at Home Park.

Tony Pulis's verdict on Argyle's performance over the first month and half of the season did not differ from that of many Pilgrims' fans: "Not good enough to stay up," he told the club's already concerned directors.

The new broom immediately swept out Taribo West, the former Nigerian international centre-back whose brief Argyle career had been beset by passport problems which had seen him exiled in Italy when the season began.

West's fellow defender Rufus Brevett was also quickly consigned to the sidelines, while midfielder Bjarni Gudjonsson also disappeared from view

after featuring in Pulis's opening three games. The Icelandic international soon severed his ties with the Pilgrims in favour of a return to his homeland.

Pulis began his tenure against Southampton at St Mary's, the goal-less draw providing something of a taster of what was to come, and 2-0 defeat at then-leaders Sheffield United, where the dug-outs uniquely contained four Argyle managers, past and present: Pulis, his coach David Kemp, United's Neil Warnock and his assistant Mick Jones.

Kemp, who managed the Pilgrims between 1990-92, had returned to Home Park with Pulis, who was also to bring in two other tried and tested fellow coaches, Lindsay Parsons and Mark O'Connor.

The footballing fates had decreed that Pulis's first home games in charge should be against Stoke City, the club he had been sacked from a few months earlier, and Sheffield Wednesday, which saw the return to Home Park of another ex-Pilgrims' boss, Paul Sturrock.

Stoke were despatched 2-1, courtesy of substitute Akos Buzsaky's late intervention, whilst a nerveless penalty from captain Paul Wotton ensured an honours-even 1-1 draw with Sturrock's Owls.

Three successive draws followed – 1-1s at Queens Park Rangers and Luton, and a Sunday afternoon 0-0 snooze in front of the telly cameras against Millwall at Home Park – before the Pilgrims were denied a possible home victory against Leicester when a waterlogged pitch forced the game's abandonment at half-time with Argyle leading 1-0 through Nick Chadwick's waterborne goal.

Pre-Christmas away form continued to be patchy – 3-1 defeats at Ipswich and Coventry, but workmanlike draws at Sheffield Wednesday (0-0) and Watford (1-1), who equalised late into injury-time – but the arrival of West Ham centre-back Elliott Ward and Norwich midfielder Jason Jarrett on loan provided a notable stiffness to the spine.

Reading gained their revenge at the end of November, but that 2-0 Home Park reversal was sandwiched between convincing home victories over Queens Park Rangers (3-1) and Crystal Palace, against who Chadwick scored the first in a 2-0 win in less than 12 seconds.

The good form maintained until the end of the year. Cardiff were beaten 2-0 at Ninian Park for the second of only three wins on the road in the entire season, while Ward's headed goal at

Wolves earned a 1-1 draw. Despite the Leicester washout and the freezing off of the home holiday game against Preston, Argyle were now well clear of the relegation places.

The new year kicked off with a season's-worst 3-0 home defeat by Leeds and an FA Cup third-round defeat at Wolves where the only goal of the game came from Leon Clarke, who was destined to end the season as an Argyle player.

Norwich, with Jarrett now back in their starting line-up, were then held 1-1 at Home Park thanks to a goal which, after much studying of video tape and an appeal to the Football League, was eventually credited to Chadwick.

Jarrett's replacement had already been found by Pulis – Frenchman Lilian Nalis, fresh from being released by Sheffield United, increased the Pilgrims' Gallic contingent and did not miss a minute of the rest of the season.

A double from Wotton in the 2-1 win at Crewe completed the set of away victories before Leicester, at the second time of asking, and Southampton were despatched on consecutive Tuesday nights at Home Park, 1-0 and 2-1 respectively.

Such had been the Pilgrims' improvement under Pulis that, far from worrying about relegation, some optimistic Argyle fans were beginning to speculate the the team were about to sneak into the play-offs.

A 1-0 defeat at Burnley, followed by 0-0 draws against Sheffield United at Home Park, and Stoke, where Pulis was afforded a warm welcome, put paid to such idle speculation, before hopes were raised again when Vincent Péricard netted a hat-trick in the 3-1 home win over Coventry, becoming only the second Pilgrim to achieve such a feat on his full home debut in eight decades (Steve Guinan, seven years previously had been the other).
Former Juventus forward Péricard had arrived on loan from Portsmouth for the final few weeks of the campaign, when one of his partners was Wolves striker Clarke, the latter being easily the least successful of Pulis's temporary additions to the Argyle squad.

Three defeats in the next four matches – with Nalis's winner in the 1-0 home victory over Brighton coming in between 1-0 away reverses at Derby and Hull and a home defeat by a similar score to Cardiff – lowered everyone's expectations before the successful negotiation of a tricky trio of games ensured Argyle's survival as a Championship club.

Goal-less draws at play-off sides Preston and Leeds, where dubious refereeing decisions thwarted the chance of achieving even more pleasing results, either side of a sweeping 2-0 best-of-the-season home victory over Wolves earned enough points to make relegation impossible with still four games to go.

Inevitably, having passed the finishing line, Argyle suffered a comedown, which undoubtedly contributed to a soul-less 1-1 draw at already-doomed Millwall, a 2-1 Easter Monday home defeat by old rivals Luton, and an insipid 1-0 loss at Leicester.

Thanks largely to one man, the season did not, however, peter out altogether.

Michael Evans' decision to leave the Pilgrims after – on and off – 15 years of service to his hometown club set the scene for a thoroughly memorable final game of the season against Ipswich.

Evans was sent from Home Park on a wave of emotion from team-mates and supporters alike.

Despite going a goal down, his team-mates rallied to ensure Evans' 432nd and final Argyle appearance was not a losing one. Tony Capaldi equalised before Evans himself reacted quickest to a flick-on by Péricard to head home the winner in a 2-1 victory that lifted Argyle to 14th place – their highest finishing position in two decades.

As Home Park went bonkers, you were left to reflect on the pleasing symmetry of a season which had ended in the same way it had begun – with an Evans' goal.

The goal was greeted by a wave of emotion so thick that you had to brush it away from your face, yet even the wealth of genuine affection

which greeted the 81st strike of Evans' career was nothing compared to the reception afforded him at the end.

Evans was not the only one with tears in his eyes as he led the Pilgrims around Home Park on what was scheduled by the club to be a lap of appreciation by the players to the fans, but which turned out to be an outpouring of love

from the terraces to the Argyle number nine.

And why not?

He thoroughly, utterly, completely deserved every scintilla of praise and thanks going.

Forget Reading, this was the high point of the season.

1 Romain Larrieu
Goalkeeper

After playing second fiddle to Luke McCormick for the second half of the 2004-05 campaign, Argyle's big French stopper cannot have imagined that the 2006-07 season would have seen such a change in his fortunes.

Larrieu, 29, was recalled by Bobby Williamson for the opener at Reading and retained his place throughout the season, missing just one league match when Tony Pulis decided to have a look at McCormick.

One of the longest-serving Pilgrims, a veteran of the 2001-02 Third Division title-winning side, Ro kept 14 clean sheets in his 45 matches and was short-listed for the Coca-Cola Championship's Player of the Month award for March.

Player Details:

Date of Birth:	31.08.1976
Place of Birth:	Mont-de-Marsan
Nationality:	French
Height:	6'2"
Weight:	14st
Foot:	Left

Player Performance 05/06

League Performance

Percentage of total possible time player was on pitch   ⊙ position in league table at end of month

Month:	Aug	Sep	Oct	Nov	Dec	Jan	Feb	Mar	Apr	Total
	100%	100%	100%	100%	100%	100%	100%	100%	83%	98%
	21	23	21	19	19	14	15	15	14	
Team Pts:	4/18	5/15	7/15	4/12	8/15	10/15	5/15	5/15	8/18	56/138
Team Gls F:	5	2	5	4	7	6	3	1	6	39
Team Gls A:	10	5	4	6	5	6	3	2	5	46
Total mins:	540	450	450	360	450	450	450	450	450	4,050
Starts (sub):	6	5	5	4	5	5	5	5	5	45
Goals:	0	0	0	0	0	0	0	0	0	0
Assists:	0	0	0	0	0	0	0	0	0	0
Clean sheets:	0	2	1	1	2	1	2	3	2	14
Cards (Y/R):	0	0	0	0	0	0	0	0	1	1

League Performance Totals

Clean Sheets

▶ Larrieu:	14
▶ Team-mates:	0
Total:	**14**

Assists

▶ Larrieu:	0
▶ Team-mates:	32
Total:	**32**

Cards

▶ Larrieu:	1
▶ Team-mates:	67
Total:	**68**

Cup Games

	Apps	CS	Cards
FA Cup	1	0	0
Carling Cup	0	0	0
Total	**1**	**0**	**0**

Career History

Career Milestones

Club Debut:
vs Bristol C. (H), W 3-0, Ft Lg Trophy

▶ **05.12.00**

Time Spent at the Club:

▶ **5.5 Seasons**

First Goal Scored for the Club:
—

▶ —

Full International:

▶ —

Championship Totals

04-06

Appearances	68
Clean Sheets	18
Assists	0
Yellow Cards	2
Red Cards	0

Clubs

Year	Club	Apps	CS
00-06	Plymouth	193	64

Off the Pitch

Age:

▶ Larrieu: 29 years, 9 months
▶ Team: 26 years, 10 months
| League: 26 years, 1 month

Height:

▶ Larrieu: 6'2"
▶ Team: 5'11"
| League: 5'11"

Weight:

▶ Larrieu: 14st
▶ Team: 12st 1lb
| League: 11st 13lb

23 Luke McCormick
Goalkeeper

Season Review 05/06

Last season was a frustrating one for goalkeeper McCormick, who sat on the substitutes' bench 42 times and made just one league start when Tony Pulis rested regular number one Romain Larrieu towards the end of the campaign.

The talented 22-year-old had shared duties equally with Larrieu the previous campaign, finishing the season as Bobby Williamson's preferred 'keeper, so it was something of a surprise when Larrieu took the gloves at Reading last August.

Larrieu's form and a lack of reserve games did nothing to help Luke to press any claim for inclusion at the Frenchman's expense.

Player Details:

Date of Birth:	15.08.1983
Place of Birth:	Coventry
Nationality:	English
Height:	6'
Weight:	13st 12lb
Foot:	Right

Player Performance 05/06

League Performance

Percentage of total possible time player was on pitch   ⊖ position in league table at end of month

Month:	Aug	Sep	Oct	Nov	Dec	Jan	Feb	Mar	Apr	Total
position	21	23	21	19	19	14	15	15	14	
%	0%	0%	0%	0%	0%	0%	0%	0%	17%	2%
Team Pts:	4/18	5/15	7/15	4/12	8/15	10/15	5/15	5/15	8/18	56/138
Team Gls F:	5	2	5	4	7	6	3	1	6	39
Team Gls A:	10	5	4	6	5	6	3	2	5	46
Total mins:	0	0	0	0	0	0	0	0	90	90
Starts (sub):	0	0	0	0	0	0	0	0	1	1
Goals:	0	0	0	0	0	0	0	0	0	0
Assists:	0	0	0	0	0	0	0	0	0	0
Clean sheets:	0	0	0	0	0	0	0	0	0	0
Cards (Y/R):	0	0	0	0	0	0	0	0	0	0

League Performance Totals

Clean Sheets
- McCormick: 0
- Team-mates: 14
- **Total: 14**

Assists
- McCormick: 0
- Team-mates: 32
- **Total: 32**

Cards
- McCormick: 0
- Team-mates: 68
- **Total: 68**

Cup Games

	Apps	CS	Cards
FA Cup	0	0	0
Carling Cup	2	0	0
Total	**2**	**0**	**0**

Career History

Career Milestones

Club Debut:
vs Rochdale (H), D 0-0, League Two

➡ 05.05.01

Time Spent at the Club:

➡ 6.5 Seasons

First Goal Scored for the Club:
—

➡ —

Full International:

➡ —

Championship Totals

04-06

Appearances	24
Clean Sheets	9
Assists	0
Yellow Cards	2
Red Cards	0

Clubs

Year	Club	Apps	CS
04-04	Boston Utd	2	0
99-06	Plymouth	76	33

Off the Pitch

Age:

- McCormick: 22 years, 9 months
- Team: 26 years, 10 months
- League: 26 years, 1 month

Height:

- McCormick: 6'
- Team: 5'11"
- League: 5'11"

Weight:

- McCormick: 13st 12lb
- Team: 12st 1lb
- League: 11st 13lb

3 Rufus Brevett
Defence

Season Review 05/06

The highlight of the former Fulham and West Ham left-back's brief Argyle career came in the first half of the first game of the 2005-06 season, when he laid on the opener for Michael Evans in the victory at eventual champions Reading.

Brought to Home Park in the close-season by Bobby Williamson, Brevett, 36, started 12 of the opening 13 games – missing only Tony Pulis's debut draw at Southampton because he had picked up five bookings in the opening nine matches.

After starting Pulis's next three matches, the only other time he saw first-team action was as a late substitute in the fourth, and he ended the season on loan at Leicester City.

Player Details:

Date of Birth:	24.09.1969
Place of Birth:	Derby
Nationality:	English
Height:	5'8"
Weight:	11st 8lb
Foot:	Left

Player Performance 05/06

League Performance

Percentage of total possible time player was on pitch   ⊖ position in league table at end of month

Month:	Aug	Sep	Oct	Nov	Dec	Jan	Feb	Mar	Apr	Total
	93%	66%	34% 21	19	19	14	15	15	14	23%
	21	23	0%	0%	0%	0%	0%	0%	0%	
Team Pts:	4/18	5/15	7/15	4/12	8/15	10/15	5/15	5/15	8/18	56/138
Team Gls F:	5	2	5	4	7	6	3	1	6	39
Team Gls A:	10	5	4	6	5	6	3	2	5	46
Total mins:	501	296	151	0	0	0	0	0	0	948
Starts (sub):	6	4	2 (1)	0	0	0	0	0	0	12 (1)
Goals:	0	0	0	0	0	0	0	0	0	0
Assists:	1	0	0	0	0	0	0	0	0	1
Clean sheets:	0	0	0	0	0	0	0	0	0	0
Cards (Y/R):	3	2	0	0	0	0	0	0	0	5

League Performance Totals

Goals

- Brevett: 0
- Team-mates: 37

Total: 37

- own goals: 2

Assists

- Brevett: 1
- Team-mates: 31

Total: 32

Cards

- Brevett: 5
- Team-mates: 63

Total: 68

Cup Games

	Apps	Goals	Cards
FA Cup	0	0	0
Carling Cup	0	0	0
Total	0	0	0

Career History

Career Milestones

Club Debut:

vs Reading (A), W 1-2, Championship

 06.08.05

Time Spent at the Club:

▶ **1 Season**

First Goal Scored for the Club:

▶ —

Full International:

▶ —

Championship Totals

04-06

Appearances	24
Goals	1
Assists	1
Yellow Cards	7
Red Cards	1

Clubs

Year	Club	Apps	Gls
06-06	Leicester	1	0
05-06	Plymouth	13	0
03-05	West Ham	29	1
98-03	Fulham	217	2
91-98	QPR	171	1
88-91	Doncaster R.	129	3

Off the Pitch

Age:

- Brevett: 36 years, 8 months
- Team: 26 years, 10 months
- League: 26 years, 1 month

Height:

- Brevett: 5'8"
- Team: 5'11"
- League: 5'11"

Weight:

- Brevett: 11st 8lb
- Team: 12st 1lb
- League: 11st 13lb

13 Mathias Doumbe
Defence

The cool Frenchman missed only three league games all season, nailing down the right centre-back position from day one – although he did play twice, with varying success, at right-back.

For the most part, though, Doumbe, 26, played alongside Elliott Ward, Hasney Aljofree or Taribo West with equal aplomb, using his main asset - his pace - to maximum advantage.

A free signing from Hibernian the previous summer, Mat also managed to get himself on the scoresheet once, slamming the ball home following a corner in the 3-1 home victory over Queens Park Rangers at Home Park.

Player Details:

Date of Birth:	28.10.1979
Place of Birth:	Dancy
Nationality:	French
Height:	6'1"
Weight:	12st 5lb
Foot:	Right

Player Performance 05/06

League Performance

Percentage of total possible time player was on pitch   ⊖ position in league table at end of month

Month:	Aug	Sep	Oct	Nov	Dec	Jan	Feb	Mar	Apr	Total
	100%	100%	100%	100%	100%	100%	80%	70%	83%	92%
	21	23	21	19	19	14	15	15	14	
Team Pts:	4/18	5/15	7/15	4/12	8/15	10/15	5/15	5/15	8/18	56/138
Team Gls F:	5	2	5	4	7	6	3	1	6	39
Team Gls A:	10	5	4	6	5	6	3	2	5	46
Total mins:	540	450	450	360	450	450	360	314	450	3,824
Starts (sub):	6	5	5	4	5	5	4	4	5	43
Goals:	0	0	0	1	0	0	0	0	0	1
Assists:	0	0	0	0	0	0	0	0	0	0
Clean sheets:	0	2	1	1	2	1	2	2	2	13
Cards (Y/R):	0	1	1	0	1	0	2	1	0	6

League Performance Totals

Goals
- Doumbe: 1
- Team-mates: 36
- Total: 37
- own goals: 2

Assists
- Doumbe: 0
- Team-mates: 32
- Total: 32

Cards
- Doumbe: 6
- Team-mates: 62
- Total: 68

Cup Games

	Apps	Goals	Cards
FA Cup	1	0	0
Carling Cup	2	0	0
Total	3	0	0

Career History

Career Milestones

Club Debut:
vs Yeovil (A), L 3-2, League Cup
▶ 24.08.04

Time Spent at the Club:
▶ 2 Seasons

First Goal Scored for the Club:
vs Preston (A), D 1-1, Championship
▶ 28.09.04

Full International:
▶ —

Championship Totals

04-06
Appearances	69
Goals	3
Assists	2
Yellow Cards	9
Red Cards	1

Clubs

Year	Club	Apps	Gls
04-06	Plymouth	74	3
	Hibernian		
	Paris-SG		

Off the Pitch

Age:
- Doumbe: 26 years, 7 months
- Team: 26 years, 10 months
- League: 26 years, 1 month

Height:
- Doumbe: 6'1"
- Team: 5'11"
- League: 5'11"

Weight:
- Doumbe: 12st 5lb
- Team: 12st 1lb
- League: 11st 13lb

18

Nuno Mendes
Defence

Season Review 05/06

Argyle's Portugeezer's time at Home Park was short and far from sweet.

Signed in the summer as a replacement for popular centre-back Graham Coughlan, Mendes, 30, played just twice in the opening month of the campaign.

He featured, out of position, as a holding midfielder in the away defeats at Crystal Palace and Brighton, before disappearing off the radar altogether.

An engaging character, Nuno was last heard of trialling for the New York-New Jersey Metro Stars in America.

Player Details:

Date of Birth:	07.04.1976
Place of Birth:	Penafiel
Nationality:	Portuguese
Height:	5'11"
Weight:	12st 13lb
Foot:	Left/Right

Player Performance 05/06

League Performance

Percentage of total possible time player was on pitch · ⊖ position in league table at end of month

Month:	Aug	Sep	Oct	Nov	Dec	Jan	Feb	Mar	Apr	Total
	24%	0%	0%	0%	0%	0%	0%	0%	0%	3%
Team Pts:	4/18	5/15	7/15	4/12	8/15	10/15	5/15	5/15	8/18	56/138
Team Gls F:	5	2	5	4	7	6	3	1	6	39
Team Gls A:	10	5	4	6	5	6	3	2	5	46
Total mins:	132	0	0	0	0	0	0	0	0	132
Starts (sub):	2	0	0	0	0	0	0	0	0	2
Goals:	0	0	0	0	0	0	0	0	0	0
Assists:	0	0	0	0	0	0	0	0	0	0
Clean sheets:	0	0	0	0	0	0	0	0	0	0
Cards (Y/R):	0	0	0	0	0	0	0	0	0	0

(Position in league table line: 21, 23, 21, 19, 19, 14, 15, 15, 14)

League Performance Totals

Goals

- Mendes: 0
- Team-mates: 37
- **Total: 37**
- own goals: 2

Assists

- Mendes: 0
- Team-mates: 32
- **Total: 32**

Cards

- Mendes: 0
- Team-mates: 68
- **Total: 68**

Cup Games

	Apps	Goals	Cards
FA Cup	0	0	0
Carling Cup	1	0	0
Total	**1**	**0**	**0**

Career History

Career Milestones

Club Debut:
vs Crystal Palace (A), L 1-0, Champ.

 20.08.05

Time Spent at the Club:

 1 Season

First Goal Scored for the Club:
—

 —

Full International:

 —

Championship Totals

04-06

Appearances	2
Goals	0
Assists	0
Yellow Cards	0
Red Cards	0

Clubs

Year	Club	Apps	Gls
05-06	Plymouth	3	0
	Santa Clara		

Off the Pitch

Age:

- Mendes: 30 years, 1 month
- Team: 26 years, 10 months
- League: 26 years, 1 month

Height:

- Mendes: 5'11"
- Team: 5'11"
- League: 5'11"

Weight:

- Mendes: 12st 13lb
- Team: 12st 1lb
- League: 11st 13lb

21 Elliott Ward
Defence

Season Review 05/06

Arguably the most successful loan signing since goalkeeper Alan Miller's temporary move from Arsenal a 20 years earlier, Ward's 15 appearances across Christmas and the New Year resonated through the rest of the campaign.

Ward, 21, was a towering presence in the centre of a defence that benefited from his experience of having won promotion from the Championship with West Ham the previous season.

By the time Ell returned to Upton Park in February, he had not only carved a niche for himself in the hearts of the Green Army, but also enhanced his reputation as one of England's best young defenders.

Player Details:

Date of Birth:	19.01.1985
Place of Birth:	Harrow
Nationality:	English
Height:	6'1"
Weight:	14st 11lb
Foot:	Right

Player Performance 05/06

League Performance

Percentage of total possible time player was on pitch — position in league table at end of month

Month:	Aug	Sep	Oct	Nov	Dec	Jan	Feb	Mar	Apr	Total
	0%	0%	0%	25%	100%	100%	80%	0%	0%	33%
	21	23	21	19	19	14	15	15	14	
Team Pts:	4/18	5/15	7/15	4/12	8/15	10/15	5/15	5/15	8/18	56/138
Team Gls F:	5	2	5	4	7	6	3	1	6	39
Team Gls A:	10	5	4	6	5	6	3	2	5	46
Total mins:	0	0	0	90	450	450	360	0	0	1,350
Starts (sub):	0	0	0	1 (1)	5	5	4	0	0	15 (1)
Goals:	0	0	0	0	1	0	0	0	0	1
Assists:	0	0	0	0	0	0	0	0	0	0
Clean sheets:	0	0	0	0	2	1	2	0	0	5
Cards (Y/R):	0	0	0	0	0	0	0	0	0	0

League Performance Totals

Goals
- Ward: 1
- Team-mates: 36
- **Total: 37**
- own goals: 2

Assists
- Ward: 0
- Team-mates: 32
- **Total: 32**

Cards
- Ward: 0
- Team-mates: 68
- **Total: 68**

Cup Games

	Apps	Goals	Cards
FA Cup	0	0	0
Carling Cup	0	0	0
Total	**0**	**0**	**0**

Career History

Career Milestones

Club Debut:
vs Sheff Wed (A), D 0-0, Champ.
 **22.11.05**

Time Spent at the Club:
0.5 Seasons

First Goal Scored for the Club:
vs Wolverhampton (A), D 1-1, Champ.
 31.12.05

Full International:
—

Championship Totals
04-06

Appearances	27
Goals	1
Assists	2
Yellow Cards	3
Red Cards	0

Clubs

Year	Club	Apps	Gls
05-06	Plymouth	16	1
04-05	Bristol Rovers	3	0
04-04	Peterborough	0	0
01-06	West Ham	21	0

Off the Pitch

Age:
- Ward: 21 years, 4 months
- Team: 26 years, 10 months
- League: 26 years, 1 month

Height:
- Ward: 6'1"
- Team: 5'11"
- League: 5'11"

Weight:
- Ward: 14st 11lb
- Team: 12st 1lb
- League: 11st 13lb

2

Anthony Barness
Defence

Season Review 05/06

Thirty-three league starts in 2005-06 speaks volumes for the staying power of 33-year-old former Charlton, Chelsea and Bolton full-back Barness, who joined the Pilgrims as a free agent during the close-season.

Barny demonstrated his versatility by playing half of those games on either side of the back four, starting on the right at the Madejski but being used more on the left after Tony Pulis's arrival.

A third of the games in which he played saw Argyle's opponents fail to score, including the draw against Neil Warnock's Sheffield United - a match in which crosses from the left-back position offered the Pilgrims' best hope of scoring.

Player Details:

Date of Birth:	25.02.1973
Place of Birth:	Lewisham
Nationality:	English
Height:	5'10"
Weight:	12st 1lb
Foot:	Right/Left

Player Performance 05/06

League Performance

Percentage of total possible time player was on pitch   ⊙ position in league table at end of month

Month:	Aug	Sep	Oct	Nov	Dec	Jan	Feb	Mar	Apr	Total
	100%	71%	54%	100%	96%	100%	77%	41%	14% / 0%	69%
	21	23	21	19	19	14	15	15	14	
Team Pts:	4/18	5/15	7/15	4/12	8/15	10/15	5/15	5/15	8/18	56/138
Team Gls F:	5	2	5	4	7	6	3	1	6	39
Team Gls A:	10	5	4	6	5	6	3	2	5	46
Total mins:	540	320	242	360	433	450	345	184	0	2,874
Starts (sub):	6	4 (1)	3	4	5	5	4	2 (2)	0	33 (3)
Goals:	0	0	0	0	0	0	0	0	0	0
Assists:	0	0	0	0	1	0	0	0	0	1
Clean sheets:	0	1	0	1	2	1	2	1	0	8
Cards (Y/R):	0	2	0	0	0	0	1	0	0	3

League Performance Totals

Goals

- Barness: 0
- Team-mates: 37
- **Total: 37**
- own goals: 2

Assists

- Barness: 1
- Team-mates: 31
- **Total: 32**

Cards

- Barness: 3
- Team-mates: 65
- **Total: 68**

Cup Games

	Apps	Goals	Cards
FA Cup	1	0	0
Carling Cup	2	0	0
Total	**3**	**0**	**0**

Career History

Career Milestones

Club Debut:

vs Reading (A), W 1-2, Championship

▶ **06.08.05**

Time Spent at the Club:

▶ **1 Season**

First Goal Scored for the Club:

—

▶ —

Full International:

▶ —

Championship Totals

04-06

Appearances	36
Goals	0
Assists	1
Yellow Cards	3
Red Cards	0

Clubs

Year	Club	Apps	Gls
05-06	Plymouth	39	0
00-05	Bolton	116	0
96-00	Charlton	107	3
96-96	Southend	5	0
93-93	Middlesbrough	1	0
92-96	Chelsea	19	0
91-92	Charlton	34	2

Off the Pitch

Age:

- Barness: 33 years, 3 months
- Team: 26 years, 10 months
- League: 26 years, 1 month

Height:

- Barness: 5'10"
- Team: 5'11"
- League: 5'11"

Weight:

- Barness: 12st 1lb
- Team: 12st 1lb
- League: 11st 13lb

16 Hasney Aljofree
Defence

Season Review 05/06

The Mancunian defender's value to the squad was shown by the fact that he failed to make the team-sheet only on a couple of occasions in his fourth – and most successful – season with the Pilgrims.

For the most part, Hasney, 28, was Mat Doumbe's regular partner in the centre of the back four but also filled in at left-back during Elliott Ward's loan spell from West Ham.

Despite not going up for corners too often, Has still managed to get on the scoresheet with a memorable goal in the home victory against Wolverhampton Wanderers.

Player Details:

Date of Birth:	11.07.1978
Place of Birth:	Manchester
Nationality:	English
Height:	6'
Weight:	12st 3lb
Foot:	Left

Player Performance 05/06

League Performance

Percentage of total possible time player was on pitch   ⊖ position in league table at end of month

Month:	Aug	Sep	Oct	Nov	Dec	Jan	Feb	Mar	Apr	Total
	60%	100%	100%	100%	34%	53%	38%	100%	100%	76%
	21	23	21	19	19	14	15	15	14	
Team Pts:	4/18	5/15	7/15	4/12	8/15	10/15	5/15	5/15	8/18	56/138
Team Gls F:	5	2	5	4	7	6	3	1	6	39
Team Gls A:	10	5	4	6	5	6	3	2	5	46
Total mins:	326	450	450	360	153	237	171	450	540	3,137
Starts (sub):	4	5	5	4	2 (1)	3	2	5	6	36 (1)
Goals:	0	0	0	0	0	0	0	0	1	1
Assists:	1	0	0	0	0	0	0	0	0	1
Clean sheets:	0	2	1	1	1	1	0	3	2	11
Cards (Y/R):	0	0	0	1	0	1	0	1	1	4

League Performance Totals

Goals
- ▶ Aljofree: 1
- ▶ Team-mates: 36
- **Total: 37**
- ▶ own goals: 2

Assists
- ▶ Aljofree: 1
- ▶ Team-mates: 31
- **Total: 32**

Cards
- ▶ Aljofree: 4
- ▶ Team-mates: 64
- **Total: 68**

Cup Games

	Apps	Goals	Cards
FA Cup	1	0	0
Carling Cup	0	0	0
Total	**1**	**0**	**0**

Career History

Career Milestones

Club Debut:
vs Q.P.R. (A), D 2-2, League One
▶ **31.08.02**

Time Spent at the Club:
▶ **4 Seasons**

First Goal Scored for the Club:
vs Notts Cty (H), W 1-0, League One
▶ **28.12.02**

Full International:
▶ —

Championship Totals
04-06

Appearances	49
Goals	2
Assists	2
Yellow Cards	5
Red Cards	0

Clubs

Year	Club	Apps	Gls
04-04	Sheff Wed	3	0
02-06	Plymouth	98	3
	Dundee Utd		
96-00	Bolton W.	22	0

Off the Pitch

Age:
- ▶ Aljofree: 27 years, 10 months
- ▶ Team: 26 years, 10 months
- | League: 26 years, 1 month

Height:
- ▶ Aljofree: 6'
- ▶ Team: 5'11"
- | League: 5'11"

Weight:
- ▶ Aljofree: 12st 3lb
- ▶ Team: 12st 1lb
- | League: 11st 13lb

22 Paul Connolly
Defence

It was not until mid-October that Connolly made his first start of last season.

The Liverpudlian defender, 22, thereafter became pretty well a regular, with Tony Pulis moving Anthony Barness to left-back to accommodate Connolly on the right.

He missed a handful of games thereafter, solely as a result of two suspensions, including one for the only red card received by an Argyle player during the campaign – at Derby in February.

Indiscretions apart, Shelly was a vital component in the Green Machine, with increasingly important contributions in the form of well-delivered crosses and corners.

Player Details:

Date of Birth:	29.09.1983
Place of Birth:	Liverpool
Nationality:	English
Height:	6'
Weight:	11st 9lb
Foot:	Right

Player Performance 05/06

League Performance

Percentage of total possible time player was on pitch   ⊖ position in league table at end of month

Month:	Aug	Sep	Oct	Nov	Dec	Jan	Feb	Mar	Apr	Total
	7%	0%	80%	75%	61%	42%	96%	75%	95%	59%
	21	23	21	19	19	14	15	15	14	
Team Pts:	4/18	5/15	7/15	4/12	8/15	10/15	5/15	5/15	8/18	56/138
Team Gls F:	5	2	5	4	7	6	3	1	6	39
Team Gls A:	10	5	4	6	5	6	3	2	5	46
Total mins:	39	0	360	270	274	189	433	338	513	2,416
Starts (sub):	0 (2)	0	4	3	3 (1)	2 (1)	5	4	6	27 (4)
Goals:	0	0	0	0	0	0	0	0	0	0
Assists:	0	0	0	0	0	0	0	0	1	1
Clean sheets:	0	0	1	1	1	0	2	2	2	9
Cards (Y/R):	0	0	2	1	0	0/1	0	0	1	6/1

League Performance Totals

Goals

- Connolly: 0
- Team-mates: 37

Total: 37

- own goals: 2

Assists

- Connolly: 1
- Team-mates: 31

Total: 32

Cards

- Connolly: 7
- Team-mates: 61

Total: 68

Cup Games

	Apps	Goals	Cards
FA Cup	1	0	0
Carling Cup	1	0	0
Total	**2**	**0**	**0**

Career History

Career Milestones

Club Debut:

Rochdale (H), D 0-0, League Two

► 05.05.01

Time Spent at the Club:

► 6 Seasons

First Goal Scored for the Club:

—

► —

Full International:

► —

Championship Totals

04-06

Appearances	50
Goals	0
Assists	4
Yellow Cards	9
Red Cards	2

Clubs

Year	Club	Apps	Gls
	Bideford		
00-06	Plymouth	86	0

Off the Pitch

Age:

- Connolly: 22 years, 8 months
- Team: 26 years, 10 months
- League: 26 years, 1 month

Height:

- Connolly: 6'
- Team: 5'11"
- League: 5'11"

Weight:

- Connolly: 11st 9lb
- Team: 12st 1lb
- League: 11st 13lb

4 Taribo West
Defence

There has never been a more colourful Argyle signing than Taribo West – twice appearing in the World Cup finals, an Olympic gold medallist, and UEFA Cup-winner.

The Nigerian international defender's stay was memorable, but a lot shorter than anticipated. Passport problems meant he was exiled in Milan when the campaign kicked off and, by the time the professed Christian returned for a debut against Hull, the absence had clearly had a debilitating affect.

Three more games – and two defeats – followed before the ex-Internazionale star's Argyle career ended at Barnet's Underhill, where Tony Pulis watched the Pilgrims' Carling Cup exit and decided West was not part of his plans.

Player Details:

Date of Birth:	26.03.1974
Place of Birth:	Port Harcourt
Nationality:	Nigerian
Height:	6'1"
Weight:	13st 10lb
Foot:	Right

Player Performance 05/06

League Performance

Percentage of total possible time player was on pitch   position in league table at end of month

Month:	Aug	Sep	Oct	Nov	Dec	Jan	Feb	Mar	Apr	Total
	33% 21	40% 23	21 0%	19 0%	19 0%	14 0%	15 0%	15 0%	14 0%	9%
Team Pts:	4/18	5/15	7/15	4/12	8/15	10/15	5/15	5/15	8/18	56/138
Team Gls F:	5	2	5	4	7	6	3	1	6	39
Team Gls A:	10	5	4	6	5	6	3	2	5	46
Total mins:	180	180	0	0	0	0	0	0	0	360
Starts (sub):	2	2	0	0	0	0	0	0	0	4
Goals:	0	0	0	0	0	0	0	0	0	0
Assists:	0	0	0	0	0	0	0	0	0	0
Clean sheets:	0	1	0	0	0	0	0	0	0	1
Cards (Y/R):	1	0	0	0	0	0	0	0	0	1

League Performance Totals

Goals

West:	0
Team-mates:	37
Total:	**37**
own goals:	2

Assists

West:	0
Team-mates:	32
Total:	**32**

Cards

West:	1
Team-mates:	67
Total:	**68**

Cup Games

	Apps	Goals	Cards
FA Cup	0	0	0
Carling Cup	1	0	0
Total	**1**	**0**	**0**

Career History

Career Milestones

Club Debut:
vs Hull (H), L 0-1, Championship
▶ 27.08.05

Time Spent at the Club:
▶ 0.5 Seasons

First Goal Scored for the Club:
—
▶ —

Full International:
▶ Nigeria

Championship Totals

04-06

Appearances	4
Goals	0
Assists	0
Yellow Cards	1
Red Cards	0

Clubs

Year	Club	Apps	Gls
05-05	Plymouth	5	0
	Al-Arabi		
	Partizan Belgrade		
	Kaiserslautern		
00-01	Derby	20	0
	AC Milan		
	Internazionale		
	AJ Auxerre		

Off the Pitch

Age:

West: 32 years, 2 months
Team: 26 years, 10 months
League: 26 years, 1 month

Height:
West: 6'1"
Team: 5'11"
League: 5'11"

Weight:
West: 13st 10lb
Team: 12st 1lb
League: 11st 13lb

8 Akos Buzsaky
Midfield

Player Details:

Date of Birth:	07.05.1982
Place of Birth:	Budapest
Nationality:	Hungarian
Height:	5'11"
Weight:	11st 9lb
Foot:	Right/Left

Season Review 05/06

A season of two halves for the Pilgrims' playmaker – if the player of the season voting had been made in January, he would have walked it.

Up until then, the 24-year-old Hungarian playmaker had proved to be a rare bright spot, scoring spectacular goals against Stoke, QPR, Ipswich and Barnet.

However, a stomach injury picked up on international duty and Lilian Nalis's arrival saw Akos relegated to some delightful cameo roles from the bench.

A summer signing after fans urged the board to make his loan spell permanent, Buzsaky is a compelling talent with plenty of tricks and a bagful of confidence in his locker.

Player Performance 05/06

League Performance

Percentage of total possible time player was on pitch   ⊕ position in league table at end of month

Month:	Aug	Sep	Oct	Nov	Dec	Jan	Feb	Mar	Apr	Total
	86%	22%	82%	76%	4%	33%	11%	17%	32%	41%
	21	23	21	19	19	14	15	15	14	
Team Pts:	4/18	5/15	7/15	4/12	8/15	10/15	5/15	5/15	8/18	56/138
Team Gls F:	5	2	5	4	7	6	3	1	6	39
Team Gls A:	10	5	4	6	5	6	3	2	5	46
Total mins:	466	100	370	274	17	150	49	76	175	1,677
Starts (sub):	5 (1)	0 (4)	4 (1)	4	0 (1)	2	0 (3)	0 (3)	1 (5)	16 (18)
Goals:	0	0	2	1	0	0	0	0	1	4
Assists:	1	0	0	1	0	0	0	0	0	2
Clean sheets:	0	0	1	1	0	0	0	0	0	2
Cards (Y/R):	0	1	0	1	0	0	0	0	1	3

League Performance Totals

Goals

- ▶ Buzsaky: 4
- ▶ Team-mates: 33
- **Total: 37**
- ▶ own goals: 2

Assists

- ▶ Buzsaky: 2
- ▶ Team-mates: 30
- **Total: 32**

Cards

- ▶ Buzsaky: 3
- ▶ Team-mates: 65
- **Total: 68**

Cup Games

	Apps	Goals	Cards
FA Cup	1	0	0
Carling Cup	2	1	0
Total	**3**	**1**	**0**

Career History

Career Milestones

Club Debut:
vs Preston (H), L 0-2, Championship
▶ **22.01.05**

First Goal Scored for the Club:
vs Watford (H), W 1-0, Championship
▶ **05.04.05**

Time Spent at the Club:
▶ **1.5 Seasons**

Full International:
▶ **Hungary**

Championship Totals

04-06

Appearances	49
Goals	5
Assists	2
Yellow Cards	5
Red Cards	0

Clubs

Year	Club	Apps	Gls
05-06	Plymouth	52	6
	FC Porto		

Off the Pitch

Age:
- ▶ Buzsaky: 24 years
- ▶ Team: 26 years, 10 months
- | League: 26 years, 1 month

Height:
- ▶ Buzsaky: 5'11"
- ▶ Team: 5'11"
- | League: 5'11"

Weight:
- ▶ Buzsaky: 11st 9lb
- ▶ Team: 12st 1lb
- | League: 11st 13lb

32

Bojan Djordjic
Midfield

Season Review 05/06

Kept Tony Capaldi on the bench until the arrival of Tony Pulis, after which he was largely restricted to a substitute's role, starting only twice on the left side of midfield when Capaldi played left-back.

Former Manchester United player Djordjic, 24, was signed by Bobby Williamson from Rangers during the summer on a three-year deal, but failed to make a compelling case to Pulis for regular inclusion.

A multi-lingual Swedish Under-21 international, Bo's finest moment undoubtedly came at Kenilworth Road, where he headed a far-post equaliser against Luton in the final of four minutes of injury-time.

Player Details:

Date of Birth:	06.02.1982
Place of Birth:	Belgrade
Nationality:	Swedish
Height:	5'10"
Weight:	11st 1lb
Foot:	Left/Right

Player Performance 05/06

League Performance

Percentage of total possible time player was on pitch   ⊙ position in league table at end of month

Month:	Aug	Sep	Oct	Nov	Dec	Jan	Feb	Mar	Apr	Total
	66%	82%	32% 21	14% 19	0% 19	8% 14	2% 15	11% 15	0% 14	24%
	21	23								
Team Pts:	4/18	5/15	7/15	4/12	8/15	10/15	5/15	5/15	8/18	56/138
Team Gls F:	5	2	5	4	7	6	3	1	6	39
Team Gls A:	10	5	4	6	5	6	3	2	5	46
Total mins:	354	367	143	50	0	35	9	49	0	1,007
Starts (sub):	4 (2)	4 (1)	1 (3)	0 (2)	0	0 (2)	0 (1)	0 (2)	0	9 (13)
Goals:	0	0	1	0	0	0	0	0	0	1
Assists:	0	0	0	0	0	0	0	0	0	0
Clean sheets:	0	1	0	0	0	0	0	0	0	1
Cards (Y/R):	1	1	1	0	0	0	0	0	0	3

League Performance Totals

Goals

▶ Djordjic:	1
▶ Team-mates:	36
Total:	**37**
▶ own goals:	2

Assists

▶ Djordjic:	0
▶ Team-mates:	32
Total:	**32**

Cards

▶ Djordjic:	3
▶ Team-mates:	65
Total:	**68**

Cup Games

	Apps	Goals	Cards
FA Cup	1	0	0
Carling Cup	2	0	0
Total	**3**	**0**	**0**

Career History

Career Milestones

Club Debut:
vs Reading (A), W 1-2, Championship

 **06.08.05**

Time Spent at the Club:

▶ **1 Season**

First Goal Scored for the Club:
vs Luton (A), D 1-1, Championship

▶ **22.10.05**

Full International:

▶ —

Championship Totals

04-06

Appearances	22
Goals	1
Assists	0
Yellow Cards	3
Red Cards	0

Clubs

Year	Club	Apps	Gls
05-06	Plymouth	25	1
	Rangers		
	Red Star Belgrade		
	Aarhus		
01-02	Sheff Wed	5	0
99-05	Man Utd	2	0
	Brommapojkarna		

Off the Pitch

Age:

▶ Djordjic: 24 years, 3 months
▶ Team: 26 years, 10 months
| League: 26 years, 1 month

Height:

▶ Djordjic: 5'10"
▶ Team: 5'11"
| League: 5'11"

Weight:

▶ Djordjic: 11st 1lb
▶ Team: 12st 1lb
| League: 11st 13lb

17
Bjarni Gudjonsson
Midfield

Season Review 05/06

The Icelandic international made just six starts for the Pilgrims last season before returning to his homeland to play for his local club and pursue a life outside football.

Midfielder Gudjonsson, 27, featured in the opening day win against Reading but had fallen out of favour by the time Tony Pulis arrived.

Having been released before by Pulis when the pair were together at Stoke, it was something of a surprise that Bjarni started – and finished – the new manager's first three games.

However, they proved to be his Home Park swansong, and Gudjonsson – whose brother Joey was Leicester's player of the season – was soon on his way back home.

Player Details:

Date of Birth:	26.02.1979
Place of Birth:	Reykjavik
Nationality:	Icelandic
Height:	5'8"
Weight:	11st 2lb
Foot:	Right

Player Performance 05/06

League Performance

Percentage of total possible time player was on pitch   ◔ position in league table at end of month

Month:	Aug	Sep	Oct	Nov	Dec	Jan	Feb	Mar	Apr	Total
	54%	32% 23	21 16%	19 0%	19 0%	14 0%	15 0%	15 0%	14 0%	12%
	21									
Team Pts:	4/18	5/15	7/15	4/12	8/15	10/15	5/15	5/15	8/18	56/138
Team Gls F:	5	2	5	4	7	6	3	1	6	39
Team Gls A:	10	5	4	6	5	6	3	2	5	46
Total mins:	289	142	73	0	0	0	0	0	0	504
Starts (sub):	3 (2)	2	1 (2)	0	0	0	0	0	0	6 (4)
Goals:	0	0	0	0	0	0	0	0	0	0
Assists:	0	0	0	0	0	0	0	0	0	0
Clean sheets:	0	1	0	0	0	0	0	0	0	1
Cards (Y/R):	0	1	0	0	0	0	0	0	0	1

League Performance Totals

Goals
- Gudjonsson: 0
- Team-mates: 37
- **Total: 37**
- own goals: 2

Assists
- Gudjonsson: 0
- Team-mates: 32
- **Total: 32**

Cards
- Gudjonsson: 1
- Team-mates: 67
- **Total: 68**

Cup Games

	Apps	Goals	Cards
FA Cup	0	0	0
Carling Cup	1	0	0
Total	**1**	**0**	**0**

Career History

Career Milestones

Club Debut:
vs Derby (H), L 0-2, Championship

 **18.12.04**

First Goal Scored for the Club:
vs Everton (H), L 1-3, FA Cup

 **08.01.05**

Time Spent at the Club:

▶ **1.5 Seasons**

Full International:

▶ **Iceland**

Championship Totals

04-06

Appearances	35
Goals	0
Assists	6
Yellow Cards	3
Red Cards	0

Clubs

Year	Club	Apps	Gls
04-06	Plymouth	27	1
04-04	Coventry	33	3
	VfL Bochum		
00-03	Stoke	161	17
	RC Genk		
97-98	Newcastle Utd	0	0
	IA Akranes		

Off the Pitch

Age:

- Gudjonsson: 27 years, 3 months
- Team: 26 years, 10 months
- League: 26 years, 1 month

Height:

- Gudjonsson: 5'8"
- Team: 5'11"
- League: 5'11"

Weight:

- Gudjonsson: 11st 2lb
- Team: 12st 1lb
- League: 11st 13lb

14 Tony Capaldi
Midfield

The Norwegian-born Northern Ireland international Brummie was one of the most consistent Pilgrims last season, his third with the club.

Capaldi, 24, was dogged by injury and Williamson's preference for Bojan Djordjic early on in the season, but his renaissance coincided with the arrival of Tony Pulis, and he missed only one game – through suspension – after Pulis's debut at Southampton.

His set-piece contributions, from long throw-ins or corners, were vital to the Argyle cause, as was his supply from the left side of midfield.

TC took his international caps to 16 before the season's end, leaving him just four short of Moses Russell's all-time Argyle record.

Player Details:

Date of Birth:	12.08.1981
Place of Birth:	Porsgrunn
Nationality:	Northern Irish
Height:	6'
Weight:	11st 6lb
Foot:	Left

Player Performance 05/06

League Performance

Percentage of total possible time player was on pitch   ↺ position in league table at end of month

Month:	Aug	Sep	Oct	Nov	Dec	Jan	Feb	Mar	Apr	Total
	31%	44%	100%	100%	100%	80%	100%	100%	94%	82%
	21	23	21	19	19	14	15	15	14	
Team Pts:	4/18	5/15	7/15	4/12	8/15	10/15	5/15	5/15	8/18	56/138
Team Gls F:	5	2	5	4	7	6	3	1	6	39
Team Gls A:	10	5	4	6	5	6	3	2	5	46
Total mins:	165	197	450	360	450	360	450	450	510	3,392
Starts (sub):	2 (1)	2 (2)	5	4	5	4	5	5	6	38 (3)
Goals:	1	0	0	0	1	0	0	0	1	3
Assists:	0	0	1	0	0	1	1	0	2	5
Clean sheets:	0	1	1	1	2	1	2	3	2	13
Cards (Y/R):	0	1	1	0	2	1	0	2	0	7

League Performance Totals

Goals

► Capaldi:	3
▪ Team-mates:	34
Total:	**37**
▪ own goals:	2

Assists

► Capaldi:	5
▪ Team-mates:	27
Total:	**32**

Cards

► Capaldi:	7
▪ Team-mates:	61
Total:	**68**

Cup Games

	Apps	Goals	Cards
FA Cup	1	0	0
Carling Cup	2	0	0
Total	**3**	**0**	**0**

Career History

Career Milestones

Club Debut:
vs Wycombe W. (H), W 1-0, Lge One

► **03.05.03**

First Goal Scored for the Club:
vs Rushden & D's (A), L 1-2, Lge One

► **16.08.03**

Time Spent at the Club:

► **3 Seasons**

Full International:

► **N. Ireland**

Championship Totals

04-06

Appearances	76
Goals	5
Assists	8
Yellow Cards	11
Red Cards	0

Clubs

Year	Club	Apps	Gls
03-06	Plymouth	117	12
01-02	Hereford Utd	14	0
98-03	Birmingham	0	0

Off the Pitch

Age:

- ► Capaldi: 24 years, 9 months
- ▪ Team: 26 years, 10 months
- | League: 26 years, 1 month

Height:

- ► Capaldi: 6'
- ▪ Team: 5'11"
- | League: 5'11"

Weight:

- ► Capaldi: 11st 6lb
- ▪ Team: 12st 1lb
- | League: 11st 13lb

20

Lee Hodges
Midfield

Season Review 05/06

For much of 2005-06, it seemed unlikely that Hodges would play for Argyle again, let alone win another contract to take him into his sixth season with the Pilgrims.

However, the 32-year-old made such a successful comeback from a long-term back injury that, by the season's end, he was the team's regular left-back and rewarded with a new deal.

Hodgy, a veteran of the 2001-02 and 2003-04 title-winning sides, made his return in January's FA Cup defeat in Wolverhampton, but had to wait the best part of two months before his league comeback at Derby.

After that, he heart-warmingly retained his place until the end of the campaign.

Player Details:

Date of Birth:	04.09.1973
Place of Birth:	Epping
Nationality:	English
Height:	6'
Weight:	12st
Foot:	Left/Right

Player Performance 05/06

League Performance

Percentage of total possible time player was on pitch   position in league table at end of month

Month:	Aug	Sep	Oct	Nov	Dec	Jan	Feb	Mar	Apr	Total
	0%	0%	0%	0%	0%	1%	14%	86%	88%	23%
(table position)	21	23	21	19	19	14	15	15	14	
Team Pts:	4/18	5/15	7/15	4/12	8/15	10/15	5/15	5/15	8/18	56/138
Team Gls F:	5	2	5	4	7	6	3	1	6	39
Team Gls A:	10	5	4	6	5	6	3	2	5	46
Total mins:	0	0	0	0	0	6	65	389	476	936
Starts (sub):	0	0	0	0	0	0 (1)	1	5	6	12 (1)
Goals:	0	0	0	0	0	0	0	0	0	0
Assists:	0	0	0	0	0	0	0	0	0	0
Clean sheets:	0	0	0	0	0	0	0	3	2	5
Cards (Y/R):	0	0	0	0	0	0	0	0	0	0

League Performance Totals

Goals
- Hodges: 0
- Team-mates: 37
- **Total: 37**
- own goals: 2

Assists
- Hodges: 0
- Team-mates: 32
- **Total: 32**

Cards
- Hodges: 0
- Team-mates: 68
- **Total: 68**

Cup Games

	Apps	Goals	Cards
FA Cup	1	0	0
Carling Cup	0	0	0
Total	**1**	**0**	**0**

Career History

Career Milestones

Club Debut:
vs Chester (A), W 1-2, League One

 **27.02.93**

Time Spent at the Club:

5.5 Seasons

First Goal Scored for the Club:
vs Chester (A), W 1-2, League One

27.02.93

Full International:

—

Championship Totals
04-06

Appearances	32
Goals	0
Assists	0
Yellow Cards	1
Red Cards	0

Clubs

Year	Club	Apps	Gls
01-06	Plymouth	169	11
97-01	Reading	98	10
94-97	Barnet	121	30
93-94	Wycombe	6	0
93-93	Plymouth	7	2
92-94	Tottenham	5	0

Off the Pitch

Age:

- Hodges: 32 years, 8 months
- Team: 26 years, 10 months
- League: 26 years, 1 month

Height:

- Hodges: 6'
- Team: 5'11"
- League: 5'11"

Weight:
- Hodges: 12st
- Team: 12st 1lb
- League: 11st 13lb

4

Lilian Nalis
Midfield

Arrived at Home Park in January and within a month had played against his previous three clubs, Leicester, Coventry and Sheffield United, who had released him from his contract to allow him to join the Pilgrims until the end of the campaign.

The 34-year-old Frenchman did not miss a minute of the season following his debut against Norwich and impressed sufficiently in his 19 starts to earn a new deal for 2006-07.

A defensive midfielder formerly with Italian Serie A side Chievo, Lil mixes his game up, alternating between being the playmaker when the Pilgrims have the ball, and the playbreaker when they have not.

Player Details:

Date of Birth:	29.09.1971
Place of Birth:	Nogent sur Marne
Nationality:	French
Height:	6'1"
Weight:	12st 3lb
Foot:	Right

Player Performance 05/06

League Performance

Percentage of total possible time player was on pitch   ⊖ position in league table at end of month

Month:	Aug	Sep	Oct	Nov	Dec	Jan	Feb	Mar	Apr	Total
						80%	100%	100%	100%	
	21	23	21	19	19	14	15	15	14	43%
	0%	0%	0%	0%	0%					
Team Pts:	4/18	5/15	7/15	4/12	8/15	10/15	5/15	5/15	8/18	56/138
Team Gls F:	5	2	5	4	7	6	3	1	6	39
Team Gls A:	10	5	4	6	5	6	3	2	5	46
Total mins:	0	0	0	0	0	360	450	450	540	1,800
Starts (sub):	0	0	0	0	0	4	5	5	6	20
Goals:	0	0	0	0	0	0	0	1	0	1
Assists:	0	0	0	0	0	0	0	0	0	0
Clean sheets:	0	0	0	0	0	1	2	3	2	8
Cards (Y/R):	0	0	0	0	0	0	1	0	2	3

League Performance Totals

Goals

Nalis:	1
Team-mates:	36
Total:	**37**
own goals:	2

Assists

Nalis:	0
Team-mates:	32
Total:	**32**

Cards

Nalis:	3
Team-mates:	65
Total:	**68**

Cup Games

	Apps	Goals	Cards
FA Cup	0	0	0
Carling Cup	0	0	0
Total	**0**	**0**	**0**

Career History

Career Milestones

Club Debut:
vs Norwich (H), D 1-1, Championship
14.01.06

Time Spent at the Club:
0.5 Seasons

First Goal Scored for the Club:
vs Brighton (H), W 1-0, Championship
04.03.06

Full International:
—

Championship Totals
04-06

Appearances	69
Goals	8
Assists	0
Yellow Cards	7
Red Cards	0

Clubs

Year	Club	Apps	Gls
06-06	Plymouth	20	1
05-05	Coventry	6	2
05-06	Sheff Utd	6	0
03-05	Leicester	66	6
	Chievo Verona		
	Bastia		

Off the Pitch

Age:

- Nalis: 34 years, 8 months
- Team: 26 years, 10 months
- League: 26 years, 1 month

Height:

- Nalis: 6'1"
- Team: 5'11"
- League: 5'11"

Weight:

- Nalis: 12st 3lb
- Team: 12st 1lb
- League: 11st 13lb

27 Jason Jarrett
Midfield

Stiffened the Pilgrims' midfield during a seven-game loan spell from Norwich over Christmas.

After an inauspicious start to his temporary Argyle career, Jarrett, 26, starred in one of the best sequences of the season - victories over Crystal Palace and at Cardiff, and draws at Watford and Wolves.

Argyle were unable to extend his stay and Jase returned to Home Park within two weeks of leaving as Norwich were held to a 1-1 draw.

Ended the season at Preston, from whose line-up he was surprisingly omitted in the second leg of their play-off defeat by Leeds.

Player Details:

Date of Birth:	14.09.1979
Place of Birth:	Bury
Nationality:	English
Height:	6'
Weight:	12st 4lb
Foot:	Right

Player Performance 05/06

League Performance

Percentage of total possible time player was on pitch   ○ position in league table at end of month

Month:	Aug	Sep	Oct	Nov	Dec	Jan	Feb	Mar	Apr	Total
					100%					
	21	23	21	19 25%	19	14 20%	15	15	14	15%
	0%	0%	0%				0%	0%	0%	
Team Pts:	4/18	5/15	7/15	4/12	8/15	10/15	5/15	5/15	8/18	56/138
Team Gls F:	5	2	5	4	7	6	3	1	6	39
Team Gls A:	10	5	4	6	5	6	3	2	5	46
Total mins:	0	0	0	90	450	90	0	0	0	630
Starts (sub):	0	0	0	1	5	1	0	0	0	7
Goals:	0	0	0	0	0	0	0	0	0	0
Assists:	0	0	0	0	0	0	0	0	0	0
Clean sheets:	0	0	0	0	2	0	0	0	0	2
Cards (Y/R):	0	0	0	0	0	0	0	0	0	0

League Performance Totals

Goals
- ▶ Jarrett: 0
- ▶ Team-mates: 37
- **Total: 37**
- ▶ own goals: 2

Assists
- ▶ Jarrett: 0
- ▶ Team-mates: 32
- **Total: 32**

Cards
- ▶ Jarrett: 0
- ▶ Team-mates: 68
- **Total: 68**

Cup Games

	Apps	Goals	Cards
FA Cup	0	0	0
Carling Cup	0	0	0
Total	**0**	**0**	**0**

Career History

Career Milestones

Club Debut:
vs Reading (H), L 0-2, Championship

▶ **26.11.05**

Time Spent at the Club:
▶ **0.5 Seasons**

First Goal Scored for the Club:
—

▶ **—**

Full International:
▶ **—**

Championship Totals

04-06

Appearances	44
Goals	1
Assists	2
Yellow Cards	5
Red Cards	0

Clubs

Year	Club	Apps	Gls
06-06	Preston	11	1
05-06	Plymouth	7	0
05-06	Norwich	15	0
05-05	Stoke	3	0
02-05	Wigan	107	4
00-02	Bury	70	5
99-00	Wrexham	1	0
98-99	Blackpool	4	0

Off the Pitch

Age:
- ▶ Jarrett: 26 years, 8 months
- ▶ Team: 26 years, 10 months
- | League: 26 years, 1 month

Height:
- ▶ Jarrett: 6'
- ▶ Team: 5'11"
- | League: 5'11"

Weight:
- ▶ Jarrett: 12st 4lb
- ▶ Team: 12st 1lb
- | League: 11st 13lb

6

Keith Lasley
Midfield

One of Bobby Williamson's many Scottish imports in the 2004 close season, former Motherwell midfielder Lasley was restricted largely to a watching brief for his two seasons at Home Park, making just 14 league starts.

All of the popular Scot's starts were in his first year, with his involvement last term restricted to just five Championship appearances, all as substitute following the arrival of Tony Pulis, although he did make the first 11 for the Carling Cup defeat at Underhill.

A cheery character who hid his frustrations well, Lasley, 26, played out the final weeks of his contract on loan to League One Blackpool.

Player Details:

Date of Birth:	21.09.1979
Place of Birth:	Glasgow
Nationality:	Scottish
Height:	5'8"
Weight:	10st 7lb
Foot:	Right/Left

Player Performance 05/06

League Performance
Percentage of total possible time player was on pitch ⟲ position in league table at end of month

Month:	Aug	Sep	Oct	Nov	Dec	Jan	Feb	Mar	Apr	Total
	21 0%	23 0%	21 0%	19 12%	19 4%	14 4%	15 0%	15 0%	14 0%	2%
Team Pts:	4/18	5/15	7/15	4/12	8/15	10/15	5/15	5/15	8/18	56/138
Team Gls F:	5	2	5	4	7	6	3	1	6	39
Team Gls A:	10	5	4	6	5	6	3	2	5	46
Total mins:	0	0	0	42	19	19	0	0	0	80
Starts (sub):	0	0	0	0 (2)	0 (2)	0 (1)	0	0	0	0 (5)
Goals:	0	0	0	0	0	0	0	0	0	0
Assists:	0	0	0	0	0	0	0	0	0	0
Clean sheets:	0	0	0	0	0	0	0	0	0	0
Cards (Y/R):	0	0	0	0	0	0	0	0	0	0

League Performance Totals

Goals

▶ Lasley:	0
▶ Team-mates:	37
Total:	**37**
▶ own goals:	2

Assists

▶ Lasley:	0
▶ Team-mates:	32
Total:	**32**

Cards

▶ Lasley:	0
▶ Team-mates:	68
Total:	**68**

Cup Games

	Apps	Goals	Cards
FA Cup	0	0	0
Carling Cup	2	0	0
Total	**2**	**0**	**0**

Career History

Career Milestones

Club Debut:
vs Millwall (H), D 0-0, Championship
 **07.08.04**

First Goal Scored for the Club:
—
▶ —

Time Spent at the Club:
▶ **2 Seasons**

Full International:
▶ —

Championship Totals
04-06

Appearances	29
Goals	0
Assists	1
Yellow Cards	1
Red Cards	0

Clubs

Year	Club	Apps	Gls
06-06	Blackpool	8	0
04-06	Plymouth	32	0
	Motherwell		

Off the Pitch

Age:

▶ Lasley: 26 years, 8 months
▶ Team: 26 years, 10 months
| League: 26 years, 1 month

Height:

▶ Lasley: 5'8"
▶ Team: 5'11"
| League: 5'11"

Weight:
▶ Lasley: 10st 7lb
▶ Team: 12st 1lb
| League: 11st 13lb

15 Paul Wotton
Midfield

Season Review 05/06

Missed just one league match, through suspension, in a season during which he celebrated his testimonial and made his 400th Argyle appearance – but remained frustratingly on 49 league goals.

Skipper Wotton, 28, was also top scorer for the second season in a row, netting six thunderstruck penalties in his nine goals.

Without his goals, Argyle would have been nine points worse off, but it was his never-say-die attitude in central midfield that truly epitomised the captain's season.

A true team-man, Wottsy also looked comfortable enough when called upon to stand in for Mat Doumbe a couple of times in his old centre-back spot.

Player Details:

Date of Birth:	17.08.1977
Place of Birth:	Plymouth
Nationality:	English
Height:	5'11"
Weight:	11st 8lb
Foot:	Right

Player Performance 05/06

League Performance

Percentage of total possible time player was on pitch   position in league table at end of month

Month:	Aug	Sep	Oct	Nov	Dec	Jan	Feb	Mar	Apr	Total
	100%	100%	100%	75%	100%	100%	100%	100%	100%	98%
	21	23	21	19	19	14	15	15	14	
Team Pts:	4/18	5/15	7/15	4/12	8/15	10/15	5/15	5/15	8/18	56/138
Team Gls F:	5	2	5	4	7	6	3	1	6	39
Team Gls A:	10	5	4	6	5	6	3	2	5	46
Total mins:	540	450	450	270	450	450	450	450	540	4,050
Starts (sub):	6	5	5	3	5	5	5	5	6	45
Goals:	1	0	1	1	1	4	0	0	0	8
Assists:	1	0	1	1	1	0	0	0	0	4
Clean sheets:	0	2	1	1	2	1	2	3	2	14
Cards (Y/R):	2	2	0	1	1	1	0	0	2	9

League Performance Totals

Goals
- Wotton: 8
- Team-mates: 29
- **Total: 37**
- own goals: 2

Assists
- Wotton: 4
- Team-mates: 28
- **Total: 32**

Cards
- Wotton: 9
- Team-mates: 59
- **Total: 68**

Cup Games

	Apps	Goals	Cards
FA Cup	1	0	0
Carling Cup	1	1	0
Total	**2**	**1**	**0**

Career History

Career Milestones

Club Debut:
vs Bradford (A), L 2-0, League One
 11.03.95

Time Spent at the Club:
 11.5 Seasons

First Goal Scored for the Club:
vs Blackpool (A), D 2-2, League One
 03.12.96

Full International:
 —

Championship Totals
04-06

Appearances	85
Goals	20
Assists	5
Yellow Cards	16
Red Cards	0

Clubs

Year	Club	Apps	Gls
95-06	Plymouth	407	58

Off the Pitch

Age:
- Wotton: 28 years, 9 months
- Team: 26 years, 10 months
- League: 26 years, 1 month

Height:
- Wotton: 5'11"
- Team: 5'11"
- League: 5'11"

Weight:
- Wotton: 11st 8lb
- Team: 12st 1lb
- League: 11st 13lb

17 Anthony Pulis
Midfield

The manager's son arrived just before the end-of-season transfer deadline, on loan from Stoke City.

The 22-year-old midfielder failed to add to his one league start, for Torquay the previous season, but featured five times from the bench in the final nine games of the campaign.

Only one of those – the final away game at Leicester – ended in defeat before Ant returned to the Britannia Stadium.

Player Details:

Date of Birth:	21.07.1984
Place of Birth:	Bristol
Nationality:	Welsh
Height:	5'10"
Weight:	10st 2lb
Foot:	Right

Player Performance 05/06

League Performance

Percentage of total possible time player was on pitch   ⊖ position in league table at end of month

Month:	Aug	Sep	Oct	Nov	Dec	Jan	Feb	Mar	Apr	Total
	21	23	21	19	19	14	15	15	14	
	0%	0%	0%	0%	0%	0%	0%	0%	9%	1%
Team Pts:	4/18	5/15	7/15	4/12	8/15	10/15	5/15	5/15	8/18	56/138
Team Gls F:	5	2	5	4	7	6	3	1	6	39
Team Gls A:	10	5	4	6	5	6	3	2	5	46
Total mins:	0	0	0	0	0	0	0	0	50	50
Starts (sub):	0	0	0	0	0	0	0	0	0 (5)	0 (5)
Goals:	0	0	0	0	0	0	0	0	0	0
Assists:	0	0	0	0	0	0	0	0	0	0
Clean sheets:	0	0	0	0	0	0	0	0	0	0
Cards (Y/R):	0	0	0	0	0	0	0	0	1	1

League Performance Totals

Goals

▶ Pulis:	0
▷ Team-mates:	37
Total:	**37**
▶ own goals:	2

Assists

▶ Pulis:	0
▷ Team-mates:	32
Total:	**32**

Cards

▶ Pulis:	1
▷ Team-mates:	67
Total:	**68**

Cup Games

	Apps	Goals	Cards
FA Cup	0	0	0
Carling Cup	0	0	0
Total	**0**	**0**	**0**

Career History

Career Milestones

Club Debut:
vs Wolverhampton (H), W 2-0, Champ.

 **01.04.06**

Time Spent at the Club:

▶ **0.5 Seasons**

First Goal Scored for the Club:
—

▶ —

Full International:

▶ —

Championship Totals

04-06

Appearances	5
Goals	0
Assists	0
Yellow Cards	1
Red Cards	0

Clubs

Year	Club	Apps	Gls
06-06	Plymouth	5	0
04-05	Torquay	3	0
04-06	Stoke	0	0
03-04	Portsmouth	1	0

Off the Pitch

Age:

▶ Pulis: 21 years, 10 months
▷ Team: 26 years, 10 months
| League: 26 years, 1 month

Height:

▶ Pulis: 5'10"
▷ Team: 5'11"
| League: 5'11"

Weight:

▶ Pulis: 10st 2lb
▷ Team: 12st 1lb
| League: 11st 13lb

29

Luke Summerfield
Midfield

Made the briefest of contributions to Argyle's season, a nine-minute substitute appearance in the 2-1 Carling Cup defeat at Barnet in September.

The 18-year-old midfielder, son of former Argyle player, Kevin Summerfield, caretaker-manager and assistant to Paul Sturrock, also featured twice as an unused substitute for the first-team as his football education continued under Tony Pulis.

Player Details:

Date of Birth:	06.12.1987
Place of Birth:	Ivybridge
Nationality:	English
Height:	6'
Weight:	11st
Foot:	Right

Player Performance 05/06

League Performance

Percentage of total possible time player was on pitch   ⟳ position in league table at end of month

Month:	Aug	Sep	Oct	Nov	Dec	Jan	Feb	Mar	Apr	Total
	0%	0%	0%	0%	0%	0%	0%	0%	0%	0%
Team Pts:	4/18	5/15	7/15	4/12	8/15	10/15	5/15	5/15	8/18	56/138
Team Gls F:	5	2	5	4	7	6	3	1	6	39
Team Gls A:	10	5	4	6	5	6	3	2	5	46
Total mins:	0	0	0	0	0	0	0	0	0	0
Starts (sub):	0	0	0	0	0	0	0	0	0	0
Goals:	0	0	0	0	0	0	0	0	0	0
Assists:	0	0	0	0	0	0	0	0	0	0
Clean sheets:	0	0	0	0	0	0	0	0	0	0
Cards (Y/R):	0	0	0	0	0	0	0	0	0	0

Position markers at end of month: 21, 23, 21, 19, 19, 14, 15, 15, 14

League Performance Totals

Goals
- ▶ Summerfield: 0
- ▶ Team-mates: 37
- **Total: 37**
- ▶ own goals: 2

Assists
- ▶ Summerfield: 0
- ▶ Team-mates: 32
- **Total: 32**

Cards
- ▶ Summerfield: 0
- ▶ Team-mates: 68
- **Total: 68**

Cup Games

	Apps	Goals	Cards
FA Cup	0	0	0
Carling Cup	1	0	0
Total	**1**	**0**	**0**

Career History

Career Milestones

Club Debut:
vs Leicester (H), D 0-0, Championship
▶ **08.05.05**

First Goal Scored for the Club:
—
▶ **—**

Time Spent at the Club:
▶ **1.5 Seasons**

Full International:
▶ **—**

Championship Totals

04-06	
Appearances	1
Goals	0
Assists	0
Yellow Cards	0
Red Cards	0

Clubs

Year	Club	Apps	Gls
05-06	Plymouth	2	0

Off the Pitch

Age:
- ▶ Summerfield: 18 years, 5 months
- ▶ Team: 26 years, 10 months
- | League: 26 years, 1 month

Height:
- ▶ Summerfield: 6'
- ▶ Team: 5'11"
- | League: 5'11"

Weight:
- ▶ Summerfield: 11st
- ▶ Team: 12st 1lb
- | League: 11st 13lb

7 David Norris
Midfield

Season Review 05/06

David Norris's contribution to Argyle's 2005-06 cause can be gauged by the landslide of votes he attracted for the club's Player of the Year award.

A Paul Sturrock Christmas present to the Pilgrims in 2002, Chuck played all but one of Argyle's league games last season, missing only the visit of Leeds to Home Park in January through suspension: his absence coincided with the Pilgrims' heaviest defeat of the campaign.

Only Norris's frustrating lack of goals cast a shadow over his season in which his value as a player continued to rise exponentially to far in excess of the £25,000 Argyle paid Bolton for him.

Player Details:

Date of Birth:	22.02.1981
Place of Birth:	Peterborough
Nationality:	English
Height:	5'7"
Weight:	11st 6lb
Foot:	Right

Player Performance 05/06

League Performance

Percentage of total possible time player was on pitch   ⊖ position in league table at end of month

Month:	Aug	Sep	Oct	Nov	Dec	Jan	Feb	Mar	Apr	Total
	85%	100%	100%	100%	100%	80%	98%	100%	100%	96%
	21	23	21	19	19	14	15	15	14	
Team Pts:	4/18	5/15	7/15	4/12	8/15	10/15	5/15	5/15	8/18	56/138
Team Gls F:	5	2	5	4	7	6	3	1	6	39
Team Gls A:	10	5	4	6	5	6	3	2	5	46
Total mins:	459	450	450	360	450	360	441	450	540	3,960
Starts (sub):	5 (1)	5	5	4	5	4	5	5	6	44 (1)
Goals:	0	0	0	0	2	0	0	0	0	2
Assists:	0	0	1	2	1	1	0	0	0	5
Clean sheets:	0	2	1	1	2	1	2	3	2	14
Cards (Y/R):	2	1	0	1	2	0	0	0	0	6

League Performance Totals

Goals
- ▶ Norris: 2
- ▷ Team-mates: 35
- **Total: 37**
- ▶ own goals: 2

Assists
- ▶ Norris: 5
- ▷ Team-mates: 27
- **Total: 32**

Cards
- ▶ Norris: 6
- ▷ Team-mates: 62
- **Total: 68**

Cup Games

	Apps	Goals	Cards
FA Cup	1	0	0
Carling Cup	1	0	0
Total	**2**	**0**	**0**

Career History

Career Milestones

Club Debut:
vs Crewe Alx (A), W 1-0, League One
▶ **19.10.02**

Time Spent at the Club:
▶ **3.5 Seasons**

First Goal Scored for the Club:
vs Crewe Alx (A), W 1-0, League One
▶ **19.10.02**

Full International:
▶ **—**

Championship Totals

04-06
Appearances	80
Goals	5
Assists	8
Yellow Cards	9
Red Cards	0

Clubs

Year	Club	Apps	Gls
02-06	Plymouth	166	16
02-02	Hull	6	1
00-01	Boston Utd	5	4
00-02	Bolton W.	5	0
	Boston Utd		

Off the Pitch

Age:

- ▶ Norris: 25 years, 3 months
- ▷ Team: 26 years, 10 months
- | League: 26 years, 1 month

Height:

- ▶ Norris: 5'7"
- ▷ Team: 5'11"
- | League: 5'11"

Weight:

- ▶ Norris: 11st 6lb
- ▷ Team: 12st 1lb
- | League: 11st 13lb

18 Leon Clarke
Forward

Season Review 05/06

Played five times for Argyle on loan from Wolves, for who he had earlier scored a third-round FA Cup winner...against the Pilgrims.

It proved to be one of only two goals all season for the Blackcountryman, who joined Argyle for the last month of the campaign.

Four of the 21-year-old striker's five appearances came away from home, during which the Pilgrims scored just once.

Leon's sole Home Park performance – having been ruled out of the clash against parent club Wolves – also ended goal-less for Clarke, and a 2-1 defeat by Luton for the Pilgrims.

Player Details:

Date of Birth:	10.02.1985
Place of Birth:	Wolverhampton
Nationality:	English
Height:	6'2"
Weight:	14st 4lb
Foot:	Right/Left

Player Performance 05/06

League Performance

Percentage of total possible time player was on pitch   ⊖ position in league table at end of month

Month:	Aug	Sep	Oct	Nov	Dec	Jan	Feb	Mar	Apr	Total
	0%	0%	0%	0%	0%	0%	0%	19%	45%	8%
	21	23	21	19	19	14	15	15	14	
Team Pts:	4/18	5/15	7/15	4/12	8/15	10/15	5/15	5/15	8/18	56/138
Team Gls F:	5	2	5	4	7	6	3	1	6	39
Team Gls A:	10	5	4	6	5	6	3	2	5	46
Total mins:	0	0	0	0	0	0	0	84	243	327
Starts (sub):	0	0	0	0	0	0	0	1	4	5
Goals:	0	0	0	0	0	0	0	0	0	0
Assists:	0	0	0	0	0	0	0	0	0	0
Clean sheets:	0	0	0	0	0	0	0	1	0	1
Cards (Y/R):	0	0	0	0	0	0	0	0	0	0

League Performance Totals

Goals

- Clarke: 0
- Team-mates: 37
- **Total: 37**
- own goals: 2

Assists

- Clarke: 0
- Team-mates: 32
- **Total: 32**

Cards

- Clarke: 0
- Team-mates: 68
- **Total: 68**

Cup Games

	Apps	Goals	Cards
FA Cup	0	0	0
Carling Cup	0	0	0
Total	**0**	**0**	**0**

Career History

Career Milestones

Club Debut:
vs Preston (A), D 0-0, Championship
▶ **25.03.06**

Time Spent at the Club:
▶ **0.5 Seasons**

First Goal Scored for the Club:
—
▶ —

Full International:
▶ —

Championship Totals

04-06

Appearances	58
Goals	8
Assists	6
Yellow Cards	6
Red Cards	0

Clubs

Year	Club	Apps	Gls
06-06	Plymouth	5	0
06-06	QPR	1	0
04-04	Kidderminster	4	0
03-06	Wolverhampton	60	10

Off the Pitch

Age:

- Clarke: 21 years, 3 months
- Team: 26 years, 10 months
- League: 26 years, 1 month

Height:

- Clarke: 6'2"
- Team: 5'11"
- League: 5'11"

Weight:

- Clarke: 14st 4lb
- Team: 12st 1lb
- League: 11st 13lb

26

Chris Zebroski
Forward

Player Details:

Date of Birth:	29.10.1986
Place of Birth:	Swindon
Nationality:	English
Height:	6'1"
Weight:	11st 8lb
Foot:	Right

Breakthrough season for one of three teenagers to be offered a professional deal for the 2006-07 season.

Zebroski, 19, made his first-team debut as a substitute in the 2-1 Carling Cup success over Peterborough in August, and followed that with his league debut, again from the bench, against Hull a few days later.

Three more substitute appearances followed for Tex, who unfortunately tasted defeat in each of his four league games.

His elevation certainly benefited his performances in the youth team, for who he scored in eight consecutive games.

Player Performance 05/06

League Performance

Percentage of total possible time player was on pitch   ⊖ position in league table at end of month

Month:	Aug	Sep	Oct	Nov	Dec	Jan	Feb	Mar	Apr	Total
(position)	21	23	21	19	19	14	15	15	14	
(percentage)	7%	0%	0%	0%	0%	0%	3%	5%	0%	2%
Team Pts:	4/18	5/15	7/15	4/12	8/15	10/15	5/15	5/15	8/18	56/138
Team Gls F:	5	2	5	4	7	6	3	1	8	39
Team Gls A:	10	5	4	6	5	6	3	2	5	46
Total mins:	38	0	0	0	0	0	14	24	0	76
Starts (sub):	0 (2)	0	0	0	0	0	0 (1)	0 (1)	0	0 (4)
Goals:	0	0	0	0	0	0	0	0	0	0
Assists:	0	0	0	0	0	0	0	0	0	0
Clean sheets:	0	0	0	0	0	0	0	0	0	0
Cards (Y/R):	0	0	0	0	0	0	0	0	0	0

League Performance Totals

Goals

- Zebroski: 0
- Team-mates: 37

Total: 37

own goals: 2

Assists

- Zebroski: 0
- Team-mates: 32

Total: 32

Cards

- Zebroski: 0
- Team-mates: 68

Total: 68

Cup Games

	Apps	Goals	Cards
FA Cup	0	0	0
Carling Cup	0	0	0
Total	**0**	**0**	**0**

Career History

Career Milestones

Club Debut:
vs Hull (H), L 0-1, Championship

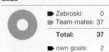 **27.08.05**

Time Spent at the Club:
 1 Season

First Goal Scored for the Club:
—

 —

Full International:
 —

Championship Totals

04-06

Appearances	4
Goals	0
Assists	0
Yellow Cards	0
Red Cards	0

Clubs

Year	Club	Apps	Gls
05-06	Plymouth	4	0

Off the Pitch

Age:
- Zebroski: 19 years, 7 months
- Team: 26 years, 10 months
- League: 26 years, 1 month

Height:
- Zebroski: 6'1"
- Team: 5'11"
- League: 5'11"

Weight:
- Zebroski: 11st 8lb
- Team: 12st 1lb
- League: 11st 13lb

19

Matt Derbyshire
Forward

Player Details:

Date of Birth:	14.04.1986
Place of Birth:	Great Harwood
Nationality:	English
Height:	5'10"
Weight:	11st 1lb
Foot:	Right

Season Review 05/06

The first of six loan players who plied their trade at Home Park last season, the Blackburn striker started just two games – both during the Jocky Scott interregnum.

Derbyshire, 20, made an immediate impact by scoring a hat-trick for the reserves on the day Bobby Williamson left the club.

However, Matt was unable to take that form into either of his starts or any of his ten substitute appearances before he was recalled to the North West.

A subsequent loan spell to Wrexham proved more productive, although 10 goals from 16 starts were not enough to help the Welsh side to promotion from League Two.

Player Performance 05/06

League Performance

Percentage of total possible time player was on pitch   ⊖ position in league table at end of month

Month:	Aug	Sep	Oct	Nov	Dec	Jan	Feb	Mar	Apr	Total
	0%	40%		3%	8%	2%	0%	0%	0%	7%
Team Pts:	4/18	5/15	7/15	4/12	8/15	10/15	5/15	5/15	8/18	56/138
Team Gls F:	5	2	5	4	7	6	3	1	6	39
Team Gls A:	10	5	4	6	5	6	3	2	5	46
Total mins:	0	182	35	9	35	11	0	0	0	272
Starts (sub):	0	2 (2)	0 (2)	0 (2)	0 (3)	0 (1)	0	0	0	2 (10)
Goals:	0	0	0	0	0	0	0	0	0	0
Assists:	0	1	1	0	0	0	0	0	0	2
Clean sheets:	0	0	0	0	0	0	0	0	0	0
Cards (Y/R):	0	0	0	0	0	0	0	0	0	0

League Performance Totals

Goals

- Derbyshire: 0
- Team-mates: 37
- **Total: 37**
- own goals: 2

Assists

- Derbyshire: 2
- Team-mates: 30
- **Total: 32**

Cards

- Derbyshire: 0
- Team-mates: 68
- **Total: 68**

Cup Games

	Apps	Goals	Cards
FA Cup	0	0	0
Carling Cup	1	0	0
Total	1	0	0

Career History

Career Milestones

Club Debut:

vs Norwich (A), L 2-0, Championship

 10.09.05

Time Spent at the Club:

▶ **0.5 Seasons**

First Goal Scored for the Club:

—

 —

Full International:

▶ —

Championship Totals

04-06

Appearances	12
Goals	0
Assists	2
Yellow Cards	0
Red Cards	0

Clubs

Year	Club	Apps	Gls
06-06	Wrexham	16	10
05-06	Plymouth	13	0
03-06	Blackburn	1	0

Off the Pitch

Age:

- Derbyshire: 20 years, 1 month
- Team: 26 years, 10 months
- League: 26 years, 1 month

Height:

- Derbyshire: 5'10"
- Team: 5'11"
- League: 5'11"

Weight:

- Derbyshire: 11st 1lb
- Team: 12st 1lb
- League: 11st 13lb

10 Vincent Pericard
Forward

Former Juventus forward who joined the Pilgrims on loan from Portsmouth for the final 15 games of the season.

The 23-year-old's finest hour came against Coventry City, when he became only the second Pilgrim in the best part of 80 years to score a hat-trick on his full home debut, the triple inspiring Argyle to a 3-1 victory.

Cameroon-qualified Frenchman Péricard netted once more during his loan from Fratton Park, in the 1-1 draw at Millwall, and his hold-up play and general forward craft added an extra dimension to the Pilgrims' cause.

Player Details:

Date of Birth:	03.10.1982
Place of Birth:	Efok
Nationality:	French
Height:	6'1"
Weight:	13st 8lb
Foot:	Right

Player Performance 05/06

League Performance

Percentage of total possible time player was on pitch   ⊖ position in league table at end of month

Month:	Aug	Sep	Oct	Nov	Dec	Jan	Feb	Mar	Apr	Total
	0%	0%	0%	0%	0%	0%	67%	100%	95%	31%
	21	23	21	19	19	14	15	15	14	
Team Pts:	4/18	5/15	7/15	4/12	8/15	10/15	5/15	5/15	8/18	56/138
Team Gls F:	5	2	5	4	7	6	3	1	6	39
Team Gls A:	10	5	4	6	5	6	3	2	5	46
Total mins:	0	0	0	0	0	0	302	450	514	1,266
Starts (sub):	0	0	0	0	0	0	3 (1)	5	6	14 (1)
Goals:	0	0	0	0	0	0	3	0	1	4
Assists:	0	0	0	0	0	0	0	0	2	2
Clean sheets:	0	0	0	0	0	0	1	3	2	6
Cards (Y/R):	0	0	0	0	0	0	0	1	0	1

League Performance Totals

Goals

▶ Pericard:	4
▷ Team-mates:	33
Total:	**37**
▷ own goals:	2

Assists

▶ Pericard:	2
▷ Team-mates:	30
Total:	**32**

Cards

▶ Pericard:	1
▷ Team-mates:	67
Total:	**68**

Cup Games

	Apps	Goals	Cards
FA Cup	0	0	0
Carling Cup	0	0	0
Total	**0**	**0**	**0**

Career History

Career Milestones

Club Debut:

vs Sheff Utd (H), D 0-0, Champ.

▶ **11.02.06**

Time Spent at the Club:

▶ **0.5 Seasons**

First Goal Scored for the Club:

vs Coventry (H), W 3-1, Champ.

▶ **18.02.06**

Full International:

▶ **—**

Championship Totals

04-06

Appearances	26
Goals	6
Assists	3
Yellow Cards	1
Red Cards	0

Clubs

Year	Club	Apps	Gls
06-06	Plymouth	15	4
05-05	Sheff Utd	11	2
02-06	Portsmouth	49	10
	Juventus		

Off the Pitch

Age:

- ▶ Pericard: 23 years, 7 months
- ▷ Team: 26 years, 10 months
- | League: 26 years, 1 month

Height:

- ▶ Pericard: 6'1"
- ▷ Team: 5'11"
- | League: 5'11"

Weight:

- ▶ Pericard: 13st 8lb
- ▷ Team: 12st 1lb
- | League: 11st 13lb

11 Nick Chadwick
Forward

The only man to score a winning goal against Reading at the Madejski last season, former Everton striker Chadwick netted six times from 27 league starts.

His other five goals came during a 13-game purple patch between November and January, and included one – against Norwich - that was awarded to him only after strenuous appeals on behalf of the club to overturn a wrongly-awarded own goal.

Capable of some truly spectacular strikes, not least of all his 12-second opener against Crystal Palace, Chadders also proved to be a willing workhorse alongside whichever of the many forward partners with which he was paired.

Player Details:

Date of Birth:	26.10.1982
Place of Birth:	Stoke
Nationality:	English
Height:	5'11"
Weight:	10st 9lb
Foot:	Right

Player Performance 05/06

League Performance

Percentage of total possible time player was on pitch   ⊖ position in league table at end of month

Month:	Aug	Sep	Oct	Nov	Dec	Jan	Feb	Mar	Apr	Total
	12%	69%	39% 21%	96%	99%	77% 14	76% 15	15 19%	14 23%	54%
	21	23		19	19					
Team Pts:	4/18	5/15	7/15	4/12	8/15	10/15	5/15	5/15	8/18	56/138
Team Gls F:	5	2	5	4	7	6	3	1	6	39
Team Gls A:	10	5	4	6	5	6	3	2	5	46
Total mins:	65	312	177	344	444	347	340	86	122	2,237
Starts (sub):	1 (1)	4 (1)	2 (3)	4	5	4	4 (1)	1 (3)	1 (2)	26 (11)
Goals:	1	0	0	1	2	2	0	0	0	6
Assists:	0	0	0	0	1	0	0	0	0	1
Clean sheets:	0	1	0	1	2	1	1	0	0	6
Cards (Y/R):	0	0	0	1	1	1	0	0	0	3

League Performance Totals

Goals

- Chadwick: 6
- Team-mates: 31
- **Total: 37**
- own goals: 2

Assists

- Chadwick: 1
- Team-mates: 31
- **Total: 32**

Cards

- Chadwick: 3
- Team-mates: 65
- **Total: 68**

Cup Games

	Apps	Goals	Cards
FA Cup	0	0	0
Carling Cup	1	0	0
Total	**1**	**0**	**0**

Career History

Career Milestones

Club Debut:
vs Rotherham (H), D 1-1, Champ.
▶ **12.02.05**

Time Spent at the Club:
▶ **1.5 Seasons**

First Goal Scored for the Club:
vs Brighton (H), W 5-1, Champ.
▶ **12.03.05**

Full International:
▶ —

Championship Totals

04-06

Appearances	52
Goals	7
Assists	3
Yellow Cards	4
Red Cards	0

Clubs

Year	Club	Apps	Gls
05-06	Plymouth	53	7
03-04	Millwall	15	4
03-03	Derby	6	0
01-05	Everton	21	6

Off the Pitch

Age:

- Chadwick: 23 years, 7 months
- Team: 26 years, 10 months
- League: 26 years, 1 month

Height:
- Chadwick: 5'11"
- Team: 5'11"
- League: 5'11"

Weight:

- Chadwick: 10st 9lb
- Team: 12st 1lb
- League: 11st 13lb

27 Reuben Reid
Forward

Season Review 05/06

A rapid rise through the Argyle ranks ended with the teenager making his league debut in the final match of last season, as a substitute against Ipswich.

Striker Reid, 18, had begun the season on trial at Manchester United but was at Argyle by the time Tony Pulis arrived as manager and immediately made an impression on the new man.

Progressed from the youth team to the reserves, and, finally, to the senior side – his introduction from the bench as Michael Evans completed his Argyle career signalling the beginning of a new era as an old one came to an end.

Player Details:

Date of Birth:	26.07.88
Place of Birth:	Bristol
Nationality:	English
Height:	6'
Weight:	12st
Foot:	Right

Player Performance 05/06

League Performance

Percentage of total possible time player was on pitch   ⊙ position in league table at end of month

Month:	Aug	Sep	Oct	Nov	Dec	Jan	Feb	Mar	Apr	Total
	21	23	21	19	19	14	15	15	14	
	0%	0%	0%	0%	0%	0%	0%	0%	2%	0%
Team Pts:	4/18	5/15	7/15	4/12	8/15	10/15	5/15	5/15	8/18	56/138
Team Gls F:	5	2	5	4	7	6	3	1	6	39
Team Gls A:	10	5	4	6	5	6	3	2	5	46
Total mins:	0	0	0	0	0	0	0	0	12	12
Starts (sub):	0	0	0	0	0	0	0	0	0 (1)	0 (1)
Goals:	0	0	0	0	0	0	0	0	0	0
Assists:	0	0	0	0	0	0	0	0	0	0
Clean sheets:	0	0	0	0	0	0	0	0	0	0
Cards (Y/R):	0	0	0	0	0	0	0	0	0	0

League Performance Totals

Goals
- Reid: 0
- Team-mates: 37

Total: 37

- own goals: 2

Assists
- Reid: 0
- Team-mates: 32

Total: 32

Cards
- Reid: 0
- Team-mates: 68

Total: 68

Cup Games

	Apps	Goals	Cards
FA Cup	0	0	0
Carling Cup	0	0	0
Total	0	0	0

Career History

Career Milestones

Club Debut:
vs Ipswich (H), W 2-1, Championship
▶ **30.04.06**

Time Spent at the Club:
▶ **0.5 Seasons**

First Goal Scored for the Club:
▶ —

Full International:
▶ —

Championship Totals

04-06

Appearances	1
Goals	0
Assists	0
Yellow Cards	0
Red Cards	0

Clubs

Year	Club	Apps	Gls
06-06	Plymouth	1	0

Off the Pitch

Age:

- Reid: 17 years, 10 months
- Team: 26 years, 10 months
- League: 26 years, 1 month

Height:
- Reid: 6'
- Team: 5'11"
- League: 5'11"

Weight:
- Reid: 12st
- Team: 12st 1lb
- League: 11st 13lb

10 Scott Taylor
Forward

Signed by Bobby Williamson on New Year's Eve 2004, Taylor never really played more than a bit-part in his year with Argyle, a fact testified to by the fact that he made more appearances from the bench, than as a starter.

Scotty, 30, cost £100,000 from Blackpool but spent much of his time at Home Park lower in the pecking order than Michael Evans and Nick Chadwick, who arrived a few weeks later from Everton.

He scored twice from 10 starts last season, including the winner in the 2-1 Carling Cup victory over Peterborough, before joining Milton Keynes in January but was unable to save the Dons from relegation to League Two.

Player Details:

Date of Birth:	05.05.1976
Place of Birth:	Chertsey
Nationality:	English
Height:	5'10"
Weight:	11st 6lb
Foot:	Left/Right

Player Performance 05/06

League Performance

Percentage of total possible time player was on pitch   ⟳ position in league table at end of month

Month:	Aug	Sep	Oct	Nov	Dec	Jan	Feb	Mar	Apr	Total
	48%	51%	59%	3%	1%	19%	0%	0%	0%	21%
	21	23	21	19	19	14	15	15	14	
Team Pts:	4/18	5/15	7/15	4/12	8/15	10/15	5/15	5/15	8/18	56/138
Team Gls F:	5	2	5	4	7	6	3	1	6	39
Team Gls A:	10	5	4	6	5	6	3	2	5	46
Total mins:	258	230	264	10	6	86	0	0	0	854
Starts (sub):	2 (3)	2 (2)	3 (2)	0 (1)	0 (1)	1 (1)	0	0	0	8 (10)
Goals:	0	1	0	0	0	0	0	0	0	1
Assists:	0	0	0	0	0	0	0	0	0	0
Clean sheets:	0	1	0	0	0	0	0	0	0	1
Cards (Y/R):	1	0	1	0	0	0	0	0	0	2

League Performance Totals

Goals
- Taylor: 1
- Team-mates: 36
- **Total: 37**
- own goals: 2

Assists
- Taylor: 0
- Team-mates: 32
- **Total: 32**

Cards
- Taylor: 2
- Team-mates: 66
- **Total: 68**

Cup Games

	Apps	Goals	Cards
FA Cup	1	0	0
Carling Cup	2	1	0
Total	3	1	0

Career History

Career Milestones

Club Debut:
vs Wolverhampton (A), D 1-1, Champ.

 **01.01.05**

Time Spent at the Club:

 1 Season

First Goal Scored for the Club:
vs Crewe (H), W 3-0, Champ.

 **26.02.05**

Full International:

 —

Championship Totals

04-06

Appearances	34
Goals	4
Assists	0
Yellow Cards	2
Red Cards	0

Clubs

Year	Club	Apps	Gls
06-06	MK Dons	17	3
04-06	Plymouth	37	5
02-04	Blackpool	138	61
01-02	Stockport	30	7
98-01	Tranmere	130	22
98-98	Blackpool	6	2
97-98	Rotherham	11	3
96-98	Bolton W.	17	3
95-96	Millwall	32	2
	Staines		

Off the Pitch

Age:

- Taylor: 30 years
- Team: 26 years, 10 months
- League: 26 years, 1 month

Height:
- Taylor: 5'10"
- Team: 5'11"
- League: 5'11"

Weight:
- Taylor: 11st 6lb
- Team: 12st 1lb
- League: 11st 13lb

9

Micky Evans
Forward

Scored the first goal of the season – in the victory at Reading – and the last, to secure a 2-1 win against Ipswich at Home Park.

The latter provoked a huge outpouring of emotion since Evans, 33, had announced that he would be leaving after the game following 432 matches for his hometown club. The popular Plymothian was not the only one with tears in his eyes during an emotional post-game lap of appreciation.

For most of the campaign, Trigger shouldered responsibility for the Pilgrims' attack, as he had done season after season, before deciding to quit with Argyle in the highest league position he had experienced.

Michael Evans – Argyle legend.

Player Details:

Date of Birth:	01.01.1973
Place of Birth:	Plymouth
Nationality:	Irish
Height:	6'
Weight:	12st 3lb
Foot:	Right/Left

Player Performance 05/06

League Performance

Percentage of total possible time player was on pitch   ⊖ position in league table at end of month

Month:	Aug	Sep	Oct	Nov	Dec	Jan	Feb	Mar	Apr	Total
	94%	83%	97%	98%	93%	100%	54%	57%	14 / 32%	78%
	21	23	21	19	19	14	15	15		
Team Pts:	4/18	5/15	7/15	4/12	8/15	10/15	5/15	5/15	8/18	56/138
Team Gls F:	5	2	5	4	7	6	3	1	6	39
Team Gls A:	10	5	4	6	5	6	3	2	5	46
Total mins:	508	374	435	351	419	450	244	256	175	3,212
Starts (sub):	6	4 (1)	5	4	5	5	3 (2)	3 (2)	1 (4)	36 (9)
Goals:	2	1	0	0	0	0	0	0	1	4
Assists:	1	0	0	0	2	2	1	0	1	7
Clean sheets:	0	2	1	1	1	1	0	1	0	7
Cards (Y/R):	1	1	0	0	0	0	0	0	0	2

League Performance Totals

Goals
- ▶ Evans: 4
- ▶ Team-mates: 33
- **Total: 37**
- ▶ own goals: 2

Assists
- ▶ Evans: 7
- ▶ Team-mates: 25
- **Total: 32**

Cards
- ▶ Evans: 2
- ▶ Team-mates: 66
- **Total: 68**

Cup Games

	Apps	Goals	Cards
FA Cup	1	0	0
Carling Cup	1	0	0
Total	2	0	0

Career History

Career Milestones

Club Debut:
vs Port Vale (A), L 5-1, Championship
▶ **01.12.90**

Time Spent at the Club:
▶ **11.5 Seasons**

First Goal Scored for the Club:
vs Millwall (H), W 4-0, ZDS Cup
▶ **22.10.91**

Full International:
▶ **Rep. Ireland**

Championship Totals

04-06

Appearances	87
Goals	8
Assists	14
Yellow Cards	7
Red Cards	0

Clubs

Year	Club	Apps	Gls
01-06	Plymouth	238	39
00-01	Bristol Rovers	26	6
97-00	West Brom	73	9
97-97	Southampton	25	5
92-92	Blackburn	0	0
90-97	Plymouth	194	43

Off the Pitch

Age:
- ▶ Evans: 33 years, 4 months
- ▮ Team: 26 years, 10 months
- ▮ League: 26 years, 1 month

Height:
- ▶ Evans: 6'
- ▮ Team: 5'11"
- ▮ League: 5'11"

Weight:
- ▶ Evans: 12st 3lb
- ▮ Team: 12st 1lb
- ▮ League: 11st 13lb

Barnsley

BARNSLEY FC

Nickname:	The Tykes
Manager:	Andy Ritchie
Chairman:	Gordon Shepherd
Website:	www.barnsleyfc.co.uk

Telephone:	01226 211 211
Ticket Office:	01226 211 200
Club Shop:	01226 211 400

Season Review 05/06

Barnsley gained promotion via the Play-offs after seeing off Huddersfield and then Swansea. Despite having been a striker himself, boss Andy Ritchie put together a defence that kept 19 clean sheets over the course of the League One season.

The Tykes were far from being defensively-minded, however, winning many admirers with some of their inventive attacking displays.

Points / Position

▶ won ▶ drawn ▶ lost H home A away

Season:	96/97	97/98	98/99	99/00	00/01	01/02	02/03	03/04	04/05	05/06
Premiership										
Division 1	2 (80pts)	19 (35pts)	13 (59pts)	4 (82pts)	16 (54pts)	23 (48pts)			17 (53pts)	14 (56pts)
Division 2	19 (54pts)	22 (49pts)					8 (65pts) 19 (52pts)	10 (90pts) 12 (62pts)	13 (61pts)	5 (72pts)
Division 3			13 (61pts)	12 (66pts)	12 (58pts)	10 (102pts)				

Date:	Result:
01.03	H 1-1
14.09	A 1-1
27.09	H 2-0
03.04	A 0-1

Champ. Head-to-Head

Facts	○ Plymouth	Barnsley ○
Games		
Points	0	0
Won	0	0
Drawn	0	0
Goals		
For	0	0
Clean Sheets	0	0
Shots on Target	0	0
Disciplinary		
Fouls	0	0
Yellow Cards	0	0
Red Cards	0	0

Goals by Area

○ Plymouth   ○ Barnsley

0		0
0		0
0		0

Goals by Position

○ Plymouth   ○ Barnsley

	Plymouth		Barnsley
▶ forward:	0	▶ forward:	0
▶ midfield:	0	▶ midfield:	0
▶ defence:	0	▶ defence:	0

Goals Scored by Period

	0	0	0	0	0	0	
0	15	30	45	60	75	90	
	0	0	0	0	0	0	

Average Attendance

All-Time Records

Total Championship Record	○ Plymouth	Barnsley ○
Played	92	0
Points	109	0
Won	27	0
Drawn	28	0
Lost	37	0
For	91	0
Against	110	0
Players Used	44	0

All-Time Record vs Plymouth

Competition	Played	Won	Drawn	Lost	For	Against
League	52	12	15	25	48	91
FA Cup	5	1	1	3	4	8
League Cup	0	0	0	0	0	0
Other	0	0	0	0	0	0
Total	**57**	**13**	**16**	**28**	**52**	**99**

Birmingham City

Nickname:	**The Blues**	Telephone:	**0871 226 1875**
Manager:	**Steve Bruce**	Ticket Office:	**0871 226 1875**
Chairman:	**David Gold**	Club Shop:	**0871 226 1875**
Website:	**www.bcfc.com**		

Season Review 05/06

Injuries played a major part as Birmingham's four-season stay in the top-flight came to an end. Manager Steve Bruce was rarely able to pick a settled team with key players such as Matthew Upson, Mikael Forssell and David Dunn all missing large chunks of the campaign.

Goals proved particularly hard to come by, with only Sunderland managing less than the 28 netted by the Blues.

Points / Position

won drawn lost H home A away

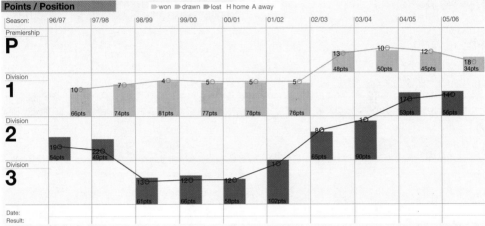

Season:	96/97	97/98	98/99	99/00	00/01	01/02	02/03	03/04	04/05	05/06
Premiership P							13 / 48pts	10 / 50pts	12 / 45pts	18 / 34pts
Division 1	10 / 66pts	7 / 74pts	4 / 81pts	5 / 77pts	5 / 78pts	5 / 76pts			17 / 53pts	14 / 56pts
Division 2	19 / 54pts	22 / 49pts					8 / 65pts	1 / 90pts		
Division 3			13 / 61pts	12 / 66pts	12 / 58pts	1 / 102pts				
Date:										
Result:										

Champ. Head-to-Head

Facts	O Plymouth	Birmingham O
Games		
Points	0	0
Won	0	0
Drawn	0	0
Goals		
For	0	0
Clean Sheets	0	0
Shots on Target	0	0
Disciplinary		
Fouls	0	0
Yellow Cards	0	0
Red Cards	0	0

Goals by Area

O Plymouth   O Birmingham

	0	0
0		0
0		0

Goals by Position

O Plymouth   O Birmingham

	forward:	0		forward:	0
	midfield:	0		midfield:	0
	defence:	0		defence:	0

Goals Scored by Period

0	0	0	0	0	0
0	15	30	45	60	75	90
0	0	0	0	0	0

Average Attendance

All-Time Records

Total Championship Record	O Plymouth	Birmingham O
Played	92	0
Points	109	0
Won	27	0
Drawn	28	0
Lost	37	0
For	91	0
Against	110	0
Players Used	44	0

All-Time Record vs Plymouth

Competition	Played	Won	Drawn	Lost	For	Against
League	24	12	7	5	51	26
FA Cup	0	0	0	0	0	0
League Cup	10	6	1	3	13	9
Other	0	0	0	0	0	0
Total	**34**	**18**	**8**	**8**	**64**	**35**

Burnley

Nickname:	The Clarets	Telephone:	0870 443 1882
Manager:	Steve Cotterill	Ticket Office:	0870 443 1914
Chairman:	Barry Kilby	Club Shop:	0870 443 1882
Website:	www.burnleyfootballclub.com		

Season Review 05/06

It was a season of little excitement at Turf Moor, with a mid-season push for the Play-offs proving to be the only real highlight. The goals of much-maligned striker Ade Akinbiyi were badly missed after he left for Sheffield United in January.

A worrying end to the campaign saw Steve Cotterill's team win just two of their final 14 Championship matches.

Points / Position

■ won ■ drawn ■ lost H home A away

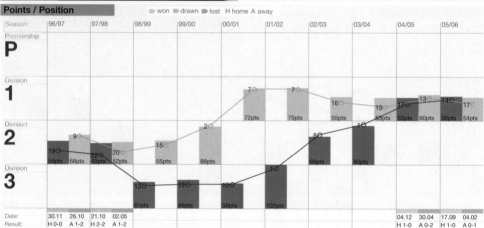

Season:	96/97	97/98	98/99	99/00	00/01	01/02	02/03	03/04	04/05	05/06
Premiership P										
Division 1						7○ 72pts	7○ 75pts	16○ 55pts	19○ 53pts / 17○ 53pts	13○ 60pts / 14○ 56pts	17○ 54pts
Division 2	19○ 54pts / 9○	68pts / 22○ 49pts	20○ 52pts	15○ 55pts	2○ 88pts		8○ 65pts	10○ 90pts		
Division 3			13○ 61pts	12○ 66pts	12○ 58pts	1○ 102pts				

Date:	30.11	26.10	21.10	02.05					04.12	30.04	17.09	04.02
Result:	H 0-0	A 1-2	H 2-2	A 1-2					H 1-0	A 0-2	H 1-0	A 0-1

Champ. Head-to-Head

Facts	○ Plymouth	Burnley ○
Games		
Points	6	6
Won	2	2
Drawn	0	0
Goals		
For	2	3
Clean Sheets	2	2
Shots on Target	32	15
Disciplinary		
Fouls	51	68
Yellow Cards	8	9
Red Cards	0	0

Goals by Area

○ Plymouth ○ Burnley

	Plymouth	Burnley
	0	0
	2	3
	0	0

Goals Scored by Period

0	0	0	1	0	1
0	15	30	45	60	75	90
0	1	0	0	0	2

Goals by Position

○ Plymouth ○ Burnley

■ forward:	1	■ forward:	1
■ midfield:	1	■ midfield:	2
■ defence:	0	■ defence:	0

Average Attendance

► **12,568**

► **12,092**

All-Time Records

Total Championship Record	○ Plymouth	Burnley ○
Played	92	92
Points	109	114
Won	27	29
Drawn	28	27
Lost	37	36
For	91	84
Against	110	93
Players Used	44	42

All-Time Record vs Plymouth

Competition	Played	Won	Drawn	Lost	For	Against
League	42	16	13	13	51	54
FA Cup	0	0	0	0	0	0
League Cup	1	0	0	1	1	2
Other	2	1	1	0	3	1
Total	45	17	14	14	55	57

Cardiff City

Nickname:	**The Bluebirds**	Telephone:	**02920 221 001**
Manager:	**Dave Jones**	Ticket Office:	**0845 345 1400**
Chairman:	**Sam Hammam**	Club Shop:	**0845 345 1485**
Website:	**www.cardiffcityfc.co.uk**		

Season Review 05/06

Cardiff spent the season on the fringes of a Play-off place, but ultimately fell away to finish 11th. On-loan midfielder Jason Koumas played a starring role, with Cameron Jerome demonstrating enough ability in attack to earn a summer move to Birmingham.

Producing consistent performances proved difficult for the Bluebirds, with back-to-back victories only achieved twice during the Championship campaign.

Points / Position

won drawn lost H home A away

Season:	96/97	97/98	98/99	99/00	00/01	01/02	02/03	03/04	04/05	05/06
Premiership **P**										
Division **1**								13 / 65pts	17 / 63pts · 16 / 54pts	14 / 56pts · 11 / 60pts
Division **2**	19 / 54pts	22 / 49pts			21 / 44pts	2 / 102pts · 1 /	4 / 83pts · 8 / 65pts · 6 / 81pts	· / 90pts		
Division **3**	7 / 69pts	21 / 50pts · 13 / 61pts	12 / 80pts	12 / 66pts	3 / 58pts	/ 82pts				

Date:			06.02	05.09	26.12	20.01	24.09	21.02	02.04	13.08	18.03	26.12
Result:			H 1-1	A 0-1	H 2-1	A 1-4	H 2-2	A 1-1	H 1-1	A 1-0	H 0-1	A 2-0

Champ. Head-to-Head

Facts	● Plymouth	Cardiff ○
Games		
Points	7	4
Won	2	1
Drawn	1	1
Goals		
For	4	2
Clean Sheets	2	1
Shots on Target	19	14
Disciplinary		
Fouls	61	76
Yellow Cards	7	9
Red Cards	0	1

Goals by Area

● Plymouth   ○ Cardiff

```
        1       0
   3            
0               1
```

Goals Scored by Period

```
    0    1    0    1    1    1
    0   15   30   45   60   75   90
    0    1    1    0    0    0
```

Goals by Position

● Plymouth   ○ Cardiff

	Plymouth		Cardiff
▶ forward:	0	▶ forward:	1
▶ midfield:	2	▶ midfield:	1
▶ defence:	1	▶ defence:	0
▶ own goals:	1		

Average Attendance

▶ **15,770**

▶ **14,550**

All-Time Records

Total Championship Record	● Plymouth	Cardiff ○
Played	92	92
Points	109	114
Won	27	29
Drawn	28	27
Lost	37	36
For	91	106
Against	110	110
Players Used	44	48

All-Time Record vs Plymouth

Competition	Played	Won	Drawn	Lost	For	Against
League	44	14	15	15	63	62
FA Cup	1	1	0	0	3	0
League Cup	4	3	0	1	8	7
Other	0	0	0	0	0	0
Total	**49**	**18**	**15**	**16**	**74**	**69**

Colchester United

Nickname:	The U's		Telephone:	0871 226 2161
Manager:	—		Ticket Office:	0871 226 2161
Chairman:	Peter Heard		Club Shop:	01206 715 309
Website:	www.cu-fc.com			

Season Review 05/06

Phil Parkinson was the toast of Colchester after leading his side to a surprise promotion, but he could not resist the overtures of Hull during the summer. The unfashionable Layer Road club overcame a shaky start and even managed a run of nine straight League One wins at home.

Amazingly, no team in the division performed in front of a lower average gate than the men from Essex.

Points / Position

won drawn lost H home A away

Season:	96/97	97/98	98/99	99/00	00/01	01/02	02/03	03/04	04/05	05/06
Premiership **P**										
Division **1**								17⊖ 53pts	14⊖ 56pts	
Division **2**	19⊖ 54pts	22⊖ 49pts	18⊖ 52pts	18⊖ 52pts	17⊖ 57pts	15⊖ 57pts	8⊖ 65pts	12⊖ 58pts	11⊖ 90pts 64pts	15⊖ 59pts	2⊖ 79pts
Division **3**	8⊖ 68pts	4⊖ 74pts	13⊖ 61pts	12⊖ 66pts	12⊖ 58pts	1⊖ 102pts				

Date:							05.04	30.11	08.05	29.11
Result:							H 0-0	A 0-0	H 2-0	A 2-0

Champ. Head-to-Head

Facts	⊙ Plymouth	Colchester ⊙
Games		
Points	0	0
Won	0	0
Drawn	0	0
Goals		
For	0	0
Clean Sheets	0	0
Shots on Target	0	0
Disciplinary		
Fouls	0	0
Yellow Cards	0	0
Red Cards	0	0

Goals by Area
⊙ Plymouth ⊙ Colchester

0   0
0   0
0   0

Goals by Position
⊙ Plymouth ⊙ Colchester

	forward:	0		forward:	0
	midfield:	0		midfield:	0
	defence:	0		defence:	0

Goals Scored by Period

0	0	0	0	0	0
0	15	30	45	60	75	90
0	0	0	0	0	0

Average Attendance

All-Time Records

Total Championship Record	⊙ Plymouth	Colchester ⊙
Played	92	0
Points	109	0
Won	27	0
Drawn	28	0
Lost	37	0
For	91	0
Against	110	0
Players Used	44	0

All-Time Record vs Plymouth

Competition	Played	Won	Drawn	Lost	For	Against
League	26	9	10	7	34	36
FA Cup	3	1	1	1	2	3
League Cup	1	1	0	0	2	1
Other	2	1	0	1	2	3
Total	**32**	**12**	**11**	**9**	**40**	**43**

Coventry City

Nickname:	The Sky Blues	Telephone:	0870 421 1987
Manager:	Micky Adams	Ticket Office:	0870 421 1987
Chairman:	Geoffrey Robinson	Club Shop:	0870 421 1987
Website:	www.ccfc.co.uk		

Season Review 05/06

Coventry made real progress over the course of the campaign, brushing aside a slow start to finish in a creditable eighth place. The brand new Ricoh Arena proved to be a happy hunting ground for the Sky Blues, with just four visiting teams emerging victorious.

Gary McSheffrey always looked dangerous, whilst Dele Adebola and Stern John struck up a decent partnership in attack.

Points / Position

won drawn lost H home A away

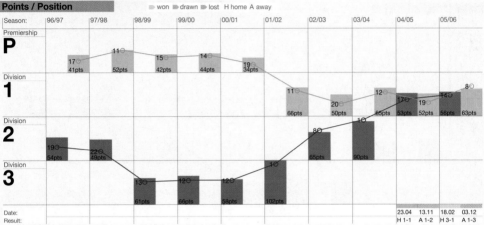

Date:									23.04	13.11	18.02	03.12
Result:									H 1-1	A 1-2	H 3-1	A 1-3

Champ. Head-to-Head

Facts	Plymouth	Coventry
Games		
Points	4	7
Won	1	2
Drawn	1	1
Goals		
For	6	7
Clean Sheets	0	0
Shots on Target	32	26
Disciplinary		
Fouls	50	59
Yellow Cards	3	10
Red Cards	0	0

Goals by Area

○ Plymouth ○ Coventry

	1	0	
	3		5
2			2

Goals Scored by Period

1	1	1	1	1	1
0	15	30	45	60	75	90
2	0	3	1	0	1

Goals by Position

○ Plymouth ○ Coventry

	Plymouth	Coventry
forward:	4	3
midfield:	2	4
defence:	0	0

Average Attendance

15,700

17,055

All-Time Records

Total Championship Record	Plymouth	Coventry
Played	92	92
Points	109	115
Won	27	29
Drawn	28	28
Lost	37	35
For	91	123
Against	110	138
Players Used	44	51

All-Time Record vs Plymouth

Competition	Played	Won	Drawn	Lost	For	Against
League	36	15	8	13	52	56
FA Cup	3	1	0	2	5	8
League Cup	0	0	0	0	0	0
Other	0	0	0	0	0	0
Total	**39**	**16**	**8**	**15**	**57**	**64**

Crystal Palace

Nickname:	The Eagles
Manager:	Peter Taylor
Chairman:	Simon Jordan
Website:	www.cpfc.co.uk

Telephone:	0208 768 6000
Ticket Office:	0871 2000 071
Club Shop:	0208 768 6100

Season Review 05/06

A campaign that began with high hopes of a return to the Premiership ended in bitter Play-off disappointment. Manager Iain Dowie then left for Charlton, with key men Andy Johnson and Fitz Hall also moving on to pastures new.

The Eagles struggled to fulfill their potential and will be hoping that new boss Peter Taylor can remedy that next season.

Points / Position

won drawn lost H home A away

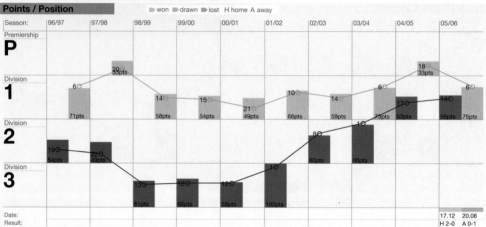

Season:	96/97	97/98	98/99	99/00	00/01	01/02	02/03	03/04	04/05	05/06

Premiership — P

Division 1:
- 97/98: 6, 71pts
- 98/99: 14, 58pts
- 99/00: 15, 54pts
- 00/01: 21, 49pts
- 01/02: 10, 66pts
- 02/03: 14, 59pts
- 03/04: 6, 73pts
- 04/05: 18, 33pts / 17, 53pts
- 05/06: 14, 58pts / 6, 75pts
- 97/98: 20, 33pts

Division 2:
- 96/97: 19, 54pts
- 97/98: 22, 49pts
- 02/03: 8, 65pts
- 03/04: 90pts (1)

Division 3:
- 98/99: 13, 61pts
- 99/00: 12, 86pts
- 00/01: 12, 58pts
- 01/02: 102pts

| Date: | | | | | | | | | 17.12 | 20.08 |
| Result: | | | | | | | | | H 2-0 | A 0-1 |

Champ. Head-to-Head

Facts	O Plymouth	C. Palace O
Games		
Points	3	3
Won	1	1
Drawn	0	0
Goals		
For	2	1
Clean Sheets	1	1
Shots on Target	7	14
Disciplinary		
Fouls	22	40
Yellow Cards	6	9
Red Cards	0	0

Goals by Area
O Plymouth O Crystal Palace

0	1
2	0
0	0

Goals by Position
O Plymouth O Crystal Palace

Plymouth		Crystal Palace	
forward:	1	forward:	0
midfield:	1	midfield:	0
defence:	0	defence:	1

Goals Scored by Period

1	0	0	0	0	1
0	15	30	45	60	75	90
0	0	0	0	1	0

Average Attendance
► **14,582**

► **18,781**

All-Time Records

Total Championship Record	O Plymouth	C. Palace O
Played	92	46
Points	109	75
Won	27	21
Drawn	28	12
Lost	37	13
For	91	67
Against	110	48
Players Used	44	23

All-Time Record vs Plymouth

Competition	Played	Won	Drawn	Lost	For	Against
League	38	16	7	15	61	69
FA Cup	2	1	0	1	4	4
League Cup	1	1	0	0	2	1
Other	0	0	0	0	0	0
Total	**41**	**18**	**7**	**16**	**67**	**74**

Derby County

Nickname:	The Rams
Manager:	Billy Davies
Chairman:	Peter Gadsby
Website:	www.dcfc.co.uk

Telephone:	0870 444 1884
Ticket Office:	0870 444 1884
Club Shop:	01332 209 000

Season Review 05/06

Derby failed to build on what had been an impressive season in 2004/05, with Phil Brown only lasting a few months in the managerial hot-seat. Caretaker replacement Terry Westley then did just enough to keep the Rams out of the relegation picture.

The summer appointment of former Preston boss Billy Davies has given many fans hope of better times to come at Pride Park.

Points / Position

■ won ■ drawn ■ lost H home A away

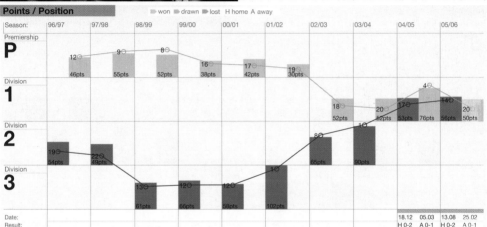

Date:									18.12	05.03	13.08	25.02
Result:									H 0-2	A 0-1	H 0-2	A 0-1

Champ. Head-to-Head

Facts	O Plymouth	Derby O
Games		
Points	0	12
Won	0	4
Drawn	0	0
Goals		
For	0	6
Clean Sheets	0	4
Shots on Target	22	20
Disciplinary		
Fouls	56	52
Yellow Cards	3	5
Red Cards	1	0

Goals by Area
O Plymouth   O Derby

	0		2	
	0			3
0				1

Goals Scored by Period

0	0	0	0	0	0
15	30	45	60	75	90
2	2	1	0	1	0

Goals by Position
O Plymouth   O Derby

	Plymouth	Derby
■ forward:	0	■ forward: 2
■ midfield:	0	■ midfield: 3
■ defence:	0	■ defence: 0
		■ own goals: 1

Average Attendance

➤ **14,807**

➤ 26,376

All-Time Records

Total Championship Record	O Plymouth	Derby O
Played	92	92
Points	109	126
Won	27	32
Drawn	28	30
Lost	37	30
For	91	124
Against	110	127
Players Used	44	47

All-Time Record vs Plymouth

Competition	Played	Won	Drawn	Lost	For	Against
League	34	18	8	8	62	45
FA Cup	6	3	1	2	8	6
League Cup	0	0	0	0	0	0
Other	0	0	0	0	0	0
Total	40	21	9	10	70	51

Hull City

Nickname:	**The Tigers**	Telephone:	**0870 837 0003**
Manager:	**Phil Parkinson**	Ticket Office:	**0870 837 0004**
Chairman:	**Adam Pearson**	Club Shop:	**0870 837 0005**
Website:	**www.hullcityafc.premiumtv.co.uk**		

Season Review 05/06

Hull enjoyed a fairly comfortable season back at Championship level and were never unduly troubled by the threat of relegation. Victory over local rivals Leeds in April was the undoubted highlight of a solid campaign.

The summer departure of popular manager Peter Taylor came as a massive blow to the club, but his youthful replacement, Phil Parkinson, has shown plenty of promise.

Points / Position

won drawn lost H home A away

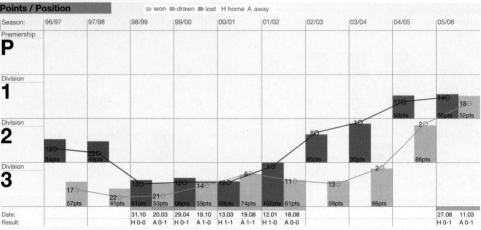

Season:	96/97	97/98	98/99	99/00	00/01	01/02	02/03	03/04	04/05	05/06
Date:			31.10	20.03	29.04	19.10	13.03	19.08	12.01	18.08			27.08	11.03
Result:			H 0-0	A 0-1	H 0-1	A 1-0	H 1-1	A 1-1	H 1-0	A 0-0			H 0-1	A 0-1

Champ. Head-to-Head

Facts	O Plymouth	Hull O
Games		
Points	0	6
Won	0	2
Drawn	0	0
Goals		
For	0	2
Clean Sheets	0	2
Shots on Target	12	13
Disciplinary		
Fouls	34	34
Yellow Cards	6	3
Red Cards	0	1

Goals by Area
O Plymouth O Hull

0		0
0		0
0		2

Goals by Position
O Plymouth O Hull

forward: 0 forward: 1
midfield: 0 midfield: 1
defence: 0 defence: 0

Goals Scored by Period

0	0	0	0	0	0
0	15	30	45	60	75	90
0	0	0	2	0	0

Average Attendance

12,329

20,137

All-Time Records

Total Championship Record	O Plymouth	Hull O
Played	92	46
Points	109	52
Won	27	12
Drawn	28	16
Lost	37	18
For	91	49
Against	110	55
Players Used	44	33

All-Time Record vs Plymouth

Competition	Played	Won	Drawn	Lost	For	Against
League	64	28	17	19	100	92
FA Cup	5	3	2	0	12	7
League Cup	0	0	0	0	0	0
Other	0	0	0	0	0	0
Total	**69**	**31**	**19**	**19**	**112**	**99**

Ipswich Town

Nickname:	The Tractor Boys	Telephone:	01473 400 500
Manager:	Jim Magilton	Ticket Office:	0870 111 0555
Chairman:	David Sheepshanks	Club Shop:	01473 400 501
Website:	www.itfc.co.uk		

Season Review 05/06

Ipswich struggled to adapt to life without Darren Bent, Shefki Kuqi, Kelvin Davis and Tommy Miller. Manager Joe Royle had little choice but to put his faith in youth and saw the Tractor Boys slump to a disappointing 15th-place finish.

Legendary skipper Jim Magilton looked set for an emotional summer exit, but instead found himself succeeding Royle as boss.

Points / Position

won ▶ drawn ▶ lost H home A away

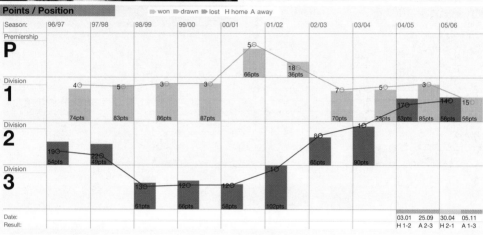

Date:	03.01	25.09	30.04	05.11
Result:	H 1-2	A 2-3	H 2-1	A 1-3

Champ. Head-to-Head

Facts	O Plymouth	Ipswich O
Games		
Points	3	9
Won	1	3
Drawn	0	0
Goals		
For	6	9
Clean Sheets	0	0
Shots on Target	27	21
Disciplinary		
Fouls	47	47
Yellow Cards	5	8
Red Cards	0	1

Goals by Area

O Plymouth   O Ipswich

```
      2     3
   3        5
 1          1
```

Goals Scored by Period

```
2    1    0    2    0    1
0   15   30   45   60   75   90
1    2    1    1    1    3
```

Goals by Position

O Plymouth   O Ipswich

▶ forward: 3   ▶ forward: 3
▶ midfield: 3   ▶ midfield: 3
▶ defence: 0   ▶ defence: 3

Average Attendance

▶ **16,922**
▶ **23,176**

All-Time Records

Total Championship Record	O Plymouth	Ipswich O
Played	92	92
Points	109	141
Won	27	38
Drawn	28	27
Lost	37	27
For	91	138
Against	110	122
Players Used	44	42

All-Time Record vs Plymouth

Competition	Played	Won	Drawn	Lost	For	Against
League	36	16	10	10	55	44
FA Cup	1	1	0	0	3	1
League Cup	0	0	0	0	0	0
Other	0	0	0	0	0	0
Total	37	17	10	10	58	45

Leeds United

Nickname:	United	Telephone:	0113 367 6000
Manager:	Kevin Blackwell	Ticket Office:	0845 121 1992
Chairman:	Ken Bates	Club Shop:	0870 125 3337
Website:	www.leedsunited.com		

Season Review 05/06

A promising campaign ended in bitter disappointment for Leeds as they missed out on promotion against Watford in the Play-off Final. Kevin Blackwell's team were a permanent fixture in the top six, but rarely threatened to go up automatically.

Rob Hulse, David Healy and Robbie Blake all contributed a decent amount of goals, with Eddie Lewis providing a number of vital assists.

Points / Position

won drawn lost H home A away

Season:	96/97	97/98	98/99	99/00	00/01	01/02	02/03	03/04	04/05	05/06

Premiership **P**

- 11○ 46pts (96/97)
- 5○ 59pts (97/98)
- 4○ 67pts (98/99)
- 3○ 69pts (99/00)
- 4○ 68pts (00/01)
- 5○ 66pts (01/02)
- 15○ 47pts (02/03)
- 19○ 33pts (03/04)

Division **1**

- 17○ 53pts
- 14 60pts
- 14○ 56pts
- 5○ 78pts

Division **2**

- 8○ 65pts
- 1○ 90pts

Division **3**

- 19○ 54pts
- 22○ 49pts
- 13○ 61pts
- 12○ 66pts
- 12○ 58pts
- 1○ 102pts

Date:			14.09	28.12	02.01	08.04
Result:			H 0-1	A 1-2	H 0-3	A 0-0

Champ. Head-to-Head

Facts	O Plymouth	Leeds O
Games		
Points	1	10
Won	0	3
Drawn	1	1
Goals		
For	1	6
Clean Sheets	1	3
Shots on Target	16	23
Disciplinary		
Fouls	51	55
Yellow Cards	5	4
Red Cards	0	0

Goals by Area

O Plymouth   O Leeds

1	4
0	1
0	1

Goals by Position

O Plymouth   O Leeds

	Plymouth	Leeds
forward:	1	4
midfield:	0	0
defence:	0	0
own goals:		2

Goals Scored by Period

0	0	0	0	0	1
0	15	30	45	60	75	90
0	0	1	3	0	2

Average Attendance

▶ **19,140**

▶ **27,573**

All-Time Records

Total Championship Record	O Plymouth	Leeds O
Played	92	92
Points	109	138
Won	27	35
Drawn	28	33
Lost	37	24
For	91	106
Against	110	90
Players Used	44	46

All-Time Record vs Plymouth

Competition	Played	Won	Drawn	Lost	For	Against
League	36	16	10	10	62	46
FA Cup	1	1	0	0	2	1
League Cup	0	0	0	0	0	0
Other	0	0	0	0	0	0
Total	37	17	10	10	64	47

Leicester City

Nickname:	The Foxes	Telephone:	0870 040 6000
Manager:	Rob Kelly	Ticket Office:	0870 499 1884
Chairman:	Andrew Taylor	Club Shop:	0870 040 6000
Website:	www.lcfc.co.uk		

Season Review 05/06

The Foxes endured a disappointing campaign, only moving away from the relegation places following the departure of manager Craig Levein. A run of 28 points from the final 16 games then helped caretaker boss Rob Kelly secure the role on a permanent basis.

Midfielder Joey Gudjonsson was very much the star performer, even managing to score from the halfway line against Hull.

Points / Position

won drawn lost H home A away

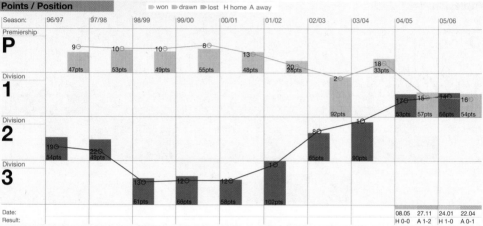

Season:	96/97	97/98	98/99	99/00	00/01	01/02	02/03	03/04	04/05	05/06
Premiership P	9 47pts	10 53pts	10 49pts	8 55pts	13 48pts	20 28pts	2 92pts	18 33pts		
Division 1									17 53pts / 15 57pts	14 66pts / 16 54pts
Division 2	19 54pts	22 49pts					8 65pts	10 90pts		
Division 3			13 61pts	12 66pts	12 58pts	1 102pts				

Date:									08.05 / 27.11	24.01 / 22.04
Result:									H 0-0 / A 1-2	H 1-0 / A 0-1

Champ. Head-to-Head

Facts	○ Plymouth	Leicester ○
Games		
Points	4	7
Won	1	2
Drawn	1	1
Goals		
For	2	3
Clean Sheets	2	2
Shots on Target	22	13
Disciplinary		
Fouls	56	70
Yellow Cards	2	7
Red Cards	0	0

Goals by Area

○ Plymouth ○ Leicester

	0		1	
	1			2
1				0

Goals by Position

○ Plymouth ○ Leicester

	Plymouth	Leicester
forward:	0	3
midfield:	2	0
defence:	0	0

Goals Scored by Period

1	0	0	1	0	0
0	15	30	45	60	75	90
0	0	0	3	0	0

Average Attendance

▶15,895

▶23,298

All-Time Records

Total Championship Record	○ Plymouth	Leicester ○
Played	92	92
Points	109	111
Won	27	25
Drawn	28	36
Lost	37	31
For	91	100
Against	110	105
Players Used	44	50

All-Time Record vs Plymouth

Competition	Played	Won	Drawn	Lost	For	Against
League	32	15	8	9	50	37
FA Cup	1	1	0	0	5	0
League Cup	2	2	0	0	4	2
Other	0	0	0	0	0	0
Total	**35**	**18**	**8**	**9**	**59**	**39**

Luton Town

Nickname:	The Hatters
Manager:	Mike Newell
Chairman:	Bill Tomlins
Website:	www.lutontown.co.uk

Telephone:	01582 411 622
Ticket Office:	01582 416 976
Club Shop:	01582 488 864

Season Review 05/06

Luton burst onto the Championship scene in spectacular fashion, rarely dropping out of the top-six until mid-December. Though the Hatters eventually finished in tenth, they won many admirers for approaching the game in such a positive fashion.

The achievements of manager Mike Newell also attracted attention, with both Leicester and Crystal Palace expressing an interest in securing his services.

Points / Position

■ won ■ drawn ■ lost H home A away

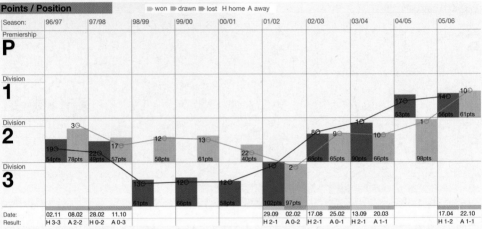

Season:	96/97	97/98	98/99	99/00	00/01	01/02	02/03	03/04	04/05	05/06
Date:	02.11	08.02	28.02	11.10		29.09	02.02	17.08	25.02	13.09	20.03		17.04	22.10
Result:	H 3-3	A 2-2	H 0-2	A 0-3		H 2-1	A 0-2	H 2-1	A 0-1	H 2-1	A 1-1		H 1-2	A 1-1

Champ. Head-to-Head

Facts	○ Plymouth	Luton ○
Games		
Points	1	4
Won	0	1
Drawn	1	1
Goals		
For	2	3
Clean Sheets	0	0
Shots on Target	5	14
Disciplinary		
Fouls	25	25
Yellow Cards	5	2
Red Cards	0	0

Goals by Area

○ Plymouth ○ Luton

	1	1
1		2
0		0

Goals Scored by Period

	0	0	0	0	1	1
0	15	30	45	60	75	90
	0	0	0	0	1	2

Goals by Position

○ Plymouth ○ Luton

	Plymouth		Luton
■ forward:	0	■ forward:	3
■ midfield:	2	■ midfield:	0
■ defence:	0	■ defence:	0

Average Attendance

► **13,486**

► **8,714**

All-Time Records

Total Championship Record	○ Plymouth	Luton ○
Played	92	46
Points	109	61
Won	27	17
Drawn	28	10
Lost	37	19
For	91	66
Against	110	67
Players Used	44	24

All-Time Record vs Plymouth

Competition	Played	Won	Drawn	Lost	For	Against
League	64	19	20	25	90	109
FA Cup	1	1	0	0	4	2
League Cup	2	0	1	1	4	5
Other	0	0	0	0	0	0
Total	**67**	**20**	**21**	**26**	**98**	**116**

Norwich City

Nickname:	The Canaries	Telephone:	01603 760 760
Manager:	Nigel Worthington	Ticket Office:	0870 444 1902
Chairman:	Roger Munby	Club Shop:	0870 444 1902
Website:	www.canaries.co.uk		

Season Review 05/06

The Canaries struggled to adjust to life back in the Championship, failing to recover from a sluggish start to the campaign. Manager Nigel Worthington came in for much criticism, particularly in light of some woeful displays away from Carrow Road.

Though the team could only manage a ninth-place finish, the club came top of the division in terms of average attendance.

Points / Position

won drawn lost H home A away

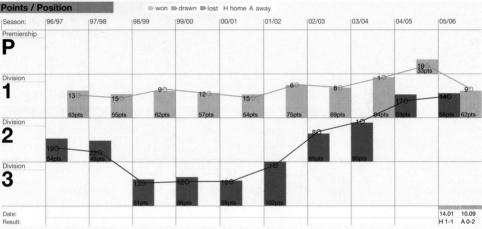

Season:	96/97	97/98	98/99	99/00	00/01	01/02	02/03	03/04	04/05	05/06
Premiership P										
Division 1	13 63pts	15 55pts	9 62pts	12 57pts	15 54pts	6 75pts	8 69pts	1 84pts	17 53pts	14 56pts / 9 62pts
Division 2	19 54pts	22 49pts					8 65pts	90pts		
Division 3			13 61pts	12 66pts	12 58pts	1 102pts				

Date:									14.01	10.09
Result:									H 1-1	A 0-2

Champ. Head-to-Head

Facts	○ Plymouth	Norwich ○
Games		
Points	1	4
Won	0	1
Drawn	1	1
Goals		
For	1	3
Clean Sheets	0	1
Shots on Target	14	12
Disciplinary		
Fouls	24	41
Yellow Cards	2	3
Red Cards	0	0

Goals by Area

● Plymouth ○ Norwich

	1	2	
0			1
0			0

Goals by Position

○ Plymouth   ○ Norwich

● forward:	1	● forward:	2
● midfield:	0	● midfield:	0
● defence:	0	● defence:	0
		● own goals:	1

Goals Scored by Period

0	1	0	0	0	0
0	15	30	45	60	75	90
0	1	1	1	0	0

Average Attendance

● 13,906

● 23,981

All-Time Records

Total Championship Record	○ Plymouth	Norwich ○
Played	92	46
Points	109	62
Won	27	18
Drawn	28	8
Lost	37	20
For	91	56
Against	110	65
Players Used	44	31

All-Time Record vs Plymouth

Competition	Played	Won	Drawn	Lost	For	Against
League	58	19	14	25	65	85
FA Cup	0	0	0	0	0	0
League Cup	0	0	0	0	0	0
Other	0	0	0	0	0	0
Total	**58**	**19**	**14**	**25**	**65**	**85**

Preston North End °

Nickname:	The Lilywhites	Telephone:	0870 442 1964
Manager:	Paul Simpson	Ticket Office:	0870 442 1966
Chairman:	Derek Shaw	Club Shop:	0870 442 1965
Website:	www.pnefc.co.uk		

Season Review 05/06

A 22-match unbeaten run midway through the season helped Preston reach the Playoffs, where they were beaten at the semi-final stage by Leeds. Manager Billy Davies then left for Derby, with Carlisle boss Paul Simpson replacing him at Deepdale.

The lilywhites kept 24 Championship clean sheets in 2005/06, but will be weakened by the departure of defender Claude Davis.

Points / Position

won drawn lost H home A away

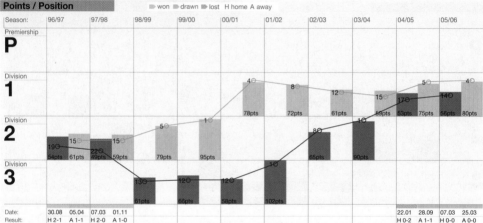

Season:	96/97	97/98	98/99	99/00	00/01	01/02	02/03	03/04	04/05	05/06

Premiership **P**

Division **1**

Division **2**

Division **3**

Date:	30.08	05.04	07.03	01.11					22.01	28.09	07.03	25.03
Result:	H 2-1	A 1-1	H 2-0	A 1-0					H 0-2	A 1-1	H 0-0	A 0-0

Champ. Head-to-Head

Facts	O Plymouth	Preston O
Games		
Points	3	6
Won	0	1
Drawn	3	3
Goals		
For	1	3
Clean Sheets	2	3
Shots on Target	23	15
Disciplinary		
Fouls	49	51
Yellow Cards	5	6
Red Cards	0	0

Goals by Area
O Plymouth   O Preston

	1	0
0		3
0		0

Goals Scored by Period

0	1	0	0	0	0
0	15	30	45	60	75	90
0	1	1	0	1	0

Goals by Position
O Plymouth   O Preston

forward:	0	forward:	2
midfield:	0	midfield:	1
defence:	1	defence:	0

Average Attendance

12,268

12,685

All-Time Records

Total Championship Record	O Plymouth	Preston O
Played	92	92
Points	109	155
Won	27	41
Drawn	28	32
Lost	37	19
For	91	126
Against	110	88
Players Used	44	50

All-Time Record vs Plymouth

Competition	Played	Won	Drawn	Lost	For	Against
League	50	20	14	16	63	60
FA Cup	2	1	0	1	3	2
League Cup	1	1	0	0	1	0
Other	0	0	0	0	0	0
Total	53	22	14	17	67	62

Nickname:	The Superhoops
Manager:	Gary Waddock
Chairman:	Gianni Paladini
Website:	www.qpr.co.uk

Telephone:	020 8743 0262
Ticket Office:	0870 112 1967
Club Shop:	020 8749 6862

Season Review 05/06

Boardroom friction did little to help matters on the pitch at Loftus Road, with Rangers finishing the season just above the relegation places. Manager Ian Holloway had been sent on "gardening leave" in February and was replaced by coach Gary Waddock.

A return of just five points from the final 11 games of the campaign highlighted the sense of uncertainty at the club. Holloway has since been appointed Argyle Manager.

Points / Position

won drawn lost H home A away

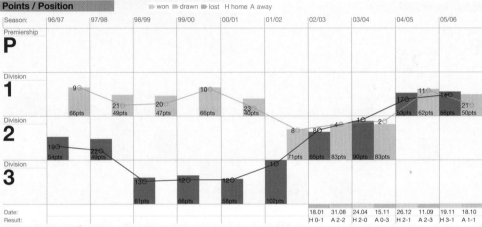

Champ. Head-to-Head

Facts	O Plymouth	QPR O
Games		
Points	7	4
Won	2	1
Drawn	1	1
Goals		
For	8	6
Clean Sheets	0	0
Shots on Target	20	19
Disciplinary		
Fouls	49	71
Yellow Cards	7	13
Red Cards	1	1

Goals by Area
O Plymouth   O QPR

Goals by Position
O Plymouth   O QPR

Plymouth		QPR	
forward:	3	forward:	6
midfield:	4	midfield:	0
defence:	1	defence:	0

Goals Scored by Period

3	0	2	2	0	1
0	15	30	45	60	75	90
0	1	0	1	3	1

Average Attendance

▶ **16,374**

▶ **13,583**

All-Time Records

Total Championship Record	O Plymouth	QPR O
Played	92	92
Points	109	112
Won	27	29
Drawn	28	25
Lost	37	38
For	91	104
Against	110	123
Players Used	44	56

All-Time Record vs Plymouth

Competition	Played	Won	Drawn	Lost	For	Against
League	40	17	2	21	54	63
FA Cup	0	0	0	0	0	0
League Cup	1	0	0	1	0	3
Other	0	0	0	0	0	0
Total	41	17	2	22	54	66

Sheff Wed

Nickname:	The Owls	Telephone:	0870 999 1867
Manager:	Paul Sturrock	Ticket Office:	0870 999 1867
Chairman:	Dave Allen	Club Shop:	0870 999 1867
Website:	www.swfc.co.uk		

Season Review 05/06

Paul Sturrock's team achieved their goal of Championship survival, helped in no small part by a terrific level of support. Things looked bleak during the early months of the campaign, but the Owls eventually found their feet.

Northern Ireland international Chris Brunt was particularly outstanding, weighing in with seven goals and six assists in the league.

Points / Position

won drawn lost H home A away

Season:	96/97	97/98	98/99	99/00	00/01	01/02	02/03	03/04	04/05	05/06
Premiership **P**	7 57pts	16 44pts	12 46pts	19 31pts						
Division **1**					17 53pts	20 50pts	22 46pts	17 53pts	14 56pts	19 52pts
Division **2**	19 54pts	22 49pts					8 65pts	16 90pts / 53pts	5 72pts	
Division **3**			13 61pts	12 66pts	12 58pts	1 102pts				

Date:								02.03 22.10		15.10 22.11
Result:								H 2-0 A 3-1		H 1-1 A 0-0

Champ. Head-to-Head

Facts	○Plymouth	Sheff Wed ○
Games		
Points	2	2
Won	0	0
Drawn	2	2
Goals		
For	1	1
Clean Sheets	1	1
Shots on Target	9	6
Disciplinary		
Fouls	21	43
Yellow Cards	2	5
Red Cards	0	0

Goals by Area
○ Plymouth ○ Sheff Wed

	0	0	
1			1
0			0

Goals by Position
○ Plymouth ○ Sheff Wed

Plymouth	Sheff Wed
forward: 0	forward: 0
midfield: 1	midfield: 0
defence: 0	defence: 0
	own goals: 1

Goals Scored by Period

	0	0	0	0	0	1
	15	30	45	60	75	90
	0	1	0	0	0	0

Average Attendance

▶ **16,534**

▶ 20,244

All-Time Records

Total Championship Record	○Plymouth	Sheff Wed ○
Played	92	46
Points	109	52
Won	27	13
Drawn	28	13
Lost	37	20
For	91	39
Against	110	52
Players Used	44	37

All-Time Record vs Plymouth

Competition	Played	Won	Drawn	Lost	For	Against
League	26	8	9	9	39	39
FA Cup	3	2	1	0	7	2
League Cup	0	0	0	0	0	0
Other	0	0	0	0	0	0
Total	29	10	10	9	46	41

Southampton

Nickname:	The Saints	Telephone:	0870 220 0000
Manager:	George Burley	Ticket Office:	0870 220 0150
Chairman:	Michael Wilde	Club Shop:	0870 220 0130
Website:	www.saintsfc.co.uk		

Season Review 05/06

Southampton failed to make an immediate return to the Premiership, paying the price for drawing 19 of their 46 games. Many fans were delighted to see Harry Redknapp desert his managerial post in December, particularly as George Burley took over.

Five wins from the final six games of the season represented a strong finish and further boosted morale in the camp.

Points / Position

▶ won ▶ drawn ▶ lost H home A away

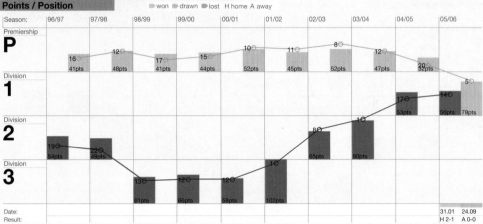

Season:	96/97	97/98	98/99	99/00	00/01	01/02	02/03	03/04	04/05	05/06
Premiership	16 / 41pts	12 / 48pts	17 / 41pts	15 / 44pts	10 / 52pts	11 / 45pts	8 / 52pts	12 / 47pts	20 / 32pts	5
Division 1								17 / 53pts	14 / 56pts	78pts
Division 2							8 / 65pts	1 / 90pts		
Division 3	19 / 54pts	22 / 49pts	13 / 61pts	12 / 66pts	12 / 58pts	1 / 102pts				

Date:	31.01	24.09
Result:	H 2-1	A 0-0

Champ. Head-to-Head

Facts	○ Plymouth	Southampton ○
Games		
Points	4	1
Won	1	0
Drawn	1	1
Goals		
For	2	1
Clean Sheets	1	1
Shots on Target	10	7
Disciplinary		
Fouls	32	28
Yellow Cards	4	3
Red Cards	0	0

Goals by Area

○ Plymouth   ○ Southampton

	0	1	
2			0
0			0

Goals by Position

○ Plymouth   ○ Southampton

	Plymouth		Southampton
▶ forward:	1	▶ forward:	0
▶ midfield:	1	▶ midfield:	1
▶ defence:	0	▶ defence:	0

Goals Scored by Period

	0	0	1	0	0	1
0	15	30	45	60	75	90
	0	0	0	0	1	0

Average Attendance

▶ **15,936**

▶ 26,331

All-Time Records

Total Championship Record	○ Plymouth	Southampton ○
Played	92	46
Points	109	58
Won	27	13
Drawn	28	19
Lost	37	14
For	91	49
Against	110	50
Players Used	44	40

All-Time Record vs Plymouth

Competition	Played	Won	Drawn	Lost	For	Against
League	56	18	16	22	75	85
FA Cup	0	0	0	0	0	0
League Cup	1	1	0	0	4	3
Other	0	0	0	0	0	0
Total	**57**	**19**	**16**	**22**	**79**	**88**

Southend United

Nickname:	The Shrimpers
Manager:	Steve Tilson
Chairman:	Ron Martin
Website:	www.southendunited.co.uk

Telephone:	01702 304 050
Ticket Office:	08444 770 077
Club Shop:	01702 351 117

Season Review 05/06

Southend took to League One like ducks to water, brushing off the tag of relegation favourites to win the division. Manager Steve Tilson continued the good work of the previous campaign, leading the team to eight straight league wins in the early part of the season.

Though the team ethic was vital to the Shrimpers' success, Freddy Eastwood's goals proved crucial.

Points / Position

▶ won ▶ drawn ▶ lost H home A away

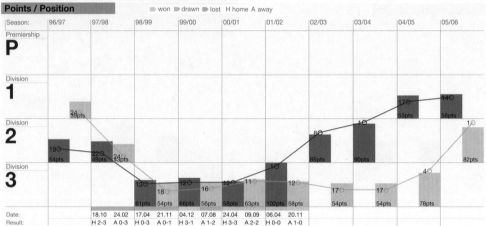

Season:	96/97	97/98	98/99	99/00	00/01	01/02	02/03	03/04	04/05	05/06

Premiership P

Division 1 — 17○ 53pts / 14○ 56pts

Division 2 — 19○ 54pts / 22○ 49pts / 24○ 43pts / 8○ 65pts / 1○ 90pts / 1○ 82pts

Division 3 — 24○ 39pts / 13○ 61pts / 18 54pts / 12○ 66pts / 16 56pts / 12○ 58pts / 11○ 63pts / 1○ 102pts / 12○ 58pts / 17○ 54pts / 17○ 54pts / 4○ 78pts

Date:	18.10	24.02	17.04	21.11	04.12	07.08	24.04	09.09	06.04	20.11
Result:	H 2-3	A 0-3	H 0-3	A 0-1	H 3-1	A 1-2	H 3-3	A 2-2	H 0-0	A 1-0

Champ. Head-to-Head

Facts	○ Plymouth	Southend ○
Games		
Points	0	0
Won	0	0
Drawn	0	0
Goals		
For	0	0
Clean Sheets	0	0
Shots on Target	0	0
Disciplinary		
Fouls	0	0
Yellow Cards	0	0
Red Cards	0	0

Goals by Area

○ Plymouth   ○ Southend

0   0
0   0
0   0
0   0

Goals by Position

○ Plymouth   ○ Southend

▶ forward:	0	▶ forward:	0
▶ midfield:	0	▶ midfield:	0
▶ defence:	0	▶ defence:	0

Goals Scored by Period

0	0	0	0	0	0
0	15	30	45	60	75	90
0	0	0	0	0	0

Average Attendance

All-Time Records

Total Championship Record	○ Plymouth	Southend ○
Played	92	0
Points	109	0
Won	27	0
Drawn	28	0
Lost	37	0
For	91	0
Against	110	0
Players Used	44	0

All-Time Record vs Plymouth

Competition	Played	Won	Drawn	Lost	For	Against
League	58	22	16	20	73	83
FA Cup	2	0	1	1	0	2
League Cup	0	0	0	0	0	0
Other	0	0	0	0	0	0
Total	60	22	17	21	73	85

Stoke City

Nickname:	**The Potters**	Telephone: **01782 592 222**
Manager:	**Tony Pulis**	Ticket Office: **01782 592 204**
Chairman:	**Peter Coates**	Club Shop: **01782 592 244**
Website:	**www.stokecityfc.com**	

Season Review 05/06

It was a season of managerial uncertainty at Stoke, with Johan Boskamp threatening to leave on several occasions prior to his summer exit. In his short time at the club, the Dutchman introduced an attacking brand of football that pleased both players and supporters alike.

Former Argyle manager Tony Pulis has since returned as boss and will be looking to turn a mid-table side into genuine Play-off contenders.

Points / Position

▶ won ▶ drawn ▶ lost H home A away

Season:	96/97	97/98	98/99	99/00	00/01	01/02	02/03	03/04	04/05	05/06
Premiership **P**										
Division **1**	12 64pts	23 46pts				21 50pts	66pts	17 53pts	12 61pts	14 56pts / 13 58pts
Division **2**	19 54pts	22 49pts	8 67pts	6 82pts	5 77pts	5 80pts	8 65pts	10 90pts		
Division **3**			13 61pts	12 66pts	12 58pts	1 102pts				

Date:								20.11	16.04	01.10	14.02
Result:								H 0-0	A 0-2	H 2-1	A 0-0

Champ. Head-to-Head

Facts	○ Plymouth	Stoke ○
Games		
Points	5	5
Won	1	1
Drawn	2	2
Goals		
For	2	3
Clean Sheets	2	3
Shots on Target	19	16
Disciplinary		
Fouls	43	58
Yellow Cards	3	7
Red Cards	0	0

Goals by Area
○ Plymouth ○ Stoke

	1	2	
1			0
0			1

Goals Scored by Period

0	0	0	0	0	1
0	15	30	45	60	75	90
0	1	1	1	0	0

Goals by Position
○ Plymouth ○ Stoke

	▶ Plymouth	▶ Stoke
▶ forward:	0	1
▶ midfield:	1	2
▶ defence:	0	0
▶ own goals:	1	

Average Attendance

▶ **13,934**

▶ **11,630**

All-Time Records

Total Championship Record	○ Plymouth	Stoke ○
Played	92	92
Points	109	119
Won	27	34
Drawn	28	17
Lost	37	41
For	91	90
Against	110	101
Players Used	44	48

All-Time Record vs Plymouth

Competition	Played	Won	Drawn	Lost	For	Against
League	34	17	9	8	52	38
FA Cup	0	0	0	0	0	0
League Cup	2	0	1	1	2	4
Other	0	0	0	0	0	0
Total	**36**	**17**	**10**	**9**	**54**	**42**

Sunderland

Nickname:	The Black Cats	Telephone:	0191 551 5000
Manager:	—	Ticket Office:	0845 671 1973
Chairman:	—	Club Shop:	0191 551 5050
Website:	www.safc.com		

Season Review 05/06

The Black Cats plumbed new depths as they collected just 15 Premiership points, breaking their own unwanted record in the process. Manager Mick McCarthy paid the price for the abject failure, but caretaker replacement Kevin Ball fared no better.

Victory against Fulham in the final home game of the season at least ensured that the fans at the Stadium of Light witnessed a league win.

Points / Position

won ▶ drawn ▶ lost H home A away

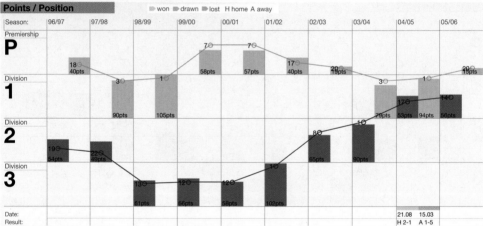

Season:	96/97	97/98	98/99	99/00	00/01	01/02	02/03	03/04	04/05	05/06

Premiership P
- 18 40pts (96/97)
- 7 58pts (99/00)
- 7 57pts (00/01)
- 17 40pts (01/02)
- 20 19pts (02/03)
- 20 15pts (05/06)

Division 1
- 3 90pts (97/98)
- 1 105pts (98/99)
- 3 79pts (03/04)
- 17 53pts (04/05)
- 1 94pts (04/05)
- 14 56pts (05/06)

Division 2
- 19 54pts (96/97)
- 22 49pts (97/98)
- 8 85pts (02/03)
- 1 90pts (03/04)

Division 3
- 13 61pts (98/99)
- 12 66pts (99/00)
- 12 58pts (00/01)
- 1 102pts (01/02)

Date:									21.08	15.03
Result:									H 2-1	A 1-5

Champ. Head-to-Head

Facts	○ Plymouth	Sunderland ○
Games		
Points	3	3
Won	1	1
Drawn	0	0
Goals		
For	3	6
Clean Sheets	0	0
Shots on Target	7	9
Disciplinary		
Fouls	28	31
Yellow Cards	2	6
Red Cards	0	0

Goals by Area
● Plymouth ○ Sunderland

0	4
1	2
2	0

Goals by Position
● Plymouth ○ Sunderland

▶ forward: 2 ▶ forward: 2
▶ midfield: 1 ▶ midfield: 3
▶ defence: 0 ▶ defence: 1

Goals Scored by Period

	1	0	1	0	0	1
	0	15	30	45	60	75	90
	0	0	3	0	2	1

Average Attendance
▶ **16,874**
▶ **25,258**

All-Time Records

Total Championship Record	○ Plymouth	Sunderland ○
Played	92	46
Points	109	94
Won	27	29
Drawn	28	7
Lost	37	10
For	91	76
Against	110	41
Players Used	44	30

All-Time Record vs Plymouth

Competition	Played	Won	Drawn	Lost	For	Against
League	22	11	4	7	40	24
FA Cup	3	3	0	0	8	2
League Cup	0	0	0	0	0	0
Other	0	0	0	0	0	0
Total	**25**	**14**	**4**	**7**	**48**	**26**

West Brom

Nickname:	The Baggies	Telephone:	08700 668 888
Manager:	Bryan Robson	Ticket Office:	08700 662 800
Chairman:	Jeremy Peace	Club Shop:	08700 662 810
Website:	www.wba.co.uk		

Season Review 05/06

Bryan Robson's men were unable to repeat the "Great Escape" of twelve months earlier, suffering relegation after a two-season Premiership stay. The Baggies were unable to recover from a crushing 6-1 loss at Fulham in February, failing to win another game from then on.

On the plus side, Albion won a new fan in the shape of 2001 Wimbledon champion Goran Ivanisevic.

Points / Position

won drawn lost H home A away

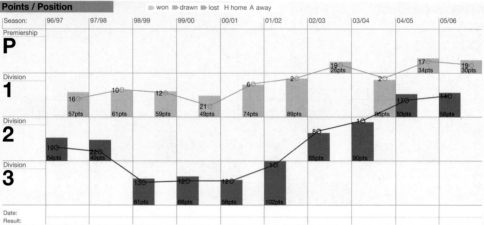

Champ. Head-to-Head

Facts	Plymouth	West Brom
Games		
Points	0	0
Won	0	0
Drawn	0	0
Goals		
For	0	0
Clean Sheets	0	0
Shots on Target	0	0
Disciplinary		
Fouls	0	0
Yellow Cards	0	0
Red Cards	0	0

Goals by Area
Plymouth   West Brom

Goals by Position
Plymouth   West Brom

forward:	0	forward:	0
midfield:	0	midfield:	0
defence:	0	defence:	0

Goals Scored by Period

0	0	0	0	0	0
0	15	30	45	60	75	90
0	0	0	0	0	0

Average Attendance

All-Time Records

Total Championship Record	Plymouth	West Brom
Played	92	0
Points	109	0
Won	27	0
Drawn	28	0
Lost	37	0
For	91	0
Against	110	0
Players Used	44	0

All-Time Record vs Plymouth

Competition	Played	Won	Drawn	Lost	For	Against
League	24	5	7	12	31	40
FA Cup	3	2	0	1	8	4
League Cup	2	1	0	1	1	2
Other	0	0	0	0	0	0
Total	29	8	7	14	40	46

Wolves °

Nickname:	Wolves	Telephone:	0870 442 0123
Manager:	–	Ticket Office:	0870 442 0123
Chairman:	Rick Hayward	Club Shop:	0870 442 0123
Website:	www.wolves.co.uk		

Season Review 05/06

Wolves were perhaps the biggest disappointment of the 2005/06 Championship season, failing even to make the Play-offs. Manager Glenn Hoddle was unable to get the most out of a talented group of players and decided to leave his post during the summer.

Expensive striker Tomasz Frankowski failed to find the net, whilst fans' favourite George Ndah was forced to hang up his boots.

Points / Position

▶ won ▶ drawn ▶ lost H home A away

Season:	96/97	97/98	98/99	99/00	00/01	01/02	02/03	03/04	04/05	05/06
Premiership **P**										
Division **1**	3○ 76pts	9○ 65pts	7○ 73pts	7○ 74pts	12○ 55pts	3○ 86pts	5○ 76pts	20○ 33pts	9○ 66pts	7○ 67pts
Division **2**	19○ 54pts	22○ 49pts					8○ 65pts	1○ 90pts	17○ 53pts	14○ 56pts
Division **3**			13○ 61pts	12○ 66pts	12○ 58pts	1○ 102pts				

Date:									18.09	01.01	01.04	31.12
Result:									H 1-2	A 1-1	H 2-0	A 1-1

Champ. Head-to-Head

Facts	○ Plymouth	Wolves ○
Games		
Points	5	5
Won	1	1
Drawn	2	2
Goals		
For	5	4
Clean Sheets	1	0
Shots on Target	18	17
Disciplinary		
Fouls	45	60
Yellow Cards	4	7
Red Cards	0	1

Goals by Area

○ Plymouth ○ Wolverhampton

	2	0	
3			3
0			1

Goals by Position

○ Plymouth ○ Wolverhampton

	Plymouth		Wolverhampton
▶ forward:	0	▶ forward:	3
▶ midfield:	2	▶ midfield:	1
▶ defence:	2	▶ defence:	0
▶ own goals:	1		

Goals Scored by Period

1	1	0	1	1	1	
0	15	30	45	60	75	90
0	1	1	0	0	2	

Average Attendance

▶ **17,253**

▶ **25,177**

All-Time Records

Total Championship Record	○ Plymouth	Wolves ○
Played	92	92
Points	109	133
Won	27	31
Drawn	28	40
Lost	37	21
For	91	122
Against	110	101
Players Used	44	39

All-Time Record vs Plymouth

Competition	Played	Won	Drawn	Lost	For	Against
League	22	10	6	6	31	27
FA Cup	4	3	1	0	7	2
League Cup	0	0	0	0	0	0
Other	0	0	0	0	0	0
Total	26	13	7	6	38	29

Fixture List 2006/07

Date	KO	v	Opponent	Competition
August				
Sat 5	**15:00**	**H**	**Wolves**	**FLC**
Tue 8	19:45	A	Colchester	FLC
Sat 12	15:00	A	Sunderland	FLC
Sat 19	**15:00**	**H**	**Sheffield Wed**	**FLC**
Sat 26	15:00	A	Stoke City	FLC
September				
Sat 9	**15:00**	**H**	**QPR**	**FLC**
Tue 12	**19:45**	**H**	**Cardiff City**	**FLC**
Sat 16	15:00	A	Southampton	FLC
Sat 23	**15:00**	**H**	**Norwich City**	**FLC**
Sat 30	15:00	A	Coventry City	FLC
October				
Sun 15	**13:15**	**H**	**Derby County**	**FLC**
Tue 17	19:45	A	Barnsley	FLC
Sat 21	**15:00**	**H**	**Burnley**	**FLC**
Sat 28	15:00	A	Crystal Palace	FLC
Tue 31	**19:45**	**H**	**Ipswich Town**	**FLC**
November				
Sat 4	**15:00**	**H**	**Birmingham**	**FLC**
Sat 11	15:00	A	Leicester City	FLC
Sat 18	15:00	A	Southend	FLC
Sat 25	**15:00**	**H**	**Leeds United**	**FLC**
Tue 28	**19:45**	**H**	**Luton Town**	**FLC**
December				
Sat 2	15:00	A	Birmingham	FLC
Sat 9	**15:00**	**H**	**Hull City**	**FLC**
Sat 16	15:00	A	Preston	FLC
Sat 23	**15:00**	**H**	**WBA**	**FLC**
Tue 26	13:00	A	Cardiff City	FLC
Sat 30	15:00	A	Derby County	FLC

Date	KO	v	Opponent	Competition
January				
Mon 1	**15:00**	**H**	**Southampton**	**FLC**
Sat 13	15:00	A	Norwich City	FLC
Sat 20	**15:00**	**H**	**Coventry City**	**FLC**
Tue 30	19:45	A	WBA	FLC
February				
Sat 3	15:00	A	Wolves	FLC
Sat 10	**15:00**	**H**	**Sunderland**	**FLC**
Sat 17	15:00	A	Sheffield Wed	FLC
Tue 20	**19:45**	**H**	**Colchester**	**FLC**
Sat 24	15:00	A	QPR	FLC
March				
Sat 3	**15:00**	**H**	**Stoke City**	**FLC**
Sat 10	15:00	A	Burnley	FLC
Tue 13	**19:45**	**H**	**Barnsley**	**FLC**
Sat 17	**15:00**	**H**	**Crystal Palace**	**FLC**
Sat 31	15:00	A	Ipswich Town	FLC
April				
Sat 7	15:00	A	Leeds United	FLC
Mon 9	**15:00**	**H**	**Leicester City**	**FLC**
Sat 14	15:00	A	Luton Town	FLC
Sat 21	**15:00**	**H**	**Southend**	**FLC**
Sat 28	**15:00**	**H**	**Preston**	**FLC**
May				
Sun 6	15:00	A	Hull City	FLC